Communicating with Our Families

Communicating with Our Families

Technology as Continuity, Interruption, and Transformation

Edited by Maryl R. McGinley, Jill K. Burk, and Joel S. Ward

LEXINGTON BOOKS
Lanham • Boulder • New York • London

Published by Lexington Books
An imprint of The Rowman & Littlefield Publishing Group, Inc.
4501 Forbes Boulevard, Suite 200, Lanham, Maryland 20706
www.rowman.com

86-90 Paul Street, London EC2A 4NE

British Library Cataloguing in Publication Information Available

Library of Congress Cataloging-in-Publication Data

Names: McGinley, Maryl R., 1980- editor. | Burk, Jill K., 1978- editor. | Ward, Joel S., 1977- editor.
Title: Communicating with our families : technology as continuity, interruption, and transformation / edited by Maryl R. McGinley, Jill K. Burk, and Joel S. Ward.
Description: Lanham : Lexington Books, [2022] | Includes bibliographical references and index.
Identifiers: LCCN 2022017880 (print) | LCCN 2022017881 (ebook) | ISBN 9781666900613 (cloth) | ISBN 9781666900637 (paper) | ISBN 9781666900620 (epub)
Subjects: LCSH: Communication in families. | Communication and technology. | Technology--Social aspects.
Classification: LCC HQ734 .C66 2022 (print) | LCC HQ734 (ebook) | DDC 306.87--dc23/eng/20220429
LC record available at https://lccn.loc.gov/2022017880
LC ebook record available at https://lccn.loc.gov/2022017881

For our families . . .

Contents

Introduction

Communicating with Our Families: Technology as Continuity, Interruption, and Transformation explores the impact of personal communication technologies on family communication. Due to the rapid pace and dissemination of new communication technologies in all spheres of our lives, we affirm an urgent call to ask questions and explore the use and impact of communication technologies on our family communication and communicative actions. We believe, as other scholars do, that families "serve as our first communication classroom" (Galvin 312; West, Turner x). We share the philosophical framework that our families model how to relate to and communicate with the world around us. Families give us context for understanding ourselves and understanding our communication patterns for making choices, showing love, and handling conflict (Galvin, Braithwaite, Bylund, 2008). For us, the family is the most influential and significant group shaping identity and providing context for our earliest interactions.

Therefore, we find it vital to examine how communication technologies are affecting families and (re)shaping family communication by exploring topics such as parental loneliness, family storytelling, family technology rules, purposeful technology usage, multigenerational communication, and community. We also recognize that these changes have already influenced our view of the family as a unit. Although some might claim that the shape families have taken for millennia simply represents a long-standing convention, others suggest that the family represents a microcosm of what a larger society might look like. Since the family is indeed the "the first communication classroom," this volume interrogates how that classroom may be changing and the implications of that change on different roles, responsibilities, and relationships within the family. Perhaps the most significant question implied by our contributors to this volume is this: Will the introduction of new communication technologies fundamentally alter familial forms, and will those new groupings that emerge resemble what has been generally assumed for several millennia?

Recognizing that binaries can be theoretically and practically troublesome, we offer three different perspectives in these collected essays. We ask whether patterns of mediated communication within the family will only generate small adjustments, interrupt communication within families in some way, or transform family communication into something different. In each of this volume's essays, we find technologies becoming more ubiquitous in the coordination and communication of family groups redefining the way family members negotiate their relationships. For example, in Sherry Turkle's most recent work, *Reclaiming Conversation,* she recounts the experience of one mother who found texting her son an easier way to resolve conflict rather than through an open and direct face-to-face conversation (Turkle 2015, 127). Turkle notes an important change in the use of technologies to mediate conflict, suggesting that although mediation offers a way to have "cleaner, calmer and more considered" conflicts, they also appear to prevent what she calls a "sentimental education" (Turkle, 129, 42). Turkle's academic observations are clearly inflected with tones of concern and positively correspond with Marshall McLuhan's categorization of communication media into hot and cold. McLuhan observes that any media promoting high participation and impersonal messages largely operates to "cool down" its participants (McLuhan 1994, 22). For McLuhan, this suggests that any electronically powered media has had cooling effects on human interaction because of the speed and breadth of its reach. Turkle views this change as a radical reorientation of conventional family conversation. Thus, suggesting that the dinner table no longer offers the opportunity for lively conversation between family members. McLuhan simply notes this as a function of the media that may have already occurred in the development of widespread literacy where many a family spent evenings reading, calmed by common and ordinary act of reading facilitated by readily available reading material for all ages. Our intent is not to offer a definitive view of how families ought to use technology to communicate. Rather, we hope that that the different topics found in the following essays offer useful examples for navigating the rapidly changing landscape of family communication.

We have organized the collection into three themes of continuity, interruption, and transformation to situate each essay within families' spectrum of responses families to the inevitable encounter with the expanding nature of digital networks. The scholars in this volume work from a human communication perspective and use various research modes of inquiry including quantitative, qualitative, and interpretive methods. Through the integration and presentation of diverse research questions tested and responded to from a variety of scholarly approaches, we feel a more nuanced exploration of communication technology utilized within a family setting is provided. We do not present this volume as a summative account. Instead, our motive lies primarily in our own desire to better understand and navigate this terrain within our own families. As parents with children, we recognize both the dangers and opportunities that new communication technologies offer. Feeling a deep obligation toward this new generation, we offer these essays to scholars, like ourselves, who might benefit from the valuable perspectives offered here.

PERSPECTIVES ON THE FAMILY AS A SOCIAL FORM

Upon collecting and reviewing the essays for this volume, we recognized that the authors, including ourselves, presuppose a particular family form or type as a foundation for their research. These presuppositions gave us pause, and we begin to ask questions such as, "what constitutes a family?" "Why do families form?" "What relationships do family members have or not have with one another?" While most of the examples of family in this collected work assume a rather conventional form of family including parents and children, we recognize that culturally this represents only one type of family and that others exist across cultures and time. Therefore, while not exhaustive, we offer a few philosophical perspectives on family as a foundation, while simultaneously providing a heuristic, for this volume.

One perspective of *family* begins with anthropology as a discipline; initiated for the most part by Claude Lévi-Strauss in *Tristes Tropiques* (1955). Lévi-Strauss argues that men and women of all cultures and all times were categorically similar. Anthropology, as a discipline, attempts to find common patterns of behavior or action between cultures separated by time or space to better define what it means to be human. While the exact reasons for why men and women form couples and bear and rear children are explained differently in cultures, the consensus in anthropology arises from a scientific understanding of the human as an advanced animal, adopting and maintaining behaviors that enhance species survival. Such a view echoes Charles Darwin's work *The Descent of Man, and Selection in Relation to Sex* (1871) in which he applies his theory of species evolution to human development. Darwin's work follows an even earlier assertion made by Jean-Jacques Rousseau, a thinker who more recently is credited with the formula for much of our contemporary thought on the nature of human relations (Trueman 2020, 124). His ideas are foundational to a modern view of human relations, since he asserts that "the earliest and only natural societies are families: yet the children remain attached to the father no longer than they have need of his protection" (Rousseau 1791, 6). This idea summarizes the anthropological view of familial relations working primarily as a system of protection from violence.

The modern view of the family suggests that human relations are built upon the necessity for protection and when such protection is no longer necessary, those relations, if sustained, are simply the following of arbitrary social conventions that could just as easily be dismissed. Ruth Benedict, another mid-twentieth-century anthropologist, defines this view in her own *Patterns of Culture*, published in 1931, in which she describes the "Science of Custom," wherein the anthropologist adopts a certain ambivalence toward different family structures, suggesting that "to the anthropologist, our customs and those of a New Guinea tribe are two possible social schemes for dealing with a common problem, and in so far as he remains an anthropologist he is bound to avoid any weighting of one in favor of the other" (Benedict 1931, 1). Though comparisons may be drawn between one cultural view of the family with another, these comparisons simply shed light on the different approaches to a similar scenario rather than indicating any hierarchy of good or better ways of relating.

As a perspective, anthropology privileges the ethnographic, even though archaeological anthropology studies culture through the study of artifacts, texts, and architecture, attempted to reconstruct a better understanding of historical human relations and the past habits of family living. Averil Cameron's history of late antiquity shows that the conventions surrounding marriage and family were heavily regulated and that marriage and family were of great concern to the civil authorities in the late Roman empire (Cameron 1993, 150). The anthropological view of the family illustrates that family relations have long been a concern of different societies and that an unregulated or disorderly familial structure contributes to disorderly politics. As Rousseau points out, "families are the first models of political societies" (Rousseau 1791, 6). This conclusion demonstrates that although the modern view of the family considers its structure largely traditional, the type and quality of such conventions have great consequence for the nature of the relations between family members.

Philosophically and theoretically, the anthropological perspective intersects with the social constructivist paradigm in communication theory. The claims made by social and linguistic structuralists propose that a change in linguistic meaning results in a change of our view of reality and that our concept of reality, personal and social, derives from normative forms of communication (Berger and Luckman 1966). Subsequently, family structure and communication arise from the conventions of its given linguistic system. If, for example, a family's sociality involves hierarchical relationships between parents and children, then the language used by each parent and child exhibits and supports the maintenance of such differences between members. This view provides a robust description of how different people organize as couples and families but refrains from positing an archetypical form of human relationships.

THEMATIC DIVISIONS AND CHAPTER DESCRIPTIONS

Communicating with Our Families: Technology as Continuity, Interruption, and Transformation is organized into three sections. Each section provides a framework for considering how novel communication technologies are forming, shaping, and impacting family communication in our age. We recognize that some chapters overflow our editorial decisions and present a perspective that engages the family as both continuous, interrupted, and transforming. However, to offer some measure of guidance, and fulfill our obligations as collectors and editors of the volume, we generated partitions to focus attention on the differing perspectives taken toward new communication technologies in research on family communication. Second, research on communication technologies could generally be divided into the positivist versus the deterministic view of technological progress. Positivists in communication technology research laud and celebrate the changes in communication technology and the opportunities it offers even if they recognize its disruptive nature. Determinists tend to take a critical view of technological progress, suggesting that these new technologies will bring about the demise of human institutions like family unity. As previously noted, we acknowledge the false dilemma that a polarity like this can generate and could be especially unhelpful for a generous analysis of the various forms families take in their patterns of interaction. For this reason, we have tried to see these essays on a continuum, beginning with the generally measured view that technologies are influential but not dangerous to families, entertaining the idea that communication technologies may interfere with family communication and then concluding with the view that families and their communication may eventually become something altogether different via new digital channels of communication.

The first section, titled *Continuity,* contains chapters whose underlying theme sees communication technologies as shaping and guiding family communication. Many of the scholars' work in this section understands communication technology as a tool which channels or filters existing communication within the family setting. In this way, communication technology provides for a continuation of existing family communication, but perhaps in a different context or setting than face-to-face communication. Some of the scholarship in this section recognizes and acknowledges challenges that novel communication technologies introduce into the family communication setting, but overall, see it as a necessity of life and work to understand the opportunities it unleashes.

In chapter 1, "Zooming through Change: The Role of Communication Technologies in Intergenerational Family Transitions during the COVID-19

Pandemic," Elizabeth B. Jones discusses how personal communication technologies offer some means for navigating intergenerational transitions during stay-at-home orders during the COVID-19 pandemic, while addressing the problem of technological ambivalence. Jones argues that although such technologies afford an acceptable means of communicating at a distance, they can also offer a false promise for maintaining closeness between family members, occasionally amplifying the feelings of loneliness rather than resolving them. Jones recommends cautious awareness about how new communication technologies interact with family communication patterns. Janie Harden Fritz argues in her chapter, "Narrative Wisdom: Implications from Literature for Family Communication Technology Engagement" (chapter 2), that narratives in literature provide useful guidance for how parents and grandparents ought to view technological change, considering its likely impact on family communication. Fritz borrows from a historic convention found in canonical literature to frame how families ought to navigate social change brought on by technological progress. Similarly, Paul Lucas discusses the potential for video game play as a new media form through which families can explore decision making and engage in mutual meaning making in chapter 3, "Rhetorical Constructions of the Reset: Video Games and Family Connections." According to Lucas, video games offer a virtual reality in which to explore different character interactions and provide family members a space to discuss failure and the possibility for second attempts. Lucas's chapter confirms the view that new media provide a recent iteration of what has always been the building block of family relations, storytelling. In chapter 4, "The Role of Communication and Information Technology in Health Information Seeking," Patty Wharton-Michael shares Jones's view that new communication technologies interact with family communication and have a distinct influence on the way families make decisions. Wharton-Michael uses the heightened discussion over COVID-19 vaccination to demonstrate that e-Health information searches and social media platforms like Facebook have complicated how family health decisions are made. The last chapter (chapter 5) in the *Continuity* section of the volume is called "With Great Power Comes Ethical Communication: Technology, Superheroes, and Family Conversations in Communication Ethics." Christina L. McDowell Marinchak and Tyrell J. Stewart-Harris provide a close reading of modern superhero stories in contemporary film and argue that the moral tales offer valuable ways for parents and children to engage contemporary media as conversational maps guiding conversation about ethical concerns.

The second section, *Interruption,* contains chapters whose underlying perspective interprets communication technologies as potentially disruptive and problematic to the family communication dynamic. While many of the authors in this section do not condemn novel communication technologies, they caution against a laissez-faire attitude toward the implementation of communication technologies in the family. They argue for increased thoughtfulness and mindfulness toward communication technology use and conscious choice-making due to technology's hegemonic nature.

Joel S. Ward, in chapter 6, "Cellular Television and the Reallocation of Familiar Attention," asks us to consider the importance of giving our attention to our families and to contemplate the deleterious effects of the divided attention encouraged by computer-mediated communication. He argues for attention to our obligation of giving attention to our parents, partners, and progeny. Anthony M. Wachs, in chapter 7, "Formative Media Consumption: Utilizing Media as Grammatical Foundations of Families," similarly discusses how both media form and the content of stories should be inspected when used in a family's communication. Wachs, echoing Postman's concern about the erosion of parents' roles as teachers, recommends applying a critical lens to new media. According to Wachs, proper criticism involves assessing both the medium and the content of the message, thus testing a story's quality for moral instruction while honing children's skills for critically reading media and messages. In chapter 8, "Motherhood and Loneliness: The Social Media Dilemma," Maryl R. McGinley and Jill K. Burk examine the connection between motherhood, feelings of loneliness, and social media usage. The authors see opportunity for connection to community in the mindful use of social spaces and the development of alloys for support.

The third section, *Transformation*, contains chapters grounded in viewpoints that understand communication technologies as transforming, and furthermore enhancing, family communication. The pieces in this section are optimistic about and hopeful for the ways in which communication technologies aid and, perhaps, make better, the family communication dynamic. They discuss ways in which communication technologies have opened doors or increased communication opportunities within the family system. Several of our authors in the following chapters suggest as much, noting that new technologies can support familiar organizations and ought to be used that way. For example, in her work, "'According to Science, This Is Who I Am': Personal Genome Testing and Adoption Reunions," Melissa Rizzo Weller describes the effect of new digital databases on communication between adopted children and their biological parents, finding that new information technologies open doors for potential reunification. In chapter 10, "Family Communication Disrupted by Incarceration and the Role of Technology: An Overview," Tiffany Petricini sees new communication technologies as a possible solution to significant disruptions to family life such as the incarceration of a parent. Petricini suggests that digital communication provides an avenue for parents to retain involvement in their children's lives while in prison. Moreover, Michelle Miller-Day, Anne E. Ray, Michael L. Hecht, and Rob Turrisi in chapter 11, "Strengthening Families through Web-Based Interventions: Developing and Assessing Feasibility of the 'Parenting Now!: Talking About Alcohol' Program," argue that families can be strengthened through web-based interventions for the reduction of harmful alcohol use by adolescents. Lastly, in chapter 12, "Embracing the Transition to Social Media in Parent–Teen Communication," Melissa Rizzo Weller, Angela M. Hosek, and Jessica Cherry argue for embracing the transition to social media as a way for parents and children to enhance communication, especially during children's teen years.

Taken as a whole, the scholarship in this edited volume raises many questions, challenges, and opportunities that novel communication technologies present to our interaction and communication within and around families. We are thankful for the work of our contributors. Their work asks and responds to thoughtful questions about family communication and the integration of communication technologies into our lives. We hope this volume provides theoretical and scholarly inspiration and presents an invitation for future thinking in family communication scholarship.

REFERENCES

Averil, Cameron. 1993. *The Mediterranean World in Late Antiquity.* London: Routledge.

Galvin, Kathleen. 2011. *Making Connections: Readings in Relational Communication.* (5th ed.) Oxford: Oxford University Press.

Galvin, Kathleen M., Dawn O. Braithwaite, and Carma L. Bylund. 2008. *Family Communication: Cohesion and Change* (7th ed.). Boston: Allyn & Bacon.

Lévi-Strauss, Claude. 1955/1992. *Triste Tropiques.* New York: Penguin Books.

McLuhan, Marshall. 1994. *Understanding Media.* Boston: First MIT Press.

Rousseau, Jean-Jacques. 1962. *The Social Contract.* New York: Hafner Publishing Co.

Trueman, Carl. 2020. *Rise and Triumph of the Modern Self.* Wheaton, IL: Crossway.

Turner, Lynn H., and Richard West. 2006. *The Family Communication Sourcebook.* Thousand Oaks, CA: Sage.

Turkle, Sherry. 2016. *Reclaiming Conversation: The Power of Talk in a Digital Age.* New York: Penguin Books.

SECTION I

Continuity

Chapter One

Zooming through Change

The Role of Communication Technologies in Intergenerational Family Transitions during the COVID-19 Pandemic

Elizabeth B. Jones

I sit in our living room on the overstuffed sofa, shifting my 38-weeks pregnant frame in an attempt to get comfortable. My husband and I are discussing the imminent birth of our fourth child with my parents. Who will ferry the older three kids to school, fix PBJs, and oversee bedtime once I go to the hospital to give birth, latch my new baby's mouth to my breast, and be flooded by a wave of hormones that paint life's contours in chiaroscuro?

My parents are unsure if they will be able to watch the big kids and encourage us to create a backup plan. We don't have family nearby, so this alternative will consist of a painstakingly assembled mélange of neighbors, babysitters, and friends who perform specific tasks at orchestrated times. On a rational level, I understand my parents' hesitation. I relax my face as I share that my partner and I can figure things out if they can't help.

But as sociologist Erving Goffman (1959) observed, within human interaction we both give information through our spoken words and "give off" information through our often inadvertent nonverbal cues. My suppressed emotions physiologically manifest and bubble through my composure. Tears sting the back of my eyes as I glance away from mom and dad. They can tell something is up.

"How do you really feel if we can't make it?" Dad asks.

The emotional dam bursts, sweeping away the competent, professional adult with a family of her own. In her place surfaces a young girl—my parents' only child.

"I feel abandoned," I respond instinctively, angry with myself for this admission of need.

I glance up to meet my parents' eyes. They too are shifting uncomfortably on their sofa, several states away. We are communing through a computer screen via video call. It is 2020, and we are in the midst of a global pandemic.

INTRODUCTION

The COVID-19 pandemic disrupted patterns of intergenerational communication common to many families, due in part to the increased risk of severe illness or death for older adults and those with underlying health conditions (CDC 2021). Thus, mundane but deeply meaningful embodied interactions previously taken for granted, such as an embrace between a grandparent and grandchild, suddenly became fraught with cost/benefit risk calculations. As the previous story of my birth plan illustrates, the pandemic also added additional layers of challenge to more complex familial negotiation practices that occur during times of transition.

Within this milieu, personal communication technologies (PCTs) emerged as lifelines that fostered intergenerational family relationship maintenance without the dangers of physical contact. As platforms used to facilitate two-way interpersonal communication, PCTs vary from one another along dimensions such as levels of synchrony, interactivity, provision of social cues and mobility (Baym 2015). Synchronous video call platforms like Zoom and FaceTime joined leaner media such as phone calls and text messages as family communication channels during the pandemic. My experiences attest that these technologies were not a panacea for relating. Rather, as media theorist Neil Postman (1992, 4–5) observed, "Every technology is both a burden and a blessing; not either-or, but this-and-that." This chapter, therefore, adopts an autoethnographic lens to explore both the opportunities and constraints provided by PCTs for intergenerational family connection during times of transition, specifically during the pandemic.

Throughout this chapter, communication is understood as an "…emergent creative activity through which human social reality is constantly being re-created, affirmed, repaired and changed" (Delia and Grossberg 1977, 36). Further, I adopt Braithwaite, Suter, and Floyd's (2018, 4) position that communication is "…the central process by which families are literally talked into being, that is, how families are co-constructed, negotiated, and legitimated in discourse." Family is broadly conceptualized here as persons who are connected by marriage, blood, or commitment for a long period and who share a common sense of identity (Galvin, Braithwaite, and Bylund 2015). More specifically, I examine the interactions fostered by PCTs among multiple generations of my extended family network. This chapter therefore: 1) discusses the autoethnographic approach adopted, 2) provides a brief overview of intergenerational family transition processes, and 3) probes the complex ways in which PCTs functioned to support, hinder, and catalyze my family's intergenerational transitions during the COVID-19 pandemic. Throughout the chapter, I couple narrative vignettes with relevant research literature for explanatory insight.

AN AUTOETHNOGRAPHIC APPROACH

Autoethnography is ". . . an autobiographical genre of academic writing that draws on and analyzes or interprets the lived experience of the author" (Poulos 2021, 4) in order to illuminate human cultural experience in all of its richness and complexity (Chang 2013; Poulos 2021). Because communication among multiple generations is multifaceted, an autoethnographic approach may be especially valuable within family communication research (Adams and Manning 2015; Berry and Adams 2016). Scholars from varying academic orientations have adopted autoethnography, including but not limited to social-scientific, humanistic, critical, and artistic perspectives (Adams and Manning 2015). Because of the wide applicability of this method, the form of the final autoethnography may manifest as a social science report, short story, poetry, or some another product (Andrew 2017; Chang 2013; Ellis 1999). I ground the autoethnography of this chapter within a social-scientific framework aligned with the interpretive tradition within the field of communication, which values a deep understanding of the lived communicative experiences of persons (Littlejohn 1989). When approaching autoethnography from a social-scientific vantage point it is valuable to report on research methods when possible, which include considerations of topic selection, autoethnographic data collection, "meaning making with collected data," and writing (Chang 2013, 119). Although these methodological considerations are separated for clarity of discussion, in actuality the autoethnographic process is highly iterative, fluid, and nonlinear (Chang 2013).

The ambivalent emotions I experienced in response to the transitions that occurred within my family during the pandemic prompted this chapter's topic. Technologies emerged as key agents of both continuity and change, underscoring the centrality of communication in family relationships during times of transition (Braithwaite, Suter, and Floyd 2018). Autoethnographic writing emerged as a vehicle to make sense of these experiences within my life story and to ground them within a larger cultural context. This storytelling impulse has been identified by autoethnographer Christopher Poulos (2008, 20) as "a call of conscience that cannot be ignored." In response to this impulse, I collected multiple forms of autoethnographic data simultaneously that included recollections, diary entries, photos, and text messages. I specifically focused on the role of PCTs from March 2020 to March 2021 within intergenerational familial interactions across four generations of my family of origin—my maternal grandparents in their 80s, my parents in their 60s, me and my spouse in our 30s, and our four children ages 0–11. Given the importance of the researcher's subjectivity in autoethnography (Muncey 2010), I engaged in systematic reflexive introspection while assembling this data (Poulos 2021), which involved adopting a posture of mindfulness toward the topic (Berry 2016) and using writing as a tool of inquiry (Poulos 2021). I noted emotions that I experienced, such as discomfort from using a style of writing stripped of the "objectivity" present in my other academic pursuits.

Meaning was made from this assemblage of data by holistically examining the bricoles of autobiographical material—"the odds and ends, the bits left over, the set of unrelated or oddly related objects of data" (Harper 1987, 74). There is no prescriptive approach to meaning-making in autoethnography (Chang 2013), and I drew upon my qualitative training in grounded theory (e.g., Charmaz 2014) for insight. I examined the individual data fragments inductively and noted overarching themes that emerged. Points of connection coalesced around three potential outcomes of communication technology use in my family during times of transition: support, hindrance, and catalyst. I acknowledge that in sharing narratives that explore these three themes, "… telling a story is rarely a benign activity" (Andrew 2017, 6). This ethical onus emerges because others' stories—people whom I love—intersect with my own. Although autoethnographies may heal and transform (Poulos 2008), they also may harm those revealed therein (Andrew 2017). Thus, to the best of my ability, I have adopted practices of relational ethics, contextuality, reflexivity, and intuitionism to mitigate potential harm (Andrew 2017). Ultimately, however, this story privileges my perspective as the authorial voice, and each of my family members may hold a different view (Poulos 2012).

INTERGENERATIONAL FAMILY TRANSITIONS

I briefly admire the botanical designs stamped in gold foil on the cover of my white journal and absentmindedly run my hand across its embossing. I gently tug the thin black satin ribbon sewn into the journal's binding to open to a blank page. I only have a few minutes to write before the kids will need me again, but I feel compelled to chronicle this moment so that I will remember it. Even though I'm 36 years old, I still address my journals the same way I did when I was six—as a sort of nonjudgmental and sympathetic friend who I keep in the loop:

> *Wow! So much has changed since my last entry. At some point in the near future I'll try to fill you in. First news is that I'm pregnant! Currently almost 13 weeks. We should find out the sex of the baby this week. Second, we are currently in the midst of a global pandemic related to Coronavirus—COVID-19. We're doing everything on Zoom...*

One of the kids yells for me to come help them connect to their online classroom. I pinch the spine of the journal, snapping its covers shut, and go.

A Life Course Perspective

Change—as my journal entry captured in miniature—is a constant in families. The life course perspective (Elder 1994), combined with insights from relationship research and intergenerational communication scholarship, is instructive in illuminating the nature and process of such change across time. This approach conceives of multigenerational families as dynamic collections of interdependent and linked individuals who function within a given sociohistorical context (Bengston and Allen 1993; Hutchinson 2021). The life course is conceptualized as "a sequence of socially defined events and roles that the individual enacts over time" from conception to death (Giele and Elder 1998, 22). In this framework, "the family as a social group provides meaning to events; through the perceptions of its members it defines as a reality, enduring and continuing over time, passed on through the lineage" (Bengston and Allen 1993, 479). The family is therefore the "primary area for experiencing the world" (Hutchinson 2021, 8), which was evidenced in my journal as I first announced my pregnancy and then situated that announcement within the context of a global pandemic.

Several life course concepts illuminate change processes; namely, transitions, life events, trajectories, and turning points. *Transitions* occur within the life course when one experiences a distinct and bounded change in role or status over time (Elder, Kirkpatrick Johnson, and Crosnoe 2003). Many life transitions are family related, such as those emerging from births and deaths, marriages and separations, and are often age-graded (e.g., new roles that emerge following graduation or retirement) (Hutchinson 2021). A transition is typically initiated by a *life event*, which is a significant occurrence that signals a relatively abrupt change to the status quo (Alwin 2012); for example, the loss of a spouse. A series of transitions constitute a given life's *trajectory*, defined as a "long-term pattern of stability and change" (Hutchinson 2021, 13). Throughout the life course, most persons experience multiple, overlapping trajectories in different spheres, such as health, work, relationships, and family (Elder 1998). A *turning point* is a life event that alters, or even reverses, a given trajectory. Turning points are often only recognized as significant change agents retrospectively, as persons make sense of life events. For instance, a particular conversation between an adult child and their parent may seem unremarkable in the moment, but upon subsequent reflection emerge as a watershed moment in relational growth or deterioration.

Dyadic relational turning points and trajectories in particular have amassed a significant amount of research within communication scholarship. Although the preponderance of studies have focused on fluctuations in closeness over time in romantic relationships (Baxter and Buchanan 2015), the approach has also proven fruitful when applied to other kinds of familial connections (Sahlstein Parcell 2013). For example, studies have examined dimensions of connectedness over time in adult child–parent relationships (Golish 2000), adult child–parent relationships during the birth of the first grandchild (Dun 2010; Dun and Sangster 2013; Dun and Sears 2017), and long-distance grandchild-grandparent relationships (Bangerter and Waldron 2014). These studies taken together confirm the dynamic nature of family relationships and the variability in potential trajectory shifts prompted by any given turning point.

Notably, transitions, life events, trajectories, and turning points may occur at any level (e.g., individual, dyadic, group) within a multigenerational family. Due to the interconnectedness of family members, a shift in any one individual's life may influence the collective in dynamic and sometimes conflicting ways. For example, an adult child may feel caught between caring for the needs of their growing children and their aging parent. Further adding to these complex undercurrents are potential challenges associated with familial intergenerational communication in general. As Giles and Gasiorek (2011, 233) noted, "across contexts, intergenerational communication is often characterized as dissatisfying or otherwise problematic." Research literature from a communication accommodation theory perspective (Giles 1973) identifies incongruent perceptions of appropriate communicative accommodation within an intergenerational interaction as a central source of dissatisfaction. Accommodation is defined as "attempts to match or meet the needs, desires, or expectations of a conversational partner's communicative preferences" (Soliz and Warner Colaner 2018, 78). Overaccomodation by younger adults of older adults is particularly prevalent and has been identified within the family (Giles and Gasiorek 2011). In this scenario, younger persons—typically with good intentions but working from implicit ageist stereotypes of mental and physical decline—engage in overly familiar and simplistic intergenerational talk (Giles and Gasiorek 2011). Older adults tend to perceive such "secondary baby talk" as patronizing (Giles and Gasiorek 2011). Both over-and under-accommodation are associated with suboptimal outcomes in intergenerational family discussions of major life events (e.g., Scott and Caughlin 2015). Further, younger adults may feel uncomfortable when older family members share painful self-disclosures during talk. Painful self-disclosures are revelations of "relatively intimate, negative information," on potentially sensitive topics such as loneliness or poor health (Giles and Gasiorek 2011, 240).

As I reflect upon the intergenerational transitions occurring within my own family during the first year of the COVID-19 pandemic, the concepts presented thus far add shape and form to the collection of events and emotions I experienced. As previously noted, the life course perspective emphasizes the dynamic interplay between the family and the larger societal environment. Within my family, the pandemic served both as a primary source of change at individual and familial levels and as an influence that colored transitions already in process. New changes introduced by the pandemic derived from social distancing efforts that reconfigured work, parenting, extended family interaction, and social engagement (McClain et al. 2021). In March 2020, the institution where I am a professor moved all courses online, so I began teaching from home. My husband was already working from home, and had been working remotely for a number of years prior to the pandemic. Our three children's schools moved their instruction online. My husband and I created an on-an-hour/off-an-hour childcare schedule so we could attempt to supervise their schooling and complete our work. In addition to these pandemic-precipitated changes, several family transitions occurred from March 2020 to March 2021 that were not caused by coronavirus but were thoroughly influenced by it. These changes included my grandfather's diagnosis of Alzheimer's disease and my fourth child's birth.

PCTs became a central means by which family connections were maintained despite social distance. Indeed, approximately 40% of Americans reported using the internet or digital technologies in "new or different ways compared with before the beginnings of the coronavirus outbreak" (McClain et al. 2021, 7). In my own family, social distancing prompted the adoption of new communication technologies and practices, such as the use of a popular messaging app by my children to communicate directly with their grandparents. However, the pandemic primarily intensified my extended family's preexisting technology usage routines. Because my extended family is geographically distributed, we have long used multiple channels such as phone and video calls, text messages, and social media to remain connected. Thus, my parents (in their 60s) and my maternal grandmother (in her 80s) were already conversant with a wide range of personal communication technologies and used them actively for keeping in touch. Taipale (2019) argued that within economically developed societies, this kind of "digital family" is common. Further, the technological disruptions of the pandemic acted upon our preexisting family culture. As Wilding (2006, 133) noted in their examination of information and communication technology (ICT) use in transnational families:

> New layers of ICTs do contribute to a stronger capacity to construct "connected presence." However, it is worth commenting on the continuities that such "connected presence" tended to serve. . . . [E]ach new ICT was incorporated into already existing expectations and practices of communication in very familiar ways. For example . . . parent–child relationships that were described as intimate prior to email remained intimate after email was introduced.

Given the intricacies of intergenerational change discussed thus far, I next explore the ways in which PCTs intersected with my family's preexisting relationships in order to support, hinder, and catalyze transitions during the COVID-19 pandemic.

COMMUNICATION TECHNOLOGIES AND INTERGENERATIONAL TRANSITIONS

I dig out a bucket from a pile in our garage, set it on the driveway, squirt in some dish soap, and fill it with water from the hose. I toss a handful of old rags and sponges into the iridescent bubbles and ask my four-year-old son if he wants to wash his "motorcycle," which is actually his small, green balance bike. Pandemic lockdowns shuttered his preschool, and although the teacher holds periodic Zoom "circle times" for the children to sing songs and read stories, an entirely online preschool curriculum is untenable. The teacher does her best to support parents and emails us handouts of hands-on learning activities to do at home—such as "bike washing." I do agree that cleaning things is a practical life skill. So here we are.

My son loves this project, and is engaged for a good 20 minutes. From my experience, a preschooler being involved with something for 20 minutes is roughly equivalent to an adult being in a state of deep flow for three hours. As he scrubs his motorcycle I look on, experiencing multiple physical and emotional sensations thrumming in the background of our interaction—anxiety about the mounting work waiting for me on my laptop, joy in this sweet and sacred time with my son, physical discomfort from pregnancy, a deep weariness. I want to mark this unremarkable moment and share it with someone who cares about the domestic, ordinary, everyday outlines of our lives. A witness to all of this and to how hard I'm trying. I snap a quick photo of my son in action and text it to my dad. A moment later, I receive a response:

Awww! He is so adorable! Tell him Papaw said great work!

We've been seen.

Support for Family Transitions

PCTs primarily functioned to support intergenerational transitions during pandemic-induced social distance indirectly by facilitating relationship maintenance. As the story of my son washing his bicycle illustrated, PCTs afforded the easy sharing of "communication that demonstrates ongoing attention to the relationship" (Baym 2015, 154). These small snippets of technologically mediated communication tended not to specifically discuss or problem-solve family transitions (though sometimes they did). Rather, these messages worked collectively to strengthen a sense of family solidarity, which in turn provided emotional ballast to weather challenging circumstances. The constellation of PCTs used by families allows them to develop what Wilding (2006) termed *virtual intimacies*; that is, the use of PCTs to transcend physical separations and to feel together, albeit temporarily. I thus next present key findings regarding the role of PCTs in familial relationship maintenance and explore two examples of mediated relationship maintenance in the support of transitions within my family: skipped-generation communication and the reconfiguration of multigenerational rituals.

A consistent finding on PCT use in relationships is that close relational partners tend to use face-to-face communication in concert with more than one PCT to maintain said relationship (Baym 2015). A number of concepts in the literature aim to capture this phenomenon, including *media multiplexity* (Haythornthwaite 2005), *mixed-media relationships* (Parks 2017) and *multimodal relationships* (Hall 2020). Evidence suggests that when new PCTs emerge, families incorporate them additively as channel options alongside earlier technologies (Caughlin and Wang 2020), and that frequent communication using multiple channels tends to be associated with relational closeness (Caughlin and Sherabi 2013). In choosing which of these PCTs to select, Baym (2015, 158) noted that "people divide their media use within a relationship based in part on their goals for that interaction." The varying affordances of phone calls, text messages, and video calls, for example, may make each more or less suitable for particular family purposes. Text messaging and video calls were two specific PCTs that were particularly important for relationship maintenance within my family during the pandemic.

Text messaging served at least two related purposes for us during lockdown. First, the mobility of smartphones enabled the regular exchange of messages that established a "connected presence" for my family (Licoppe 2004). Research literature suggests that this sense of constant connectivity can promote feelings of "emotional connection and psychological propinquity" (Tong and Walther 2011, 112). Although the substance of any given text message may seem inconsequential or even trivial, the phatic communication that occurs has "an important social function in establishing, maintaining and renewing bonds between interlocutors" (Taipale 2019, 95). Second, messaging proved useful in the more instrumental function of micro-coordinating daily actions and encounters among family members (Caughlin and Wang 2020; Ling and Lai 2016). For example, during the pandemic lockdown, my parents, grandparents and I would often use text messaging to coordinate phone or video calls.

Somewhat differently, synchronous video calls as enabled by platforms such as Zoom, FaceTime and Skype provided my family with rich cues—contextual, visual and auditory—by which to interpret our communicative encounters (Baym 2015, 10). Although Zoom specifically came to the fore during the pandemic as a valuable "stand-in" for face-to-face social contact (McClain et al. 2021), these PCTs had already received scholarly attention for their role in familial relationship for some time prior. For example, video calls have been found to be particularly important in communication among transnational families (e.g., Madianou and Miller 2012a). Video calls in grandparent–young grandchild relationships have also received research attention, due in part to the increased prevalence of long-distance grandparent-grandchild relationships (Taipale 2019). The visual nature of video calls tend to make them more engaging to and suited for young children than voice-only phone calls (Seares 2018). Thus, these calls were already a regular feature of everyday life for many families prior to the pandemic—mine included (Seares 2018). In terms of the substance of such calls, grandparent-grandchild video calls are usually arranged as "talking-heads" on each party's respective screen (Licoppe and Morel 2012). During calls grandparents and grandchildren engage in activities such as informal, collaboratively produced "shows" in which the grandchild displays an object or portion of the environment to the grandparent (Seares 2018). During the pandemic, grandparent-grandchild video calls generated significant grandparent enjoyment, and were associated with increased closeness in the relationship (Kakulla et al. 2021).

The ease and convenience of text messaging merged with the richness of video calls in a popular children's messaging app, Facebook Kids, which was adopted by my two elementary-aged children during the pandemic. My children used the app to engage in skipped-generation communication (i.e., direct interaction without an intermediary) with my parents through a messaging group the children dubbed "The Cool Club." The use of this messaging app developed within a preexisting long-distance grandparent-grandchild

PCT ecosystem that frequently used PCTs for relationship maintenance (e.g., Skype calls, phone updates). However, the skipped-generation communication—as necessitated by pandemic separation and enabled by the app's playful features—fostered a unique relational culture among them. The asynchronous flow of messages included GIFs, inside jokes, and photos taken by the children of their daily lives. Synchronous video calls also occurred directly through the app, often overlaid to the kids' delight with funny filters such as a computer-generated cat face. Through this app, my parents provided important emotional support for my children. This was in part due in part to the fresh perspective they brought to tense situations such as sibling conflicts arising from my nuclear family's close physical proximity as well as to the fact that they (almost) always answered the kids' video call requests and thus were accessible and available. This supportive communication was bidirectional, with the kids frequently messaging encouragements such as "love you" and "miss you so much" to my parents. The children also used the app instrumentally to coordinate family communication via other PCTs; for example, scheduling a phone call with my mom for math homework help or setting up a whole-family FaceTime to share pregnancy updates with my parents. Though the early pandemic experience was challenging for my children, the communication with my parents via "The Cool Club" was a welcome respite.

Last, PCTs helped to maintain family solidarity through the reconfiguration of family rituals, which involve symbolic words and actions enacted in order to "bestow protected time and space to stop and reflect on life's transformations" (Imber-Black and Roberts 1998, 3). For many Americans during the pandemic, family rituals as significant as weddings and funerals were transformed into virtual interactions (McClain et al. 2021, 12). Within my own family, rituals surrounding the arrival of my fourth child as well as family holidays were reimagined. For example, our pregnancy announcement to my parents occurred through Skype and involved displaying an early ultrasound photo in front of our laptop's webcam. Further, because I am an only child, my parents usually travel to our home to celebrate Christmas morning with us. However, in 2020—our new baby's first Christmas—they instead virtually participated in our festivities through the laptop we positioned in our living room. The children seated themselves on the floor in front of the laptop so their grandparents could watch them unwrap gifts. After opening the present, they would hold it up in front of the webcam for further excited examination and exclamation. These virtual rites were bittersweet in their simultaneous concretization of distance and unity.

My iPhone alerts me of an incoming text message in its staccato tri-tone. I glance down and see the message is from Grammy, my maternal grandmother. She's sorry she's missed my call, but she's been busy with Boppa. She's been on FaceTime with Boppa's doctor about the acceleration of his Alzheimer's. Boppa is my grandfather—a kind and handsome man who was born in a tent during the Great Depression as the third-youngest of eight children. He went on to serve in the Korean War, put himself through college, and provide for his wife and three children. He is a man of faith who dresses to the nines, sings like an angel, and dotes on his grandchildren and great-grandchildren. I've grown up hearing the story of the time when, on a family vacation, he was the only adult who could soothe me in the middle of the night as a feverish infant. He positioned the weight of my tiny body on his chest in just such a way that the strain on my infected lungs lessened and my labored breathing eased. I've adored him ever since.

I've been trying to reach Gram to see if they need groceries. Older adults have been advised to avoid shopping in stores. Even if shopping wasn't risky, Gram can't leave Boppa alone, and she doesn't really have anyone who can help her. Although I live several hours away from my grandparents, and can't provide the day-in, day-out support Gram needs, my husband and I can order groceries for them on a delivery app. Our clicks will manifest real food on their doorstep—a mundane miracle. It feels like the very least we can do. It doesn't feel like enough. She eventually calls and shares a Spartan shopping list. I add the requested groceries to the virtual cart plus a few more items on my own to pad the list's austere edges. Many stores are having trouble keeping meat, cleaning supplies, paper products and other staples in stock, so I'm unsure of what will actually arrive. I text her later:

> *"Did you get everything?"*
>
> *"Yes we did. Got a big ham bread and cheese. Thank you so much. You know I remember having ration stamps and due to my parents I didn't even know we were in a crisis!"*

I wonder if my own kids will eventually send such a message to their grandchildren about what we're experiencing now.

Hindrance to Family Transitions

Although PCTs served to indirectly support family transitions during the pandemic through their facilitation of relationship maintenance, they also at times proved unsatisfactory in coping with the more challenging and complex facets of change. These hindrances arose for my family from PCTs' mediated nature, usage challenges, and enablement of painful protection. The nature of PCTs as mediated and therefore qualitatively different from face-to-face communication became evident during family transitions that required the provision of instrumental support. As illustrated by the vignette of my grandparents provided previously, Wilding (2006, 134–135) noted:

> Although "connected presence" gives the appearance of the annihilation of distance, it can also result in increased guilt and anxiety when the distance becomes evident again through tragedy. The very real limitations of distance are also clear when someone becomes ill and requires personal care. In some circumstances, a telephone call or email is simply not sufficient to show care for kin in need.

Along these lines, during the first year of the pandemic my grandfather suffered a medical crisis from which we thought we not he would never recover. No family members were allowed to be at the hospital with him. Even if they had been permitted, my parents did not feel it would be safe to travel. My mom called me through tears saying that she never thought she would be absent when one of her parents died. Thankfully, my grandfather rallied, and my parents and I were subsequently able to see him again face-to-face. However, these experiences emphasized the potential inadequacy of PCTs when tangible support is required.

A distinctly different type of family transition that highlighted the mediated nature of PCTs involved the sharing of good news. Specifically, during my pregnancy some celebratory rituals felt flattened or were absent altogether. For example, prenatal genetic testing revealed early in the pregnancy that the biological sex of the baby was male. My oldest child was excited to share this news with their grandparents and arranged a Skype call to tell them. However, once we connected one of my parents informed us that other parent was too busy working to join the conversation. After my oldest shared the update, the available parent responded that the news was in line with their predictions. The entire call lasted only a few minutes. My parents were assuredly thrilled about their new grandchild, regardless of its biological sex. Yet the interaction felt dampened. My disappointment stemmed not from the substance of the conversation but rather from the disconnect between my expectations for and my parents' enactment of celebratory support (McCullough and Burleson 2012) through this digital channel. Although I had hoped that updates provided on this important life event would be greeted with enthusiasm and amplification, the intermediary of a screen coupled with the stress of the pandemic instead muted communal joy. Indeed, as previously alluded to in the discussion of reconfigured family rituals, PCTs sometimes dampened celebration by highlighting physical separation. Although counterintuitive, rich media such as video calls may particularly emphasize distance. As Hall et al. (2021, 13) found, participants who used video calls for relationship maintenance in the early phases of the pandemic were lonelier than those who did not, perhaps because "…the embodied reminders of an absent loved one on screen may exacerbate, rather than alleviate, loneliness."

A second way that in which PCTs acted as a hindrance to family transitions involved challenges associated with fully integrating PCTs into my nuclear family's daily digital ecosystem. As previously noted, PCTs afforded relatively convenient tools for relationship maintenance among multiple generations of my family. However, further infusing the use of these PCT into daily lives during a time of stress was sometimes challenging. For example, although my children often wanted to video call with my parents, sometimes they were preoccupied or not in the mood. This tendency seemed to increase as the pandemic dragged on, spurred in part by the lack of new experiences for my children to share. The children also sometimes unsurprisingly acted like kids during video calls and bickered with one another or goofed around instead of engaging in conversation. These behaviors placed my spouse and me in the uncomfortable position of feeling a need to mouth admonishments in hushed whispers off-screen during video calls in an attempt to enforce intergenerational respect. As Strouse et al. (2021, 554) noted in their study of grandparent-grandchild video call use during the pandemic, "Because of the need to manage video chats and direct the interactions . . . parents and grandparents sometimes found them emotionally taxing, especially when children appeared disengaged despite the adults' best efforts." Further, my nuclear family experienced what has been termed "Zoom fatigue"; namely, a weariness that emerged from the prolonged use of video calls across multiple domains of life (McClain et al. 2021). Given that we engaged in work, school, worship, and socialization via Zoom, this experience was unsurprising. Thus, though I desired to maintain intergenerational connections via video calls, at times these technologies themselves felt draining and stifled a desire to engage.

A third way that PCTs hindered family transitions involved these channels' enablement of what I term *painful protection.* Although I present this concept here in its three dimensions as a hindrance to family transitions, this conversational coping strategy was complex in its benefits and drawbacks. First, painful protection provided the resiliency to use PCTs for relationship maintenance despite their challenges because of a recognition of my extended family's mutual commitment to shield one another from the virus. Even though this physical distance often proved to be emotionally and instrumentally difficult, we all were altruistically protecting one another. Second, painful protection manifested when, during conversations, I avoided certain challenging questions related to transitions (e.g., if my parents were going to travel to assist with childcare while my husband and I were at the hospital) or concealed personal struggles I was encountering in order to prevent causing further stress to my parents and grandparents. In this scenario, I tried to protect my loved ones from pain. I believe that my parents and grandparents also avoided sharing potentially troubling information with me for the same reasons. Although this strategy was valuable for preserving daily functioning and reducing conflicts, it also enervated mutuality.

Third, painful protection transpired when I avoided intergenerational communication via PCTs altogether. In this instance, I protected myself from emotional pain and energy depletion. For example, I was frustrated when I would share a struggle and a family member would respond not by validating my challenges, but rather by sharing their own. A lack of emotional margin for all of us resulting from challenging circumstances made it difficult to respond to each other's' painful self-disclosures (Giles and Gasiorek 2011). For example, frequent expressions of the bleakness of the pandemic by family members were understandable but became taxing on repeat. Thus, at times it was easier to avoid unsatisfying support by temporarily refraining from PCT use. Although facets of painful protection could certainly present in face-to-face interactions, the curated nature of conversation via PCTs eased this kind of mutual concealment and revelation.

It is early morning, and I'm half awoken from sleep by the realization that I'm lying in something damp. Have I had an accident? I'm a day or two shy of being 12 weeks pregnant with my fourth child. Pregnancy has a habit of stripping a mother's body of polite delicacy, so I wouldn't be shocked. I groggily touch the sheets to confirm my hypothesis and my fingers meet slick viscosity. My eyes widen as I bolt upright. I'm lying in a pool of blood. I quickly wake my husband who is asleep next to me.

"Oh my God, oh my God, oh my God," I repeat in shock and prayer.

"I'm having a miscarriage."

I call my midwife through tears. She is calm and kind and tells me we need to gather more information to understand what is happening before jumping to the worst-case scenario. She doesn't want to send anyone to the hospital now because stay-at-home orders have begun today, but it can't be helped—I need to go to the obstetric emergency department immediately. Because we don't live near family, my husband calls our friend to watch our older three children. I sit heavily on the glider in our bedroom and call my parents. They immediately notice the stifled sob and ask me what's wrong. I share my dreaded expectation with them and sense that they are also experiencing my pain through the tripartite genetic, emotional, and spiritual tether that binds us together. They offer words of comfort. I don't have the emotional energy to say more than a few words so I hand the phone to my spouse to further relate our prescribed plan. We drop our children off and head to the hospital, where

I am examined and monitored for hours. I finally see the baby moving actively on the ultrasound screen, its heart a strong, pulsing flicker. They don't know why I hemorrhaged—we're told it's just one of those things that happens sometimes. It could very well happen again. But the baby is fine. I am profoundly relieved, bone tired, terrified this will happen again, and hopeful we didn't catch the new virus at the hospital.

Catalyst for Family Transitions

As previously discussed, PCTs interacted with the pandemic context to both support and hinder family transitions. However, PCTs also catalyzed new family transitions by paradoxically initiating shifts in both intergenerational distance and closeness. First, the social distance that necessitated the exclusive use of PCTs forced my nuclear family to find our own path forward in situations such as my pregnancy complication without the tangible support of geographically proximal kin. This lack of instrumental support was challenging and indicative of larger societal trends and shortfalls. However, the distance from intergenerational family members afforded by the selective nature of PCTs also allowed for a disruption in normal communication patterns in a manner that enabled us to cast our nuclear family's trajectory in a manner aligned with our values. Thus, in contrast to the preponderance of communication literature that frames family distancing as uniformly negative (Scharp and Dorrance Hall 2019), in this instance distance brought opportunities for fresh perspective and reflection. Indeed, this renewed perspective both included firmer boundaries related to family communication than existed pre-pandemic and invited continued interaction and emotional connection among our family's multiple generations.

Second, although PCTs are not relationally impoverished communication channels, they do differ from the embodiment of face-to-face interaction (Baym 2015). The use of PCTs was necessary during the pandemic and often beneficial, but the ache to hug a loved one remained. After I was fully vaccinated against COVID-19 in March 2021, I went to visit my grandfather. The appreciation of this embodied encounter was intense. Although he didn't remember me due to his Alzheimer's disease, he knew that he loved me and was happy to see me. I sat next to him holding his hand for a long time, not needing to say anything, and cried happy tears.

IMPLICATIONS

As an autoethnography situated within the interpretive communication tradition, the previous explorations are solely my own (Poulos, 2012), and are not intended to be generalized. Indeed, each individual's experience of PCT use during the COVID-19 pandemic for family transitions likely varied considerably. For example, many families experienced highly stressful and traumatic life events during the pandemic, such as job loss, extreme social isolation, COVID-19 "long hauler" symptoms, or the death of a loved one (Yong 2021). Further, positionality within historically marginalized communities tended to exacerbate the frequency or acuteness of such stressors (Miller 2020). The manner in which PCTs potentially facilitated family transitions also likely varied according to issues of media access, affordability and literacy within families (Madianou and Miller 2012b). Further, families may have faced conflicts when attempting to adopt PCTs as family communication channels. For example, Ivan and Nimrod (2021) found that intergenerational tensions emerged within families when older adults asked their adult children for technological assistance. Interestingly, those tensions dissipated when the older adult instead requested help from a grandchild (Ivan and Nimrod 2012). Last, the role of PCTs in family transitions was likely also strongly influenced by the preexisting culture and structure of the specific family. Although particularities may shape a given family's experience of PCT use in intergenerational change, this autoethnography suggests several potential areas of exploration for future investigation that may be applicable to a variety of family situations. Specifically, autoethnography as a valuable approach to family communication, the variability of PCT processes in family transitions, and the benefits of a life course perspective will be discussed.

First, I echo other scholars (e.g., Adams and Manning 2015; Berry and Adams 2016) in their affirmation of the benefits of autoethnography in family communication research, as it is well-suited to explore complex family communication processes. Further, the writing of this account has also provided personally meaningful space wherein to reflect upon a challenging time. My experience aligns with several related bodies of literature that suggest the benefits of storytelling for sense-making, including expressive writing (e.g., Pennebaker and Smyth 2016), autobiography (e.g., Birren and Svensson 2013), life stories (e.g., McAdams and McLean 2013) and reminiscence (e.g., Armstrong 2017). Thus, autoethnography as both a process and a product (Adams and Manning 2015, 354) may provide rich, socially situated explanations of personally meaningful communication experiences.

Second, afforded by autoethnography's ability to capture the gradations of complex communicative phenomena, this exploration revealed that technology use within my family context was neither uniformly good nor bad. Instead, PCTs emerged as supports, hindrances, and catalysts to family transitions. Although I separated these three themes for clarity of discussion, in reality they were co-occurring, interactive, and sometimes contradictory. The multiplicity of PCT outcomes contrasts with common cultural scripts related to new technology that are "formulaic and hyperbolic" and that cast PCTs as either a hero or a villain (Baym 2015, 32). This exploration thus suggests that adopting a wider lens to examine the complex factors that may influence PCT outcomes in families may help to explain some of the ambivalence reflected in relevant research literature. For example, Shufford et al. (2021) examined the effects of computer-mediated communication (CMC) on positive affect during the early phases of COVID-19 pandemic and found that greater frequency of CMC mediated the relationship between social distancing and positive affect. They concluded that CMC may be a fruitful way to engage with others despite social distance (Shufford et al. 2021). Conversely, Hall et al. (2021) reported that the use of video calls during the pandemic was associated with higher levels of loneliness, and Noone et al. (2020) noted that little current evidence suggests video calling ameliorates loneliness for older adults. Further, McClain et al. (2021, 13) observed that "Even as tech helped some to stay connected, a quarter of Americans say they feel less close to close family members now compared with before the pandemic." Thus, when suggesting PCTs to families as a means of connection, it appears important to note the complexities of potential outcomes rather than to make blanket recommendations to accept or reject these channels.

Third, this autoethnography adopted a life course perspective as a lens by which to understand intergenerational family transitions. As other scholars have also suggested (e.g., Sahlstein Parcell 2013), the communication discipline would benefit from attending to dynamic change across time. As the life course perspective details, each of us lives within a stream of time that is shaped by historic and social forces, such as the COVID-19 pandemic. Within the larger societal context, intergenerational families live inextricably linked lives that influence each other's subsequent life trajectories over time. Within this autoethnography, several linkages between PCTs and key life span concepts emerged. First, the widespread use of PCTs as a primary means of connection was necessitated by the social influence of the COVID-19 pandemic. However, COVID-19-related PCT use operated within the framework of our intergenerational family's prior media use and general family culture. Second, due to the linkages among lives, dyadic communication facilitated by PCTs—such as between my children and parents or me and my grandparents—influenced the communicative trajectory of the family as a whole. Although a few studies have examined the role of PCTs in dyadic family relationships' turning points and trajectories (e.g., Bangerter and Waldron

2014), it would be worthwhile to explore if similar concepts can be captured within larger family systems.

A final concept related to the life course involves the role of human agency in positive growth and development (Hutchinson 2021). Similarly, the social shaping of technology perspective (Baym 2015) reminds us that the effects of PCT use are not deterministic; rather, although the technological and social features of a given PCT are consequential, *how* we adopt and use them matters. Thus, in closing, we are capable of acknowledging the constraints of PCTs during times of transition even as we foster their opportunities for intergenerational family connection.

REFERENCES

Adams, Tony E., and Jimmie Manning. 2015. "Autoethnography and Family Research." *Journal of Family Theory & Review* 7 (4): 350–66. https://doi.org/10.1111/jftr.12116.

Alwin, Duane F. 2012. "Integrating Varieties of Life Course Concepts." *Journals of Gerontology. Series B, Psychological Sciences and Social Sciences* 67 (2): 206–20. https://doi.org/10.1093/geronb/gbr146.

Andrew, Stephen. 2017. *Searching for an Autoethnographic Ethic*. New York: Routledge.

Armstrong, Catherine. 2017. "Combining Reminiscence Therapy with Oral History to Intervene in the Lives of Isolated Older People." *Counselling Psychology Review* 32 (1): 26–32.

Bangerter, Lauren R., and Vincent R. Waldron. 2014. "Turning Points in Long Distance Grandparent-Grandchild Relationships." *Journal of Aging Studies* 29: 88–97. https://doi.org/10.1016/j.jaging.2014.01.004.

Baxter, Leslie. A. and Lauren-Ashley Buchanan. 2015. "Relational Turning Points." In *The International Encyclopedia of Interpersonal Communication*, edited by Charles R. Berger, Michael E. Roloff, Steve R. Wilson, James Price Dillard, John Caughlin, and Denise Solomon, 1469–1473. Hoboken, NJ: Wiley-Blackwell. https://doi.org/10.1002/9781118540190.wbeic018.

Baym, Nancy K. 2015. *Personal Connections in the Digital Age, Second Edition*. Malden, MA: Polity.

Bengtson, Verne L., and Katherine R. Allen. 1993. "The Life Course Perspective Applied to Families over Time." In *Sourcebook of Family Theories and Methods: A Contextual Approach*, edited by Pauline G. Boss, William J. Doherty, Ralph LaRossa, Walter R. Schumm, and Suzanne K. Steinmetz, 469–504. New York: Plenum Press. https://doi.org/10.1007/978-0-387-85764-0_19.

Berry, Keith. 2016. *Bullied: Tales of Torment, Identity, and Youth*. New York: Routledge.

Berry, Keith, and Tony E. Adams. 2016. "Family Bullies." *Journal of Family Communication* 16 (1): 51–63. https://doi.org/10.1080/15267431.2015.1111217.

Birren, James E., and Cheryl Svensson, 2013. "Reminiscence, Life Review, and Autobiography: Emergence of a New Era." *International Journal of Reminiscence and Life Review* 1: 1–6.

Braithwaite, Dawn O., Elizabeth A. Sutter, and Kory Floyd. 2018. "Introduction: The Landscape of Meta-Theory and Theory in Family Communication Research." In *Engaging Theories in Family Communication, Second Edition*, edited by Dawn O. Braithwaite, Elizabeth A. Sutter, and Kory Floyd, 1–16. New York: Routledge.

Caughlin, John P., and Liesel L. Sharabi. 2013. "A Communicative Interdependence Perspective of Close Relationships: The Connections Between Mediated and Unmediated Interactions Matter." *Journal of Communication* 63 (5): 873–93. https://doi.org/10.1111/jcom.12046.

Caughlin, John P., and Ningxin Wang. 2020. "Relationship Maintenance in the Age of Technology." In *Relationship Maintenance: Theory, Process, and Context*, edited by Brian G. Ogolsky and J. Kale Monk, 304–22. Cambridge, UK: Cambridge.

Centers for Disease Control. 2021. "People with Certain Medical Conditions." Accessed October 1, 2021. https://www.cdc.gov/coronavirus/2019-ncov/need-extra-precautions/people-with-medical-conditions.html.

Chang, Heewon. 2013. "Individual and Collaborative Autoethnography as Method." In *Handbook of Autoethnography*, edited by Stacy Holman Jones, Tony E. Adams, and Carolyn Ellis, 107–22. Walnut Creek, CA: Left Coast Press.

Charmaz, Kathy. 2014. *Constructing Grounded Theory, Second Edition*. Thousand Oaks, CA: Sage.

Delia, Jesse G., and Lawrence Grossberg. 1977. "Interpretation and Evidence." *Western Journal of Speech Communication* 41 (1): 32–42.

Dun, Tim. 2010. "Turning Points in Parent-Grandparent Relationships During the Start of a New Generation." *Journal of Family Communication* 10 (3): 194–210. https://doi.org/10.1080/15267431.2010.489218.

Dun, Tim, and Laura Sangster. 2013. "Family Trajectories: Intergenerational Relationships During the Birth of a New Generation." *Qualitative Communication Research* 2 (3): 255–80. https://doi.org/10.1525/qcr.2013.2.3.255.

Dun, Tim, and Claire Sears. 2017. "Relational Trajectories from Parent and Child to Grandparent and New Parent." *Journal of Family Communication* 17 (2): 185–201. https://doi.org/10.1080/15267431.2017.1281281.

Elder, Glen H., Jr. 1994. "Time, Human Agency, and Social Change: Perspectives on the Life Course." *Social Psychology Quarterly* 57 (1): 4–15. https://doi.org/10.2307/2786971.

———. 1998. "The Life Course as Developmental Theory." *Child Development* 69 (1): 1–12. https://doi.org/10.2307/1132065.

Elder, Glen H., Jr., Monica Kirkpatrick Johnson, and Robert Crosnoe. 2003. "The Emergence and Development of Life Course Theory." In *Handbook of the Life Course*, edited by Jeylan T. Mortimer and Michael J. Shanahan, 3–19. Boston: Springer.

Ellis, Carolyn. 1999. "Heartful Autoethnography." *Qualitative Health Research* 9 (5): 669–83. https://doi.org/10.1177/104973299129122153.

Galvin, Kathleen M., Dawn O. Braithwaite, and Carma L. Bylund. 2015. *Family Communication: Cohesion and Change, Ninth Edition.* New York: Routledge.

Giele, Janet Z., and Glen H. Elder, Jr. 1998. *Methods of Life Course Research: Qualitative and Quantitative Approaches*. Thousand Oaks, CA: Sage.

Giles, Howard. 1973. “Accent Mobility: A Model and Some Data.” *Anthropological Linguistics* 15: 87–109.

Giles, Howard, and Jessica Gasiorek. 2011. “Intergenerational Communication Practices.” In *Handbook of the Psychology of Aging*, edited by K. Warner Schaie and Sherry L. Willis, 233–247. London, UK: Elsevier Academic Press.

Goffman, Erving. 1959. *The Presentation of Self in Everyday Life*. New York: Anchor Books.

Golish, Tamara D. 2000. “Changes in Closeness between Adult Children and Their Parents: A Turning Point Analysis.” *Communication Reports* 13 (2): 79–97. https://doi.org/10.1080/08934210009367727.

Hall, Jeffrey A. 2020. *Relating Through Technology.* Cambridge, UK: Cambridge.

Hall, Jeffrey A., Natalie Pennington, and Amanda Holmstrom. 2021. “Connecting Through Technology During COVID-19.” *Human Communication and Technology* 2 (1): 1–18. https://doi.org/10.17161/hct.v3i1.15026.

Harper, Douglas. 1987. *Working Knowledge: Skill and Community in a Small Shop.* Chicago, IL: University of Chicago Press.

Haythornthwaite, Caroline. 2005. “Social Networks and Internet Connectivity Effects.” *Information, Communication & Society* 8 (2): 125–47. https://doi.org/10.1080/13691180500146185.

Hutchinson, Elizabeth. 2021. *Dimensions of Human Behavior: The Changing Life Course.* Thousand Oaks, CA: Sage.

Imber-Black, Evan, and Janine Roberts. 1998. *Rituals for Our Times: Celebrating, Healing, and Changing Our Lives and Our Relationships.* Lanham, MD: Rowman & Littlefield.

Ivan, Loredana, and Galit Nimrod. 2021. “Family Conflicts and Technology Use: The Voices of Grandmothers.” *Family Relations* 70: 104–119. https://doi.org/10.1111/fare.12530.

Kakulla, Brittne, Rachel Barr, Jennifer Zosh, Gabrielle Strouse, Lauren Myers, Georgene Troseth, and Elisabeth McClure. 2021. “Boomers and Zoomers: Grandparents Using Video Chat to Connect With Young Grandchildren During the Pandemic.” *AARP Research*, June 2021. https://doi.org/10.26419/res.00468.001.

Licoppe, Christian. 2004. “‘Connected’ Presence: The Emergence of a New Repertoire for Managing Social Relationships in a Changing Communication Technoscape.” *Environment and Planning D: Society and Space* 22 (1): 135–56. https://doi.org/10.1068/d323t.

Licoppe, Christian, and Julien Morel. 2012. “Video-in-Interaction: ‘Talking Heads’ and the Multimodal Organization of Mobile and Skype Video Calls.” *Research on Language and Social Interaction* 45 (4): 399–429. https://doi.org/10.1080/08351813.2012.724996.

Ling, Rich, and Chih-Hui Lai. 2016. "Microcoordination 2.0: Social Coordination in the Age of Smartphones and Messaging Apps." *Journal of Communication* 66 (5): 834–56. https://doi.org/10.1111/jcom.12251.

Littlejohn, Stephen W. 1989. "Interpretive and Critical Theories." In *Theories of Human Communication, Third Edition*, edited by Stephen Littlejohn, 134–149. Belmont, CA: Wadsworth.

Madianou, Mirca, and Daniel Miller. 2012a. *Migration and New Media: Transnational Families and Polymedia.* New York: Routledge.

———. 2012b. "Polymedia: Towards a New Theory of Digital Media in Interpersonal Communication." *International Journal of Cultural Studies* 16 (2): 169–87. https://doi.org/10.1177/1367877912452486.

McAdams, Dan P., and Kate C. McLean. 2013. "Narrative Identity." *Current Directions in Psychological Science* 22 (3): 233–38. https://doi.org/10.1177/0963721413475622.

McClain, Colleen, Emily A. Vogels, Andrew Perrin, Stella Sechopoulos, and Lee Rainie. 2021. "The Internet and the Pandemic." *Pew Research Center,* September 2021.

McCullough, Jennifer, and Brant R. Burleson. 2012. "Celebratory Support: Messages that Enhance the Effects of Positive Experiences." In *The Positive Side of Interpersonal Communication*, edited by Thomas J. Socha and Margaret Pitts, 229–245. New York: Peter Lang.

Miller, Eric D. 2020. "The COVID-19 Pandemic Crisis: The Loss and Trauma Event of Our Time." *Journal of Loss and Trauma* 25 (6–7): 560–72. https://doi.org/10.1080/15325024.2020.1759217.

Muncey, Tessa. 2010. *Creating Autoethnographies*. Thousand Oaks, CA: Sage.

Noone, Chris, Jenny McSharry, Mike Smalle, Annette Burns, Kerry Dwan, Declan Devane, and Eimear C. Morrissey. "Video Calls for Reducing Social Isolation and Loneliness in Older People: a Rapid Review." *The Cochrane Database of Systematic Reviews* 5 (5): CD013632.

Parks, Malcolm R. 2017. "Embracing the Challenges and Opportunities of Mixed-Media Relationships." *Human Communication Research* 43 (4): 505–17. https://doi.org/10.1111/hcre.12125.

Pennebaker, James W., Joshua M. Smyth. 2016. *Opening Up by Writing It Down, Third Edition.* New York: Guilford.

Postman, Neil. 1992. *Technopoly: The Surrender of Culture to Technology*. New York: Knopf.

Poulos, Christopher N. 2008. *Accidental Ethnography: An Inquiry into Family Secrecy.* Walnut Creek, CA: Left Coast Press.

———. 2012. "Life, Interrupted." *Qualitative Inquiry* 18 (4): 323–32. https://doi.org/10.1177/1077800411431565.

———. 2021. *Essentials of Autoethnography.* Washington, DC: American Psychological Association.

Sahlstein Parcell, Erin. 2013. "Trajectories Research in Family Communication: Toward the Identification of Alternative Pathways for Inquiry." *Journal of Family Communication* 13 (3): 167–77.

Scharp, Kristina M., and Elizabeth Dorrance Hall. 2019. "Reconsidering Family Closeness: A Review and Call for Research on Family Distancing." *Journal of Family Communication* 19 (1): 1–14. https://doi.org/10.1080/15267431.2018.1544563.

Scott, Allison M., and John P. Caughlin. 2015. "Communication Nonaccommodation in Family Conversations about End-of-Life Health Decisions." *Health Communication* 30 (2): 144–53. https://doi.org/10.1080/10410236.2014.974128.

Searles, Darcey K. 2018. "'Look It Daddy': Shows in Family Facetime Calls." *Research on Children and Social Interaction* 2 (1): 98–119. https://doi.org/10.1558/rcsi.32576.

Shufford, Kevin N., Deborah L. Hall, Ashley K. Randall, Bailey M. Braunstein, Mary M. O'Brien, and Kristin D. Mickelson. 2021. "Connected While Apart: Associations between Social Distancing, Computer-Mediated Communication Frequency, and Positive Affect during the Early Phases of COVID-19." *Journal of Social and Personal Relationships* 38 (10): 2906–20. https://doi.org/10.1177/02654075211041316. Singer 2004.

Soliz, Jordan, and Colleen Warner Colaner. 2018. "Communication Accommodation Theory and Communication Theory of Identity: Theories of Communication and Identity." In *Engaging Theories in Family Communication, Second Edition*, edited by Braithwaite, Dawn O., Elizabeth A. Sutter, and Kory Floyd, 75–86. New York: Routledge.

Strouse, Gabrielle A., Elisabeth McClure, Lauren J. Myers, Jennifer M. Zosh, Georgene L. Troseth, Olivia Blanchfield, Ellen Roche, Subul Malik, and Rachel Barr. 2021. "Zooming through Development: Using Video Chat to Support Family Connections." *Human Behavior and Emerging Technologies* 3 (4): 552–71. https://doi.org/10.1002/hbe2.268.

Taipale, Sakari. 2019. *Intergenerational Connections in Digital Families*. Cham, Switzerland: Springer.

Tong, Stephanie, and Joseph B. Walther. 2011. "Relational Maintenance and CMC." In *Computer-Mediated Communication in Personal Relationships*, edited by Kevin B. Wright and Lynne M. Webb, 98–118. New York: Peter Lang.

Wilding, Raelene. 2006. "'Virtual' Intimacies? Families Communicating across Transnational Contexts." *Global Networks* 6 (2): 125–42.

Yong, Ed. 2021. "What Happens When Americans Can Finally Exhale." *The Atlantic*, May 20, 2021.

Chapter Two

Narrative Wisdom

Implications from Literature for Family Communication Technology Engagement

Janie Harden Fritz

The explosive growth of communication technologies holds implications for how families communicate within and beyond the family system. Although features of current technologies have different affordances than those in the past, prior practices as depicted in fictional literature, with or without (communication) technology as part of the context, featuring families either already formed or to be in the future, provide insights for contemporary family communication embedded within a context replete with continually emerging opportunities for engagement through technology. Stories grounded in larger narratives offer guidance through enduring principles that can enrich family well-being. This chapter explores selected fictional works to draw insights for family communication in this historical moment.

This treatment emerges at the intersection of family communication, narrative, worldview, and media ecology. First, I situate this chapter within media ecology as represented by Neil Postman's (1993) understanding of technology's interaction with society and culture. Then I turn to representative findings from the growing literature on the family as a context for engagement of communication technology, with a brief reflection on the Amish community as a tool-using culture. From there, I turn to literature as a reflection of worldview and associated communication practices, directing attention to three authors—George MacDonald, Flannery O'Connor, and Charles Williams—writing within a faith tradition, whose fictional portrayals of families highlight enduring issues relevant to families' engagement with communication technologies today, stressing continuity in the face of change. These works are sources of narrative wisdom for families in an age of disruption and uncertainty. Throughout that section, I offer connecting points to findings about communication technology and the family as touchpoints for learning. I end with directions for future research.

TECHNOLOGY: A MEDIA ECOLOGY APPROACH

Technology is part of the human condition, an existential element tied to survival, growth, and development of human societies (Strate 2017). From clothing, shelter, and means of producing fire to the plow, weapons of war and industry, the printing press, multitudinous forms of transportation and communication, and the internet, technologies have accompanied human communities, with both creative and destructive effects. Technologies have been welcomed and feared, prompting reflection on their relationship to human culture throughout the ages, from ancient myth to contemporary scholarship in the domain of media ecology (e.g., Strate 2006). Technologies intersect and interact with human purposes and practices in consequential ways, with implications for human cultures and societies. Technologies can bring about fundamental changes in the way people think and take in the world around them, propelling corresponding changes in culture (e.g., Carr 2011, McCluhan 1962, Ong 1967). Research identifies the shaping influence of technology on thought patterns, information processing, and communication expectations, all of which hold implications for how we think about and engage relationships (e.g., Montgomery 2015). In this context, Spitzberg (2006) developed a model of computer-mediated communication competence, which suggests factors to take into account when considering questions of appropriateness and effectiveness in relational communication taking place through "computer assisted technologies" (631).

Technologies may be disciplined productively to work within the guidelines of culture, serving the meaning structures of culture rather than overwhelming, colonizing, or eclipsing them (Postman 1993). Reflective engagement of technology is necessary to ensure its contribution to the good of families, slowing the pace of change to permit course corrections as needed to preserve valued traditions, even if adapted in key aspects. For instance, Jeffrey Bogaczyk (2016) examines mediated communication practices in the context of churches, exploring implications for just those issues. For this reason, past practices emerging in storied form serve as helpful reminders that whatever changes happen in the technological landscape, fundamental guidelines tied to larger narrative structures oriented toward human flourishing remain as resources for current and future family relationships and communication practices, supporting continuity in changing times.

THE FAMILY AS CONTEXT FOR COMMUNICATION TECHNOLOGY

Family Communication

The study of family communication emerged as an outgrowth of interpersonal communication (Galvin and Braithwaite 2014). Family communication examines how families make meaning through symbolic processes (Braithwaite, Suter, and Floyd 2018). Family relationships form our character and direct our actions, although they do not determine them, teaching us appropriate and effective communication practices (Caughlin et al. 2002) through schemata tied to family communication (Schrodt et al. 2009). Families shape our worldviews, meaning structures that situate the human being within existence (Regnerus 2003).

Family Communication and Technology

Communication technologies, with their affordances for connection, information sharing, and co-participation in events and activities, as well as for surveillance, intrusion, and deception, hold implications for family processes and relationships (e.g., Bruess et al. 2015). Communication technologies can direct a family's trajectory over time, influencing the negotiation of boundaries within and beyond the family unit or system (e.g., Child and Petronio 2015). Communication technologies join the ranks of the broad category of technologies emerging throughout history that have shaped family communication and meaning patterns as part of their influence on the larger culture. For example, in his treatment of the influences of technology on the meaning structures of society, Neil Postman (1993) explores changes in society brought about by technologies such as the telescope, printing press, and mechanical clock through reconfigurations of larger worldviews, availability of knowledge, and the temporal demarcation of experience, with implications for how entire cultures, including the families that constituted them, understood their place in the universe through changes in perspective.

In addition to granting access to new domains of knowledge and control in the external, natural world, technologies reconfigure perspectives on the relational level as well, with implications for how family members understand each other's lifeworlds. During the mid-twentieth century, as Joshua Meyrowitz (1985) argued in *No Sense of Place*, television opened vistas hithertofore unseen, permitting viewers to witness events once shrouded in mystery, interactions transcending viewers' experience because of limitations tied to group standpoint. For instance, television shows featuring parental conversations behind closed doors permitted children a glimpse into the world of adult experience; women and men became privy to depictions of each other's conversations and to practices particular to men's and women's lived experience in the company of other men or women (Meyrowitz 1985). This change in phenomenological sense of place made possible by technology followed close on the heels of new engagements of physical space. Changes in micro-level family practices were shaped by technologies permitting distance and privacy from centralized family control and authority. For example, the car made it possible for courting couples to escape parental surveillance (O'Neal 2006), contributing to shifting norms and expectations for behavior connected to family participation and formation.

Our current historical moment offers a rich, dynamic, and complex context for interaction between technologies and family systems, particularly communication technologies, due to their sheer ubiquity and rapid proliferation. Communication technologies have the potential to contribute constructively to family relationships through both expressive and instrumental affordances (Christensen 2009). There is a paradox in such technologies, which complicates assessment of their effects. For example, when families are physically distant, technologies can bring them closer, but when they are physically close, the same technologies can separate them due to a divided focus of attention (Christensen 2009). This paradox is highlighted by Sherry Turkle (2011) in her work *Alone Together*.

As families confront and engage new communication technologies, researchers strive to assess the mutual influence of technology use and family communication practices. As indicated by Ramsey et al. (2013), however, technological forms and usage change rapidly, and findings may vary from one moment to the next. For instance, a 2009 study discussed in Ramsey et al. (2013) reported student use of social networking sites (SNS) with a parent to be associated with loneliness, whereas data from 2011 showed no such association. These studies also showed consistent use of communication by telephone, but an increase in frequency of text messaging and SNS use from 2009 to 2011. In both studies, communication in person or by telephone was associated with more positive outcomes, which suggests the power of traditional approaches to communication despite the availability of new options (Ramsey et al. 2013). Furthermore, it appears as though technology is additive and does not reduce time spent in face-to-face interaction with families (Baym, Zhang, and Lin 2004, Webb 2015).

Evidence from studies of parental mediation of children's digital media use points to the wisdom of reflection on implications of technology as parents seek to help children benefit from the internet as a resource while keeping them safe from harm (Livingstone et al. 2017). A style of mediation that engages and works actively with children through co-participation suggests the importance of modeling technology use and a responsibility for developing skills for such engagement. The digital realm is more complex than television viewing, calling for enhanced skills from both children and parents (Livingstone et al. 2017)—the desired outcome is "agents making constructive choices in a mediated world" (Livingstone et al. 2017, 84). Parents can create a safe context for children's internet engagement, encouraging thoughtful use of this technology as a potentially valuable tool (Livingstone et al. 2017).

Other family relationships may be shaped by communication technologies. Lindell, Campione-Barr, and Killoren (2021) investigated sibling communication through various modalities during the transition to college. Self-disclosure about potentially risky behaviors emerged for siblings who used a wide range of internet communication technologies. Such disclosures offer opportunities for intervention and assistance, potentially averting negative outcomes for at-risk young adult siblings (Lindell et al. 2021).

Dating partners have the potential to form family relationships. Communication technologies make the dialectic of interdependence and autonomy particularly salient, providing opportunities for working through issues that may affect the trajectory and future health of future family relationships when a couple marries. Duran, Kelly, and Rotaru (2011) investigated the cell phone's role in the outworking of this dialectic, noting conflict around expectations for frequency of contact and other factors relevant to the possibility of constant connection. In this context, communication technologies become a shaping force for relational development or, potentially, dissolution.

Family norms and patterns affect how technology is engaged. Rudi et al. (2015) report that families appear to choose communication technologies according to their preferred approach to social reality, supporting and maintaining conversational or conforming orientations, two different family communication patterns, through choice of technology. If this is the case, families may be demonstrating Postman's (1993) tool-using orientation rather than one of a technocracy or a technopoly. A tool-using culture is one in which technology serves the needs of the culture and does not threaten norms and values of that culture. A technocracy marks a point at which technology makes inroads into the thinking patterns and practices of the culture to the point of threatening long-standing traditions. Traditions are not eradicated or completely replaced, but they are under attack; technology threatens "to *become* the culture" [emphasis in the original] (Postman 1993, 28). In a techopoly, technology becomes a god, subsuming and directing cultural meaning; the supreme human achievement is "technical progress" (Postman 1993, 71), which is believed to solve all problems. Traditional thought-worlds are completely replaced by a technological worldview; a technopoly "is totalitarian technocracy" (Postman 1993, 48).

Considering rapid change in practices of technology use and evidence that at least some parents seek to stay involved with their children through mediation of communication technology use, we may draw the conclusion that families are implicitly aware of the affordances and risks of various forms of communication technologies and alter their approach to these tools accordingly. Evidence from a transnational study (Wilding 2006), though dated, suggests that the cultural and social context within which families are embedded has a strong influence on use of communication technologies, as well. This evidence points again to an inclination of engagement of technology as a tool serving the culture of the family rather than as an irresistible force redefining the family.

Other studies of family communication patterns appear to provide some support for this position. For instance, evidence suggests that appropriateness norms for face-to-face communication transfers to technological forms of communication (Wang et al 2019), although competence in each of these domains may best be represented by different constructs (Wang 2019). As Spitzberg (2006) notes, face-to-face and computer-mediated communication may be more similar than they are different. For this reason, we must be alert for effects of technology on family processes, but we must also remain attentive to enduring concerns for relational connection, development, growth, and sustenance provided by families. Rather than engulfing the field of our attention, communication technologies can take their place along with other emerging developments in life and the larger world that confront families as a larger unit and the members that constitute them. Because of their ubiquity, however, technologies cannot be ignored, assumed to be uniformly or unequivocally benign, or adopted unthinkingly. New communication technologies create a context that makes issues perennially confronted by families assume new dimensions. Questions of identity and self-presentation, belonging and group membership, worldview and standpoint diversity, connection and independence, public and private information, and other issues gain heightened salience in this moment, calling for careful consideration of the implications of communication technologies for families.

Technology and Tradition: The Amish Family

Thoughtful engagement of technology is evident in the Amish community. This tradition-grounded culture encourages reflective, cautious use of technology in ways that support family flourishing and integrity within a virtue structure tied to a religious narrative. An excellent example of Postman's tool-using culture, the Amish restrict technology to uses that undergird practices of involvement and participation across the generations—for example, on the family farm (Hostetler 1993; Kraybill 2001).

A high level of efficiency made possible by technology is not the goal of the Amish. Useful involvement in a labor that is also Arendtian work (Arendt 1958) is an ontological element of human life for the Amish that subordinates efficiency to goods of collaborative participation in a common project. Far from merely sustaining life, the Amish family's tilling of the ground and harvesting crops with modest technologies that take time creates an environment of humility and recognition of the interdependence of members of the community (Kraybill and Olshan 1994). Just as parents concerned for children's benefit and safety with internet use mediate their children's online practices and model wise internet use, Amish parents model for children how to work with technology such that technology works for them, preserving and passing their traditional way of life on to the next generation (e.g., Regnery 2003). As Amish parents engage work with limited technologies and encourage children to contribute as they are able, each person's value is seen as part of the larger effort, and the good of work itself manifests through skilled practice. The technology they do use enables the practice, the context, and the outcome as the family—and community—directs. This same practical caution guides the uses of communication technologies, as well, which the Amish see as promoting individualism if used indiscriminately (Kraybill and Olshan 1994).

The religious worldview of the Amish underwrites their decision to adopt, restrict, or discourage a given technology (Hostetler 1993; Kraybill 2001; Kraybill and Olshan 1994). Each potential change is held up to tradition, potential for community health, and a sense of what is required as a faithful adherent to guidelines of the Amish religious tradition. These considerations prevent the Amish community from moving from a tool-using culture to a technocracy or a technopoly. Community and family are closely tied together within this larger worldview; families draw insight and wisdom from the larger community and tradition, and those structures gain life from the families that make them up. Perhaps one implication of keeping technology in its place, for the Amish, is the recognition that God is the framer of reality, not technology, and the mediating role human beings play in engaging the world through technology gives human beings the responsibility for managing meaning and guiding the appropriate operation of technology in human experience.

What we see in the living community of the Amish we also witness in narrative portrayals of families from the nineteenth and early twentieth century. These fictional families, or nascent families, working with a much less complex system of communication technologies than we see in contemporary times, must make communicative choices as they engage each other relative to the technologies at hand, however minimalistic. These families, as have others throughout the centuries, face historical, social, and technological changes that call for wisdom and discernment. An examination of contexts from the past, portrayed in story form, in which persons find meaning within human relationships, may, through perspective by incongruity (Burke 1968), inform our current practices by moving us imaginatively out of the current moment to a temporally prior time. In this fashion, we may identify underlying themes that endure as we consider how to help families flourish in an age of ever-abounding communication technologies.

NARRATIVE WISDOM: LOOKING TO LITERATURE

George MacDonald's Spiritual Fiction: Transformative Family Communication

George MacDonald (1823–1901), a Scottish writer, authored a number of spiritual and theological books, as well as several volumes of fantasy for children and adult readers. Although less well known than his children's books, MacDonald's romance novels, which feature people in various stages of spiritual search and development, remain available in their original form and became quite popular in the 1980s in redacted form due to the work of popular author Michael Phillips (Fritz 2013). These novels offer insights for relational communication in the family in the context of a Christian worldview. MacDonald's spiritual fiction highlights the growth and development of the soul in the context of significant relationships, primarily family relationships manifesting varying degrees of health or close relationships that move toward family status. These relationships become channels of grace in everyday life manifested through the conversation and action of family members and of friends who eventually became family. From the communication interaction among pre-family and current family members, we can glean principles relevant to current engagement of families with communication technologies.

One of MacDonald's novels, *Heather and Snow*, originally published in 1893, focuses on the means by which family relationships, ranging in degree of health and spiritual strength, play a role in the spiritual development of the human person. This story serves as a reminder of the purposes of family relationships that must be maintained in the face of new developments in communication technologies. *Heather and Snow* features several characters: Kirsty Barclay; her father and mother, David and Marion Barclay; Kirsty's brother, Stephen, nicknamed Steenie, who appears to have a developmental disability; Francis (Francie) Gordon, the son of Mrs. Gordon, whose land the

Barclays work and whose husband and Francie's father, Colonel Archibald Gordon, had served with (Sergeant) David Barclay in the army; and a widowed schoolmaster, Mr. Craig, and Phemy, his daughter.

Several themes emerge in this work. In an age of proliferating communication technologies, as well as other technologies that offer opportunities to redefine the self, a moment in which identities are fluid and ever changing, we are reminded that, from a faith-grounded perspective, our true identity is tied to a destiny known and directed by God. To that end, family relationships work to call forth that destiny through development of virtuous character traits (Simon 1997). This fictional portrayal reminds us that communication technologies' use, when directed toward the end of destiny and human flourishing, serve the purposes of a larger narrative. As parents work with children to tap affordances and benefits of communication technologies (e.g., Livingstone et al. 2017), they are encouraging character traits that will help children achieve their destinies—or compromise their pursuit of those destinies.

The novel begins with Kirsty's chastising of Francie, who seems to consider himself much more highly than he ought. The conversation could be considered a precursor to family communication because of the eventual marriage of the pair. "He [Francie] was giving the girl to understand that he meant to be a soldier like his father, and quite as good a one as he" (1). Being young and thoughtless, he assumes that success will simply happen, and he is propelled solely by self-motivated ambition, which Kirsty finds problematic. Upon Francie's insistence that the world should not fail to take him seriously ("lichtly . . . me," MacDonald 2004, 1), Kirsty suggests that perhaps the world will not trouble itself about him at all, or even think about him. He becomes offended and asks why she replies in such a way. She explains why he is "scoffing" at him: "I wadna be girdin at ye, Francie, but that I care ower muckle aboot ye to lat ye think I haud the same opingon o' ye 'at ye hae o' yersel" (MacDonald 2004, 2). She goes on to explain to him that deeds are needed to prove excellence. She explains that she believes him, but does not yet believe *in* him, which are two different things. "What hae ye ever dune to gie a body ony richt to believe in ye? Ye're a guid rider, and a guid shot for a laddie, and ye rin middlin fest—I canna say like a deer, for I reckon I cud lick ye mysel at rinnin!" (MacDonald 2004, 3). Kirsty goes on to prove her words with her deeds by defeating Francie in a footrace. McDonald goes on to say that Kirsty "had been doing her best to make the boy practical like herself" (MacDonald 2004, 5). She wants him to be what he is capable of being—worthy of note because accomplishing something of note.

This principle is a reminder of how identities can be framed and altered by the affordances of technology (e.g., Brandtzaeg and Heim 2009; Brunskill 2014; Lane et al. 2019; Valkenburg 2017), such as seeing oneself as having efficacy in the sphere of politics (e.g., Lane et al. 2019). However, self-deception is also a possibility. While it is possible to deceive others in online contexts (Caspi and Gorsky 2006, Donath 1999), the potential for technological platforms to encourage alternative identities may make it more likely to anchor self-understandings in unrealistic creations or images of who one is or can be (Brunskill 2014). In the context of family communication, parents can discuss identity development and portrayal with their children, considering implications of accurate or inaccurate characteristics, differences between playful or imaginary depictions of self, and the contextual appropriateness of self-portrayals. Likewise, consideration of how others' identities may be presented selectively may help children avoid problematic or dangerous interactions. Seeing ourselves rightly in both face-to-face and online contexts allows us to view others rightly, as well, and contribute to their well-being and achievement of their destinies (Simon, 1997).

In similar fashion, parents may be reminded of the importance of loving discipline for children as their sons and/or daughters seek to be liked, recognized, and appreciated by others. The correction of a caring sibling, spouse, or parent who works with sensitive honesty to speak a hard truth (e.g., Fritz 2020) may work better in a face-to-face setting, given the importance of nonverbal cues for texturing relational messages (e.g., Daft and L'Engle 1986, Short, Williams, and Christie 1976), or a virtual meeting with a visual platform if a face-to-face meeting is impossible. Communication about weighty issues is more likely to succeed with sufficient nonverbal cues to support development of shared meaning (Trevino, Daft, and Lengle 1990), particularly regarding relational aspects of the message. However, research by Laitinen and Valo (2018) suggests that relational elements of messages can be carried by communication technologies—although message equivocality may still prompt the need for cues available in richer media (Walther, Loh, and Granka 2005).

As Caroline Simon (1997) notes, love contains a paradox. We love, though there is much in the beloved (and in ourselves) not to love. We are not to ignore those elements in need of change, but rather to stimulate and encourage virtues in the beloved that emerge in real or potential attributes moving that person toward a destiny, a future part of the personal story taking place within the larger narrative of God's story. Throughout *Heather and Snow*, Kirsty calls Francie to his better self, from this initial naming of his vice of pride to striking him with his father's own riding crop upon his insult to a young girl with whose feelings he was cavalier, to insisting that he care for an alcoholic mother whose habits were ruining both his own future and that of the property and land, affecting all those who worked it. Near the end of the book, he says that he does not think nearly as much of himself now as he did then: "'A' I can say is—'at I dinna think nearhan sae muckle o' myself as I did than'" (MacDonald 2004, 312–13). Kirsty replies that she thinks much more of him than she did back then: "And I think a heap mair o' ye" (MacDonald 2004, 312–13). Kirsty helped correct Francie's image of himself, and she also shaped his relationship with his mother, inspiring in him the courage to love his mother enough to intervene in her addiction to alcohol.

McDonald here highlights a theme that he returns to over and over in his novels and children's stories—that is, the need for corrective shaping action on both humans and animals to bring out the true, higher created nature of the creature. Neither children nor adults are born being all they can be. In the case of Kirsty, her good parents shaped her natural inclination toward the good. We see here the truth of the finding that parents have a strong influence on children's understanding and practices of communication (Caughlin et al. 2002; Schrodt et al. 2009), a reminder of the need for parental guidance in all contexts of communication. Such guidance is particularly in contexts where multiple surrounding influences may offer opportunities without narrative mooring. Parents who seek to support faith-grounded virtues and practices on the frontiers of communication technologies offering endless options answering only to a "Can we?" may help children ask, "Should we?" (Ellul 1989) when faced with such options. The schoolmaster's relationship to his daughter, Phemy, stands in stark contrast. He never disciplines her, and the result is her eventual death.

Flannery O'Connor: Self-deception, Family Communication, and Technology's (Al)lure

Narrative lessons in the context of minimal technology use remind us of enduring principles that transfer to contexts rich with technology or its looming presence. For consideration of contexts where technology's lure compromises family flourishing, I turn to Flannery O'Connor's short story "A View of the Woods." This story reminds us of the potential for technology to promise progress that effaces relational goods and reinforces false views of self, a theme echoed in another O'Connor story, "The Lame Shall Enter First," in which the "technology" is a psychological theory applied without consideration of the particular, the error of a technician of goodness (Arnett 1996).

Flannery O'Connor (1925–1964) was a Catholic writer whose fiction reflected a sacramental worldview (May 1976, Edmondson 2018, Getz 1980). Her stories and novels address, in often grotesque form, issues of God's grace, the fallen human condition, and divine mercy. Family and human relationships are central to her work, although these relationships are often distorted (Gordon 2003). Her stories "cast doubt on the consensus assumptions of the modern age" (Wood 2004, 9), reminding us of the imperfectability of human nature and implicitly warning against faith in technology as a cure.

In "A View of the Woods," we see a family consisting of a dad (Mr. Pitts), his wife (Mrs. Pitts), Grandpa Fortune (father of Mrs. Pitts), and Mary Fortune Pitts, daughter of Mr. and Mrs. Pitts, referred to in the story as "Mary Fortune." Mary Fortune is the apple of her grandfather's eye, his protégé and veritable image, sharing his materialistic, progressive orientation to the world until the day in which a disagreement over the meaning of a patch of ground dissolves their unity. Mr. Fortune plans to sell some of the property, the section that Mary Fortune considers "the lawn" (O'Connor 1965, 63), for construction of a gas station. The gas station is the embodiment of progress, fuel for a new era of machines and power. Mr. Fortune has said as much to his granddaughter: "'The Pittses are the kind that would let a cow pasture interfere with the future . . . but not you and me'" (O'Connor 1965, 58). In his focus on embracing the new as central to his identity and thereby, in his view, of his granddaughter's, he ignores her as tied to the Pitts family, with its backward ways and inferior approach to life. Mr. Fortune's hoped-for conversion of the piece of ground used by his son-in-law to graze his calves into a place of convenience consistent with contemporary times denied the reality of his granddaughter's connection to her father. In this way, the father–daughter relational identity was destined for effacement, with Mary Fortune's identity engulfed and consumed by that of her grandfather. This dispute over technology had dire consequences, as we see at the end of the story.

The learning for families derived from this story points to challenges emerging when relationships become instrumentalized as supports for one's own self-importance. Virtues of humility and recognition of the intrinsic value of others, as well as one's dependence on others, stand in contrast to the vices of pride, lack of recognition of the intrinsic value of others, and failure to see our interconnectedness with other human beings. In this context, technology and its promise appears to have encouraged this instrumental approach, with Mary Fortune's identity subordinated, along with the "field of weeds" (O'Connor 1965, 63), to Mr. Fortune's purposes. A technology that was designed to bring Mr. Fortune and his granddaughter into even closer alignment drove them apart, an echo of Christensen's (2009) reflection on technology's paradox.

Interestingly, Mr. Fortune denied Mr. Pitts the opportunity to dig a deeper well for the family's use when the first well ran dry, insisting that they pipe water from a stream, for fear that Mr. Pitts would claim credit for this technology and its contribution to the family (O'Connor 1965, 56). These technologies, although not strictly communicative in nature, held communicative implications and became a central point of contention and struggle in this family. One can also see these technologies' role in Mr. Fortune's creation of a false image of himself, assuming to himself a control over nature, self, and others that was unrealistic and deceptive. In this case, the primary technology in question, represented by the gas station, rested within the legitimate sphere of human activity (Strate 2017), although it was used for a problematic end and was not engaged in a way that helped Mary Fortune benefit from technology while still remaining safe (e.g., Livingstone et al. 2017). Mr. Fortune had no one to call him to account while he was in the thrall to technology's vision of an unrealistic, illusory identity (e.g., Brunskill 2014, 395), and his final action toward his granddaughter was greatly disinhibited, an effect noted as characteristic of an "e-personality" (Brunskill 2014, 397, 399, 410).

Charles Williams: Human Limits

Charles Williams was a member of the Oxford Literary group known as "The Inklings," along with C. S. Lewis, J. R. R. Tolkien, and Owen Barfield. Williams, a poet, literary critic, dramatist, theologian, and novelist, wrote a series of novels about ordinary people encountering spiritual entities and realities in various contexts. Praised by C. S. Lewis (Lindop 2015, 258), these novels were Christian fantasy thrillers, exploring theological, supernatural, and philosophical motifs. Each novel portrays families or future families (or even former family members who have died) in the context of uncanny, unexpected events that reveal the heart and have the potential to prompt spiritual learning.

In *The Greater Trumps*, we see how a technological attitude toward nature and the spiritual realm, in which human beings attempt to control forces beyond their realistic sphere of influence, leads to hubris and family endangerment. Family communication, in this portrayal, leads to a happy outcome, as family members are called out to intervene and recall members to humility and recognition of their dependence on the Divine and interdependence with each other. The turning point in this story comes about because of one character's responsiveness to the communicative efforts of another—a persuasive effort inviting her to think, reflect, learn, grow, and love.

A young man, Henry, and his grandfather, Aaron, learn that the father of Henry's girlfriend, Nancy, inherited a pack of tarot cards that turn out to be the original, long-lost deck mystically connected—tied in a relational correspondence—with a set of figures continually in motion on a board (much like a chess board). The cards and figures contain within their being a microcosm of the Dance, the entire movement and meaning of the universe; when united, the cards and figures would lend great power to those who would wield them, opening "'a way to all knowledge and all prophecy" (Williams 1976, 51), apparently derived from the idea of "principle" in Plato's Symposium (Medcalf 1996, 30); the cards themselves have power independent of the union of cards and figures. Henry greatly desires the creative power and control possible with the reuniting of cards and figures. He begins to see Nancy as an “instrument . . . a complex and delicate piece of machinery” (Williams 1976, 50), a means to secure the cards. When Nancy’s father is reluctant to part with the cards, Henry secretes the cards away and taps their power, starting a deadly snowstorm designed to kill Nancy’s father so he can keep the cards, but the forces he put into play quickly spiral out of control. Thanks to the intervention of Nancy’s aunt Sybil, the one person in the story who is completely self-possessed and calm, who does not wish to see the future, but who is uncannily attuned to the board and the images, including the central figure, the Fool, which she alone can view in motion, all is put right, and “the presentation of the dance was for ever done” (Williams 1976, 230).

This story illustrates the ultimate technological temptation—to instrumentalize the Divine and created nature, through attempts to control, putting ourselves in the place of the Divine Creator. In the process, technology overcomes us, or threatens to do so, and the only remedy is a return to the fitting order of the human in relation to the Divine and to the natural world—a world that is charged with the supernatural for those who have eyes to see. We see also how instrumentalizing the Divine leads to instrumentalization of other human beings, as well.

A key theme emerges in this story as Sybil teaches Nancy a fitting attitude toward these greater powers, one of adoring the “‘truth of Love’” (Williams 1976, 143), and encourages her to love Henry, despite his misdirected efforts. An acceptance of not knowing, of refusing to pry secrets from the universe, honors the boundaries of our temporally situated selves in relation to the eternal and infinite; not only do people have boundaries protecting privacy that extend to online contexts (Child and Petronio 2015), but nature and the Divine have them, as well. Forcing the universe to yield its secrets by making use of a power that transcends technology demonstrates a lack of recognition of the reality of limits; the ethical question of “should we” is eclipsed (Ellul 1989). The importance of “persons and of personal relations” (Medcalf 1996, 20), which are threatened by the principles’ unleashing, stands out as a concern for the particularity of human beings.

The Greater Trumps highlights the wisdom of a return to larger stories of significance and meaning that encourage us to find our true identities as partakers of and participants in something larger than ourselves that we cannot control—and which our technologies cannot control. Findings from ongoing studies of family practices in relation to communication technologies point us in a constructive direction; the very studies themselves place the human being as investigator in a place of thoughtful understanding and learning in a context appropriate for the responsibilities and tasks of the existential human condition. As research on family engagement with communication technologies continues, this cautionary tale provides hope as well as a warning.

CONCLUSION

Whatever the modality, the intentionality and purpose of communication remain vital to family flourishing. The attentiveness to others so necessary for development and growth is still a vital human responsibility as part of a family and in relationships that will eventually constitute a family. Family members can resist the lure of technology that knows no limits, that encourages self-deception and mere image, and that instrumentalizes others and human relationships. The Amish, with families embedded in tradition and seeking to work within that tradition to guide and contain technological developments, offer a living embodiment of the importance of communication technology as subjected to culture rather than controlling it. Literature from earlier times echoes principles that correspond to contemporary efforts to reflect on and study family communication practices carried through and by technology.

Future research in the area of family and social communication technology would do well to consider the ethical and philosophical basis on which such engagement rests. Integrating humanities scholarship with quantitative and qualitative social science research yields textured, rich insights for scholarship and guidance in the face of great uncertainty. Although technology brings change, this change can be guided by continuity of human needs and concerns, prompting perennial questions across historical moments. Without falling prey to dystopian fears, we can acknowledge and honor concerns raised by communities like the Amish and reflect on principles from literature resting on assumptions tied to frameworks for human flourishing. Communication technologies are here to stay; by exploring their affordances and risks, communication scholars will provide avenues for meaningful engagement with these tools in ways that assist families, communities, and the larger human project.

REFERENCES

Arendt, Hannah. 1958. *The Human Condition*. Chicago: University of Chicago Press.

Arnett, Ronald C. 1996. "Technicians of Goodness: Ignoring the Narrative Life of Dialogue." In *Responsible Communication Ethical Issues in Business, Industry and the Professions*, edited by James A. Jaska and Michael S. Pritchard, 339–55. Cresskill, NJ: Hampton.

Baym, Nancy K., Yan Bing Zhang, and Mei-Chin Lin. 2004. "Social Interactions Across Media: Interpersonal Communication on the Internet, Telephone, and Face-to-face." *New Media and Society* 6 (3): 299–318. https://doi.org/10.1177/1461444804041438.

Bogaczyk, Jeffrey. 2016. "Building a House of Worship One (Agnostic) Platform at a Time." In *Communication and the Global Landscape of Faith*, edited by Adrienne Hacker Daniels. Lanham, MD: Lexington Books.

Brandtzæg, Petter Bae, and Jan Heim. 2009. "Why People Use Social Networking Sites." In *International Conference on Online Communities and Social Computing*, edited by A. Ant Ozok and Panayiotis Zaphiris, 143–52. Berlin: Springer.

Braithwate, Dawn O., Elizabeth A. Suter, and Kory Floyd. 2018. *Engaging Theories in Family Communication: Multiple Perspectives*, 2nd ed. New York: Routledge.

Bruess, Carol, ed. 2015. *Family Communication in the Age of Digital and Social Media.* New York: Peter Lang.

Brunskill, David. 2014. "The Dangers of Social Media for the Psyche." *Journal of Current Issues in Media & Telecommunications* 6 (4): 391–415.

Burke, Kenneth. 1968. *Counter-Statement*. Berkeley, CA: University of California Press.

Carr, Nicholas. 2011. *The Shallows: What the Internet Is Doing to Our Brains.* New York: W. W. Norton.

Caspi, Avner, and Paul Gorsky. 2006. "Online Deception: Prevalence, Motivation, and Emotion." *CyberPsychology & Behavior* 9 (1): 54–9. https://doi.org/10.1089/cpb.2006.9.54

Caughlin, John, Tamara Golish, Loreen Olson, Jack Sargent, Jeff Cook, and Sandra Petronio. 2000. "Intrafamily Secrets in Various Family Configurations: A Communication Boundary Management Perspective." *Communication Studies* 51 (2): 116–134.

Child, Jeffrey T., and Sandra Petronio. 2015. "Privacy Management Matters in Digital Family Communication." In *Family Communication in the Age of Digital and Social Media*, edited by Carol J. Bruess, 32–54. New York: Peter Lang.

Christensen, Toke. 2009. "'Connected Presence' in Distributed Family Life." *New Media & Society* 11 (3): 433–451. https://doi.org/10.1177/1461444808101620.

Daft, Richard L., and Robert H. Lengel. 1986. "Organizational Information Requirements, Media Richness, and Structural Design." *Management Science* 32 (5): 554–71. https://doi.org/10.1287/mnsc.32.5.554.

Donath, Judith. S. 1998. "Identity and Deception in the Virtual Community." In *Communities in Cyberspace*, edited by Peter Kollock and Marc Smith, 29–59. London: Routledge. https://doi.org/10.4324/9780203194959.

Duran, Robert L., Lynne Kelly, and Teodora Rotaru. 2011. "Mobile Phones in Romantic Relationships and the Dialectic of Autonomy Versus Connection." *Communication Quarterly* 59 (1): 19–36. https://doi.org/10.1080/01463373.2011.541336.

Edmondson III, Henry T. 2018. "Tantum Ergo (Ridiculum) Sacramentum: Flannery O'Connor on the Meaning of Sacrament." *Listening: Journal of Communication Ethics, Religion, and Culture* 53 (3): 137–51.

Ellul, Jaques. 1989. *The Presence of the Kingdom*. Colorado Springs, CO: Helmers & Howard.

Fritz, Janie Marie Harden. 2013. "A Prophecy Fulfilled: George MacDonald and Evangelical Popular Culture." In *Evangelical Christians and Popular Culture,* edited by Robert H. Woods Jr., 36–53. Santa Barbara, CA: Praeger.

———. 2020. "Honesty as Ethical Communicative Practice: A Framework for Analysis." In *Integrity, Honesty, and Truth-Seeking,* edited by Christian B. Miller and Ryan West, 127–52. New York: Oxford University Press.

Galvin, Kathleen M., and Dawn O. Braithwaite. 2014. "Family Communication Theory and Research from the Field of Family Communication: Discourses that Constitute and Reflect Families." *Journal of Family Theory & Review* 6 (1): 97–111. https://doi.org/10.1111/jftr.12030.

Getz, Lorine M. 1980. *Flannery O'Connor: Her Life, Library and Book Reviews.* New York: Edwin Mellen Press.

Gordon, Sarah. 2003. *Flannery O' Connor: The Obedient Imagination.* Athens, GA: University of Georgia Press.

Gurstein, Rochelle. 1996. *The Repeal of Reticence: A History of America's Cultural and Legal Struggles over Free Speech, Obscenity, Sexual Liberation, and Modern Art*. New York: Hill and Wang.

Hostetler, John A. 1993. *Amish Society.* 4th ed. Baltimore, MD: Johns Hopkins University Press.

Kraybill, Donald B. 2001. *The Riddle of Amish Culture*. Revised Edition. Baltimore, MD: Johns Hopkins University Press.

Kraybill, Donald B., and Marc A. Olshan. 1994. *The Amish Struggle with Modernity.* Hanover, NH: University Press of New England.

Laitinen, Kaisa, and Maarit Valo. 2018. "Meanings of Communication Technology in Virtual Team Meetings: Framing Technology-Related Interaction." *International Journal of Human-Computer Studies* 111: 12–22. https://doi.org/10.1016/j.ijhcs.2017.10.012.

Lane, Daniel S., Sigi S. Lee, Fan Liang, Dam Hee Kim, Liwei Shen, Brian E. Weeks, and Nojin Kwak. 2019. "Social Media Expression and the Political Self." *Journal of Communication* 69 (1): 49–72. https://doi.org/10.1093/joc/jqy064.

Lindell, Anna K., Nicole Campione-Barr, and Sarah E. Killoren. 2015. "Technologically-Mediated Communication with Siblings During the Transition to College: Associations with Relationship Positivity and Self-Disclosure." *Family Relations: An Interdisciplinary Journal of Applied Family Studies* 64 (4): 563–78. https://www.doi.org/10.1111/fare.12133.

Lindop, Grevel. 2015. *Charles Williams: The Third Inkling*. Oxford: Oxford University Press.

Livingstone, Sonya, Kjarton Ólafsson, Ellen Helsper, Francisco Lupiáñez-Villanueva, Guiseppe Veltri, and Frans Folkvord. 2017. "Maximizing Opportunities and Minimizing Risks for Children Online: The Role of Digital Skills in Emerging Strategies of Parental Mediation." *Journal of Communication* 67 (1): 82–105. https://doi.org/10.1111/jcom.12277.

MacDonald, George. 2004. *Heather and Snow* (2nd ed.). Whitethorn, CA: Johannesen. Original work published 1893/1896.

May, John R. 1976. *The Pruning Word: The Parables of Flannery O'Connor.* Notre Dame, IN: University of Notre Dame Press.

McLuhan, Marshall. 1962. *The Gutenberg Galaxy.* Toronto: The University of Toronto Press.

Medcalf, Stephen. 1996. "Athanasian Principles in Williams's Use of Images." In *The Rhetoric of Vision: Essays on Charles Williams*, edited by Charles A. Huttar and Peter J. Schakel, 27–43. Lewisburg, PA: Bucknell University Press.

Meyrowitz, Joshua. 1985. *No Sense of Place: The Impact of Electronic Media on Social Behavior*. New York: Oxford University Press.

Montgomery, Kathryn. 2015. "Children's Media Culture in a Big Data World." *Journal of Children and Media* 9 (2): 266–71. https://doi.org/10.1080/17482798.2015.1021197.

O'Connor, Flannery. 1956. "A View of the Woods." In *Everything that Rises Must Converge*, by Flannery O'Connor. New York: Farrar, Straus and Giroux.

O'Neal, Michael J. 2005. *Decades of American History: America in the 1920s.* New York: Facts on File.

Ong, Walter. 1967. *The Presence of the Word.* New Haven, CT: Yale University Press.

Postman, Neil. 1993. *Technopoloy: The Surrender of Culture to Technology*. New York: Vintage Books.

Ramsey, Meagan, Amy Gentzler, Jennifer Morey, Ann Oberhauser, and David Westerman. 2013. "College Students' Use of Communication Technology with Parents: Comparisons Between Two Cohorts in 2009 and 2011." *Cyberpsychology, Behavior, and Social Networking* 16 (10): 747–52. https://doi.org/10.1089/cyber.2012.0534.

Regnerus, Mark. 2003. "Religion and Positive Adolescent Outcomes: A Review of Research and Theory." *Review of Religious Research* 44 (4): 394–413. https://doi.org/10.2307/3512217.

Rudi, Jessie, Amy Walkner, and Jodi Dworkin. 2015. "Adolescent-Parent Communication in a Digital World: Differences by Family Communication Patterns." *Youth & Society* 47 (6): 811–28. https://doi.org/10.1177/0044118X14560334.

Sheer, Vivian C., and Ling Chen. 2004. "Improving Media Richness Theory: A Study of Interaction Goals, Message Valence, and Task Complexity in Manager–Subordinate Communication." *Management Communication Quarterly* 18 (1): 76–93.

Short, John, Ederyn Williams, and Bruce Christie. 1976. *The Social Psychology of Telecommunications*. London: John Wiley & Sons.

Simon, Caroline. 1997. *The Disciplined Heart: Love, Destiny, and Imagination.* Grand Rapids, MI: Wm. B. Eerdmans Publishing Company.

Spitzberg, Brian. 2006. "Preliminary Development of a Model and Measure of Computer-Mediated Communication (CMC) Competence." *Journal of Computer-Mediated Communication* 11 (2): 629–66. https://doi.org/10.1111/j.1083-6101.2006.00030.x.

Strate, Lance. 2006. *Echoes and Reflections: Media Ecology as a Field of Study.* Creskill, NJ: Hampton Press.

———. 2017. "The Human Condition as the Subject of Media Ecological Investigation." *Review of Communication* 17 (4): 240–56. https://doi.org/10.1080/15358593.2017.1367829.

Trevino, Linda Klebe, Richard L. Daft, and Robert H. Lengel. 1990. "Understanding Managers' Media Choices: A Symbolic Interactionist Perspective." In *Organizations and Communication Technology*, edited by Janet Fulk and Charles Steinfield, 71–94. Thousand Oaks, CA: Sage Publications, Inc.

Turkle, Sherry. 2011. *Alone Together: Why We Expect More from Technology and Less from Each Other.* New York: Basic Books.

Valkenburg, Patti M. 2017. "Understanding Self-Effects in Social Media." *Human Communication Research* 43 (4): 477–90. https://doi.org/10.1111/hcre.12113.

Walther, Joseph B., Tracy Loh, and Laura Granka. 2005. "Let Me Count the Ways: The Interchange of Verbal and Nonverbal Cues in Computer-Mediated and Face-to-Face Affinity." *Journal of Language and Social Psychology* 24 (1): 36–65. https://doi.org/10.1177/0261927X04273036.

Wilding, Raelene. 2006. "'Virtual' Intimacies? Families Communicating Across Transnational Contexts." *Global Networks* 6 (2): 125–42. https://doi.org/10.1111/j.1471-0374.2006.00137.x.

Williams, Charles. 1976. *The Greater Trumps*. Grand Rapids, MI: William B. Eerdmans. Original work published 1932 by Victor Gollancz Limited.

Wood, Ralph C. 2004. *Flannery O'Connor and the Christ-Haunted South*. Grand Rapids, MI: William B. Eerdmans.

Chapter Three

Rhetorical Constructions of the Reset

Video Games and Family Connections

Paul Lucas

Video games are often the recipient of misperception and demonization, being seen as a medium that has more negative impact than anything else. In general, there is a thought process that entertainment media has the potential to put "social development at risk" (Chory and Banfield 2009, 42). Significant levels of "media dependence could . . . lead to less frequent relational maintenance" (Chory and Banfield 2009, 44). Video games in particular are "quickly vilified" (Williams 2003, 524). In more recent history, though, video games have "earned some measure of redemption" (Williams 2003, 524). In that regard, I would like to examine how video games have not only been able to 'redeem' themselves, but how their specific functionality and storytelling capabilities can actually assist 'social development,' namely as it applies to contexts within the family.

There is very little debate left about the unique features of the video game medium and its capacity for storytelling. Video game storylines can be complex and interesting, though they are further distinguished from other media because of their participatory nature; within the storytelling capacity video games have, there is the ever-present and medium-defining sense of interactivity. Interactivity in video games can be defined as "the affordance that allows the user to make real-time changes in content to the medium" (Sundar and Limperos 2013, 515).

Since players take an interactive role in gameplay and plot, the video game experience is active, hinging on "player's agency" (Kjeldgaard-Christiansen 2020, 68) as important to plot progression. It is the act of "*being* a media character" (Klimmt, Hefner, and Vorderer 2009, 354). Especially within video games that are nonlinear, the player will have a direct impact on how and to what extent the storyline unfolds. Video games can importantly be characterized according to Gerl's (2016) idea of "dream worlds," as "'I can do anything' places" (14).

By assuming the role of playable characters, players can take on tasks and abilities that allow them to become fully immersed in the narrative structure, learning of plots and environments as the characters do. In video games, the player "can literally get into a character's skin and see the world from the character's point of view" (Simpson 2005, 21). Ultimately, "in video games, curiosity may refer to the progress of the story, but also to the action possibilities that players can try out ('What will happen if I do this?')" (Klimmt, et al. 2012, 193). Players are therefore able to make a number of different attempts at their gameplay, with a number of different approaches and additional chances at success.

With that in mind, I want to talk about playing video games as a family activity; as, yes, something that can be enjoyed for fun, but also as something that can ultimately be viewed as a learning opportunity for shaping worldviews. Specifically, in this work, I would like to explore the ways in which video game experiences allow for a literal and also symbolic 'reset,' where players are meant to understand the relevance of second chances. Ultimately, stories can be experienced and explored because of the active roles players take, but a number of attempts, failures, and retries are perfectly acceptable. Since video games are, after all, just games, it is okay to make mistakes and fail. Video games do have consequences—players can lose, characters can die—but the game's consequences, the punishments, are negligible and, at worst, short-lived.

Steel's (1998) notion of how "the ascendancy of simplicity over complexity is evident in almost every form of human endeavor, although strangely people's perceptions are almost exactly the opposite" (151) is central to my argument. Regardless of how 'simplistic' a message can appear at the surface level, the way in which people will interpret messages can be extremely complex. For families, video games are therefore a medium well-suited for a basis of an understanding of parental caring. Arnett and Arneson (1999) pointed out that "we make sense of the world together through stories created in common experience" (210). If that 'common experience' is one that families can share together when it comes to playing video games, then children might actually better perceive the family dynamic. Video games, after all, "provide an invaluable support for identity formation" (Persico et al. 2019, 1700) and are therefore relevant for study when they attempt to deal with complex and personal challenges.

Yes, video games have an "education potential" (Persico 2019, 1688). That potential, though, is manifested uniquely through video games, though, because "the individual is the fulcrum of [the] environment, and generally controls it, even if sometimes it can be overwhelming" (Persico 2019, 1690). 'Control' is, of course, the operative word because the player is in the position of guiding both the gameplay and plot.

Now, consider this idea from the standpoint of negotiating understanding. For children who are able to interact with, and at least partially impact, a game environment, which sometimes might be 'overwhelming' and in which they can ultimately be defeated, they take a hands-on approach to a gaming experience that can be appear tough at times and not always result in victory. That is exactly where family support can be shown as valuable to real-life challenges and losses.

The Game World

I would argue that learning is part of a reward in video gameplay, as, in many cases, "the goals of the game are interrelated with the unfolding of the story, requiring players to solve problems in order to advance the plot" (Lieberman 2006, 382). Since critical thinking and learning are often central to meeting objectives in video games, and since progressing through the story is often only achieved through meeting those objectives, it then stands to reason that thought-provoking elements of gameplay could also serve as a prompt for additional learning and reflection to take place within lived experience.

I would also argue that the real influence video games have on audiences is through the ways in which they allow players a temporary escape that is also categorized by the active role. Smuts (2008) even went as far as to say that video games are largely devoid of suspense because "suspense only arises when our ability to make a difference is radically diminished" (284). Suspense is felt in instances and scenes when players are "taken out of control" (Smuts 2008, 286), which, for your standard video game, would obviously not be often. While those watching a game might feel suspense, the player's ability to act and react within the game world makes them a direct participant who is therefore less likely to feel suspense due to an amount of control they have.

The active versus passive characteristic to video games also extends into how the games can serve as a means of escape. According to Klug and Schell (2006), "Rather than simply escape, as [people] do when they read a novel or when they watch a movie, games allow players to become actively involved in the world they escape into" (92). Video games can take hold of players because they are not the passive, more relaxed form of escape compared with other forms of media, and, as described by Geigner (2020), "A little escapism is nearly medicine."

Just because there is an active role for a player, though, does not mean video games should be viewed as punishing for poor or wrong decisions. Video games are a means of escape that allow the player to live out fantasy through character interactivity, but they also have little to no concern of implications for consequence—the story is molded in large part by the player, but can also be retried. It is in the interactive character and plot engagement, combined with the low risk of consequence, that video games may well be one of the most beneficial points of activity and conversation for families when juxtaposed against other forms of media entertainment.

To illustrate the point further, I would like to point out how video games lend themselves to these kinds of conversations in large part because of the characteristic of repeated tries as a form of exploration. Unlike other media, "Video games . . . encourage multiple attempts at problem-solving and decision-making" (Wood and Szymanski 2020, 130). Video games, "by contrast to the allocentricity of literature and film . . . may be said to offer principally *egocentric* experience: experience that is of and about the self" (Kjeldgaard-Christiansen 2020, 68). While other media can be accurately viewed as kinds of vicarious experiences, in that learning takes place passively through characters and plots, video games combine "interactivity and storytelling" (Crawford 2003, 262) for an experience that is much more active and hands-on, with players able to influence plot directions and character decisions. Part of that characteristic level of control puts the player in a position for do-overs. Players can take risks and then decide if they want to try again with different strategies.

The minimal consequence to gaming decisions hinges on the idea that "a low cost for failure [in video games] ensures that players will take risks, explore and try new things" (Gee 2010, 52). Video games can be started again, video games can be reset, and video game efforts can be tried once more. By allowing for 'resets,' or additional chances to succeed within both casual and competitive gameplay, children can learn that they may make mistakes, and yet still be allowed do-overs within the mindset of the family—that love from parents, and other family members, is just not fragile. Video games can be considered "learning ecologies . . . especially for younger people" (Persico et al. 2019, 1689), therefore playing key roles both in leisure activity and self-reflection.

It is here that the parental and familial discussions can become relevant to families. Through decisions made within video games, and with additional chances, parents have an opportunity to help their children think through choice and to show support for decisions. In this way, "Parents and children of high conversation-oriented families are free to interact with one another as they share ideas, express concerns, and participate in decision making" (Thompson and Schrodt 2014, 407). Video games, then, can be a catalyst. Further to the point, as evidenced in a study by Nash (2016), children viewed "belonging as the most important need within the Maslow hierarchy" (125). Players tend not to fully succeed at video games on their first tries, after all, so there is an opportunity to be explored in terms of the importance of learning from inevitable failure and mistakes but also how subsequent support can be received in light of mistakes—which may well be of particular importance for children to understand.

Fiction and Function for the Family

To explain it more clearly, video games can be used as a basis for reference when dealing with complex and personal challenges in life. While game world experiences are much more superficial than what will occur in real life, derived meanings from gameplay can and should be applied to contexts that are exceedingly more complicated. Chances for restarts are afforded to video game characters because they are integral to the plot and gaming experience, while opportunities for restarts for people in real life are key to strong relationships—including familial relationships.

In Fisher's (1984) perception of the ways in which narratives can be critiqued, he discussed the importance of "probability, what constitutes a coherent story" and a "constant habit of testing narrative fidelity, whether the stories they experience ring true with the stories they know to be true in their lives" (8). While coherent stories are important for video game appeal, it is the fidelity, the application for what is true in life, that is central to the current discussion. Lieberman (2006) noted that "interactive games are powerful environments for learninglearning. . . . Players learn new skills, knowledge, insights, attitudes, or even behaviors in games that challenge them to think, explore, and respond" (379). An application to real life, from that 'powerful environment for learning,' should not be lost on the player, especially if families have conversations surrounding video games as they are played.

I would agree with Gee (2010) when he commented on how "video games are not content-driven media though they do have content. They are driven by choices and problem solving. Content is there to motivate player choices about how to solve problems" (52). If we accept the premise that "video games may be full of nonnarrative material, like philosophical reflections, descriptions unrelated to the narrative core" (Grodal 2003, 133), then we can also accept that, as explained previously, while video games have compelling storylines that players seek to progress by accomplishing in-game objectives, there is the opportunity for much deeper thought and more detailed thought processes. While the 'narrative core' might well be related to internal plot dynamics, it is the 'fidelity' that shows the real value of narrative to an external application in our lives.

In summation, video games, as compared with other kinds of games, allow for an immersion into fictional worlds with characters on a more significant level. Contrasted with other media, video games have an important element of active participation, which may well be appealing to families because of the level at which family members can engage with the gameplay. Though this may, at face value, appear to be a stretch because it is an unconventional way of approaching and understanding video games, it is worthwhile as a discussion point for how the unique medium might be understood. It is almost by the nature of what they are that video games can be valued in this respect. That 'common experience' for families could allow for some reality world-building, in addition to the ability players have "to create or live in an alternate world and build narrative out of that world" (Klug and Schell 2006, 92).

Although video game stories are obviously works of fiction, and although the threat of consequence to player choice and action in video games is minimal, they should not be discounted in terms of how truly thought-provoking they can be. Video games are, quite simply, fictional manifestations of how people can understand the real world because they have the potential for considerable and serious reflection from experience on the part of the player—again, primarily because they must complete decisions and actions in the role of the character.

Before I get into some specific recommendations about types of games and applications that might be effective in drawing a familial comparison to the game world, I would like to concretely express why video games can be of particular importance in their family appeal in the first place. In recent history, there has been a prevailing notion that "policy makers, regulators, and video game marketers might all benefit from a deeper understanding of the influence of family dynamics in video game demand" (Bassiouni, Hackley, and Meshreki 2018, 1377). Though Bassiouni, Hackley, and Meshreki (2018) in their study speculated as to the benefits of video games outside the realm of a medium of entertainment, they claimed that "shared identity had a direct influence on children's behaviour towards video games from the perspective of their parents, as they were seen to seek potential social gains such as group membership and inclusion from its ownership and usage" (1390). Again—the authors here were suggesting that people/friends can bond over having video gameplay and knowledge in common, but I would like to offer the premise that the seeking of 'social gains and group membership' can also have a correlation to families bonding over video game experiences, as well.

Games and Guidelines

I am hesitant to recommend exact game titles that could be ideal for family activity for two reasons. The first is reason is I see a close-to universal benefit of enjoying video games with family. I similarly want to reinforce the concept that it is the importance of 'resets,' of do-overs, and even of failed attempts that matter. Failing and trying again are far from exclusive to any particular titles, so I again would not want to limit the issue by giving precise titles.

The second reason I am hesitant to recommend particular titles is because I want to avoid putting an exact range of age parameters on what I mean when I say 'children.' Certainly, there is an argument to be made that younger children would see the most benefit in understanding how they can make mistakes and be supported and forgiven by family. At the same time, teenagers and young adults could see benefit, as well. Trying to fit in within peers in high school and college, while also trying to make decisions such as major and career path, can cause significant stress. Enjoying video games with family at those life stages could be a therapeutic experience since it is a low-stakes chance to spend time with family in a fun activity—that more importantly allows for do-overs, second chances, and exploration, all things that young adults may lose sight of as they make such critical decisions in their lives.

Additionally, teenagers and young adults would likely want to play more mature-rated video game titles as compared with younger children. Mature-rated games are typically more challenging, with deeper, more complex plotlines and decision making; that could be important, as parents could then show their children they are capable of playing and knowing more popular video games. It could also be a clear demonstration to older children that the family activity is more designed for them, as opposed to being 'for kids.'

Having said that, I would still like to make some very measured arguments and offer up possible genres to consider. This idea of a reset that is rhetorically constructed through video games, of a learning experience where children can determine that mistakes and failures are okay and that families allow for second chances—not expecting perfection—is important. It does not hold much weight, however, without application that removes the suggestion from purely theoretical speculation.

Video game characters have the capability to function as "supernatural ambassadors of agency" (Rehak 2003, 106), which is why they can be a factor in meaningful family activity and discussion. Characters are representative of 'supernatural agency' because they are like stand-ins for players; they are a way to live out player desire and choice, all within the confines of that low-stakes game world. As playable characters progress and struggle, fail and achieve, they can be a basis for some real thought-provoking conversations among family members. 'Why did the character/player make that choice?' 'Why is the character struggling?' 'What is currently motivating the character?' Most importantly, if and when the player fails, there can be meaningful conversation about how additional chances are afforded; the emphasis on how failure and mistakes are okay, especially in the eyes of family when it comes to the worth of family members.

I would again like to emphasize the importance of these significant kinds of discussions coupled with playing video games as a family activity. Without it, some of the "narrative fidelity" (Fisher 1984, 8) may not resonate or could be lost. Klimmt, Hefner, and Vorderer (2009) depicted the dichotomy between players and characters as "a moment of intense identification and substantial change of self-perception through adoption of character attributes [that] may be followed by an episode of greater perceived distance between the player and the character" (360). In the absence of substantive conversations with families, video games, characters, and their application to reality may not have longevity—even though there is likely a strong level of player-character empathy during the gameplay experience. For all the learning that is possible through video games, they are still entertaining works of fiction. It is that genuine connection with family, both through the bonding over gameplay and through thoughtful dialogue, which has permanence.

Because video games are part of popular culture and because they do have such appeal as a form of entertainment, they can be a useful way to spark conversation. Perhaps most importantly, Lieberman (2006) explained video game relevance by saying that "interactive games can motivate people to learn, including those who at first are not particularly interested in the subject matter" (380). Even beyond the fact that video games can be used as an entry point to family discussion, I would suggest that they should be. For any children interested in video games, some talk about family support and inner workings might be bolstered because of the connection to video games. While some may argue that doing so creates a level of superficiality to serious conversation, I would counter by saying it is the conversation that matters in the long term.

Given the right opportunity, video games and their characters can make a difference. As characters have that 'supernatural agency' ascribed to them, they can function like change agents for children looking to comprehend that failure and mistakes are okay; that family will ultimately be there and will forgive, allowing for more chances. It is a form of what Miliard (2014) called "gamification," which is "using computer game design and mechanics to teach people, or encourage them to change their behavioral patterns." I would also then speculate that, if family members can learn some important lessons about family dynamics and relationships through the video game experience, change is a possibility in family members and their way of thinking.

To put it plainly, the player to character relationship and the nonlinear gameplay toward story experience are exactly what can bring about a change of thinking grounded in reality. Video games "do not deal with what happened or is happening, but with what may happen. Unlike narrative and drama, its essence lays on a basic assumption: change is possible" (Frasca 2003, 233). Players can look at the potential for what can be achieved in the game world as a future prospect, both in terms of character behavior and decision making that can be applied to a forward trajectory.

Since video games are characterized by what the player can do to push the storylines forward, a future, forward thinking about how the player can change and shape the fictional world becomes more important than what is happening currently or in the past in terms of the plot. The same case, though, could be made for what can be learned from the gaming experience. The 'intense identification' might be fleeting because it is intrinsically tied to the character as the narrative evolves, but then change can also be possible in terms of how the individual might move forward with greater knowledge and understanding of what it means to be part of and supported by family. The key characteristics of 'what may happen' and 'change is possible' can be logically linked to how one might move forward with a greater understanding of familial place—so, 'what may happen' now? For children of a variety of ages, who might embrace a variety of different games, there exists a possibility that they can learn about family and change their perspective and way of thinking, as brought on by families playing video games together and discussing elements of story and gameplay.

Genres and Guidelines

In order to create a more exact frame of reference, then, I would like to recommend two genres of video games that could prove the most worthwhile. While, again, I am hesitant to recommend particular titles, I would like to suggest two genres that can help put theory into practice and for specific reasons. For those unfamiliar with video games, I will also provide brief descriptive points as to why these genres might be effective.

As stressed throughout this work, the 'reset' is the best feature games have for family discussion. By emphasizing with children that do-overs, second chances, and additional tries are welcome within family life, too, children can benefit from not taking video game mistakes and failures so seriously, while also grasping that family will love and support them through real-life failures and mistakes, as well. To build on that train of thought, role-playing video games and visual novels may be ideal genres for family gameplay. At the very least, they could be well-suited for family activity because they are generally not quite as brutal as some other genres, such as first-person shooters. For anyone newer to video games and learning to play them, they may also be ideal because they do not generally require the same skill set as some other genres, such as platformers. Both role-playing games and visual novels also tend toward intricate storylines with well-developed characters, which may frequently hold appeal over puzzle and strategy-based games.

Role-playing video games have a key feature that is valuable for discussion. In addition to the fact that characters progress, they also level up as part of their advancement through the game. The characters are meant to grow stronger, increase in stats, and even gain new skills and abilities. The subsequent talk around the role-playing games, then, can concentrate on learning and gaining different skills and knowledge throughout life. Of course, as is consistent with games in general, certain failures and mistakes come with the territory of that kind of personal growth.

Really, the objective in role-playing games is often some kind of big-picture achievement. Sellers (2006) described role-playing games as "allowing the player to take on the role of a hero on a quest to right a wrong or achieve a great destiny" (11). Since characters try to do what is 'right,' they may face certain challenges and certain adversities as a direct result of that goal. They may also experience failure. When trying to map out for a child the distinctions between right and wrong, it could be explained that sometimes doing what is right is more difficult and may come with struggle.

As a caveat to my recommendation of role-playing games, I want to address the issue of permadeath, a reference to a game characteristic when a character's death is final—which can be found in role-playing video games, though it is possible to locate it in other types of games, as well. For example, maybe a player would have a playable character in his or her party who then does not survive a battle; with the permadeath feature active, that character will be permanently gone/dead, no longer able to be used and perhaps even no longer having a role within the game's narrative. Permadeath creates much greater risk and consequence, so there are a few things to think about when confronted with it.

First, permadeath, for the games that even have it to begin with, in some role-playing games is optional, available to be disabled. In those cases, permadeath does not have to be a part of the gameplay at all if not wanted. Second, depending on the age of the child, permadeath may present an opportunity to discuss death. Third and most importantly, however, video games should always be viewed as fun and entertaining; as having low stakes. Even if a character falls in battle and permadeath makes them gone forever, the battle/game can be retried. It can be 'reset.' There is a level of forgiveness and second chance to error, which I cannot stress enough as a critical component to this work.

For the other genre, I would like to advocate for visual novels. Visual novels are often overlooked by players overall because they deviate from standard gameplay. Rather than focusing so much on character action, visual novels instead mostly put players in the position of characters who make decisions and dialogue choices when conversing with other characters. Since visual novels do not usually require the same level of video game knowledge and ability that other genres do, they can serve as origin points for parents, or other family members, who may be looking to play video games with family but do not know where to start.

It is with the dialogue, though, that visual novels have their real value with families. As opposed to many other video games where success and failure are gauged through character action, success and failure in visual novels are customarily more dependent on what is said. There is a chance to talk about second chances and forgiveness/support from family when the mistake made by a family member is not based in action, but rather is based in what is said. We all sometimes say things we do not mean, which is why visual novels may hold a special place in the greater context of family activity and subsequent connection.

Visual novels and their "lack of action" means they can "unfold at a deliberate pace" (Cavallaro 2010, 9)—which also means a 'deliberate pace' for thought. As players, for characters, think through decisions in their dialogue choices, they can take their time because they are not pressured based on action-based decisions. More critical thinking can therefore be enacted, as well, which matches up with the lesson in real life that we need to be careful and conscious in what we say to others.

Sometimes, visual novels constrain the player's ability to take too long lost in thought, by adding a timer that either runs out and results in the character not saying anything at all, or runs out and then forces the character into a default line of dialogue—often in response to another character. In those cases, some conversation with children about how we sometimes gut-level react, without thinking things through fully, can lead to saying what we do not mean. Again, though, the game can always be retried, much in the same way as, hopefully, future interactions with family members can be, as well, if the relationship is not dismantled because of missteps within conversation.

What it comes down to for both role-playing video games and visual novels is that there is significant reliance on story for the games' marketability and appeal. Role-playing games and visual novels function because "for the game itself to become a narrative, the player's imagination and interpretive skills must be consistently stimulated" (Cavallaro 2010, 78). What the player can 'imagine' will play a functional part in how the stories are viewed and 'interpreted,' as well as how the stories progress and end.

In role-playing games, which skills and abilities will the player choose to instill in the playable characters? How will players strategically approach challenges on the path to doing what is right? In visual novels, what kinds of dialogue choices will players make? How will those choices impact character conversations and relationships in the game?

Unsurprisingly, these kinds of questions can then correlate directly to how players might ask questions in reality, particularly as ascribed to family. Which skills and abilities will a child choose to develop in life? How will the child strategically use skills and knowledge to try and do what is right? What kinds of choices will a child make when interacting and talking with family? How will those choices impact individual conversations, as well as overall relationships among family? There are a number of rhetorical constructions from video games that can then be used as informational in life.

Again, though, each of these questions can lead to discussions about how second chances, metaphorical 'resets,' can be afforded to family members. If children work in life to develop certain skills and abilities, they can always backtrack, perhaps toward different skill sets and a different career path. If children try and have an intention to do what is right, and either fail or make things worse, they are not lost but can be put back on track. If children make the wrong decisions in what they say, they can be forgiven—either in the moment or in the grand scheme of the entire familial relationship. The value of role-playing video games and visual novels cannot be overstated for making these levels of associations.

Conclusion

There will likely always be disagreement over the extent to which reality mirrors the media and media mirror reality. Just because that disagreement takes place, however, is an indication that media provide important talking points and chances for reflection. Video games occupy a unique space within entertainment media, distinguished by interactive storytelling that establishes objectives and moves the story along in accordance with player action.

Since active participation is intertwined in progressing video game stories, failures within gameplay can derail or cease the story progression either through altering the narrative completely or ceasing it. While players would obviously like to succeed at video games, failures and repeated attempts are a normal and standard part of the video game decision making experience. Though video game failure can be frustrating, it is part of the challenge and enjoyment of playing video games, with do-overs and retries characteristically letting players learn from their mistakes through subsequent attempts.

As a more obvious point, it can be important to have conversations with children about how they should not take failure within video games too seriously—video games are meant for fun entertainment, after all. As a less obvious point, though, playing video games as a family activity may present an occasion to open up a larger conversation with children, letting them know that failure and mistakes in life can be forgiven by family, and that the family will continue to provide support. In this way, video games can be a jumping off point to some really critical discussions about how retries, metaphorical kinds of 'resets' or second chances, are given when children have missteps and make mistakes, especially when they are motivated and trying to do their best.

While I would argue that video games, near universally, can be these meaning generators with families who play video games together as a bonding experience, I would mainly want to draw attention to video games that have characters and plot central to the gameplay. The interactivity and plot/character progression are starting points to why video games can be an engaging medium for family enjoyment, but these characteristics also help make the case that video games are distinct from other kinds of family activities and even other kinds of games, as well. They give families a chance to rhetorically construct meanings within families and how relationships among family members should be perceived, including when some family members are struggling, making mistakes, or failing.

As a prescriptive feature to this work, I would recommend considering role-playing video games and visual novels as possible genres that could prove effective for engaging with family through video gameplay. At the same time, I would like to suggest that nearly all video games have the capability of encouraging important conversation. My expectation is that families can make sound judgments regarding what kinds of video games work best to be shared, with attention to individual family member interests and age ranges. There is rich storytelling available out there in video game worlds, but there is rich storytelling that should occur within the family, as well.

REFERENCES

Arnett, Ronald C., and Pat Arneson. 1999. *Dialogic Civility in a Cynical Age: Community, Hope, and Interpersonal Relationships.* Albany, NY: State University of New York Press.

Bassiouni, Dina. H., Chris Hackley, and Hakim Meshreki. 2018. "The Integration of Video Games in Family-life Dynamics: An Adapted Technology Acceptance Model of Family Intention to Consume Video Games." *Information Technology & People* 32, no. 6: 1376–96.

Cavallaro, Dani. 2010. *Anime and the Visual Novel: Narrative Structure, Design and Play at the Crossroads of Animation and Computer Games.* Jefferson, NC: McFarland & Company, Inc.

Chory, Rebecca M., and Sara Banfield. 2009. "Media Dependence and Relational Maintenance in Interpersonal Relationships." *Communication Reports* 22, no. 1: 41–53.

Crawford, Chris. (2003). "Interactive Storytelling." In *The Video Game Theory Reader,* ed. Mark J. P. Wolf and Bernard Perron. 259–273. New York: Routledge.

Fisher, Walter. R. 1984. "Narration as a Human Communication Paradigm: The Case of Public Moral Argument." *Communication Monographs* 51: 8–22.

Frasca, Gonzalo. 2003. "Simulation Versus Narrative: Introduction to Ludology." In *The Video Game Theory Reader,* ed. Mark J. P. Wolf and Bernard Perron. 221–235. New York: Routledge.

Gee, James Paul. 2010. "Video Games: What They Can Teach Us about Audience Engagement." *Nieman Reports* 52–54.

Geigner, Timothy. 2020, March 25. "After Years of Being Blamed for Everything, the World Turns to Video Games to Escape During Coronavirus Shut-in." *techdirt* https://www.techdirt.com/articles/20200324/16255544164/after-years-being-blamed-everything-world-turns-to-video-games-to-escape-during-coronavirus-shut-in.shtml.

Gerl, Ellen. J. 2016. "Survivors and Dreamers: A Rhetorical Vision of *Teen Voices* Magazine." *Journal of Magazine & New Media Research* 17, no. 1: 1–26.

Grodal, Torben. 2003. "Stories for Eye, Ear, and Muscles: Video Games, Media, and Embodied Experiences." In *The Video Game Theory Reader,* ed. Mark J. P. Wolf and Bernard Perron. 129–55. New York: Routledge.

Kjeldgaard-Christiansen, Jens. 2020. "Narrative Video Game Aesthetics and Egocentric Ethics." *Journal of Media and Communication Research* 68: 88–106.

Klimmt, Christoph, Dorothée Hefner, and Peter Vorderer. 2009. "The Video Game as 'True' Identification: A Theory of Enjoyable Alterations of Players' Self-perception." *Communication Theory* 19: 351–73.

Klimmt, Christoph, Christian Roth, Ivar Vermeulen, Peter Vorderer, and Franziska Susanne Roth. 2012. "Forecasting the Experience of Future Entertainment Technology: 'Interactive Storytelling' and Media Enjoyment." *Games and Culture* 7, no. 3: 187–208.

Klug, G. Christopher, and Jesse Schell. 2006. "Why People Play Games: An Industry Perspective." In *Playing Video Games: Motives, Responses, and Consequences,* ed. Peter Vorderer and Jennings Bryant. 91–100. Mahwah, NJ: Lawrence Erlbaum Associates, Inc.

Lieberman, Debra. A. 2006. "What Can We Learn from Playing Interactive Games?" In *Playing Video Games: Motives, Responses, and Consequences,* ed. Peter Vorderer and Jennings Bryant. 379–97. Mahwah, NJ: Lawrence Erlbaum Associates, Inc.

Miliard, Mike. 2014. "Gamification Comes to Clinicians." *Healthcare IT News' Website* http://www.healthcareitnews.com/news/gamification-comes-clinicians.

Nash, Sally. 2016. "Message in a Bottle: A Comparative Study of Spiritual Needs of Children Both in and Out of the Hospital." *International Journal of Children's Spirituality* 21, no. 2: 116–27.

Persico, Donatella, Marcello Passarelli, Francesca Pozzi, Jeffrey Earp, Francesca Maria Dagnino, and Flavio Manganello. 2019. "Meeting Players Where They Are: Digital Games and Learning Ecologies." *British Journal of Educational Technology* 50, no. 4: 1687–1712.

Rehak, Bob. 2003. "Playing at Being: Psychoanalysis and the Avatar." In *The Video Game Theory Reader*, ed. Mark J. P. Wolf and Bernard Perron. 103–27. New York: Routledge.

Sellers, Michael. 2006. "Designing the Experience of Interactive Play." In *Playing Video Games: Motives, Responses, and Consequences,* ed. Peter Vorderer and Jennings Bryant. 9–22. Mahwah, NJ: Lawrence Erlbaum Associates, Inc.

Simpson, Elizabeth S. 2005. "Evolution in the Classroom: What Teachers Need to Know about the Video Game Generation." *TechTrends: Linking Research & Practice to Improve Learning* 49, no. 5: 17–22.

Smuts, Aaron. 2008. "The Desire-frustration Theory of Suspense." *Journal of Aesthetics and Art Criticism* 66, no. 3: 281–90.

Steel, Jon. 1998. *Truth, Lies, and Advertising: The Art of Account Planning.* New York: John Wiley & Sons, Inc.

Sundar, S. Shyam, and Anthony M. Limperos. 2013. "Uses and Grats 2.0: New Gratifications for New Media." *Journal of Broadcasting and Electronic Media* 57, no. 4: 504–25.

Thompson, Patty Ann, and Schrodt, Paul. 2015. "Perceptions of Joint Family Storytelling as Mediators of Family Communication Patterns and Family Strengths." *Communication Quarterly* 63, no. 4: 405–26.

Williams, Dmitri. 2003. "The Video Game Lightning Rod: Constructions of a New Media Technology, 1970–2000." *Information, Communication, and Technology* 6, no. 4: 523–50.

Wood, Susannah M., and Antonia Szymanski. 2020. "'The Me I Want You to See': The Use of Video Game Avatars to Explore Identity in Gifted Adolescents." *Gifted Child Today* 43, no. 2: 124–34.

Chapter Four

The Role of Communication and Information Technology in Health Information Seeking

Patty Wharton-Michael

Family life is increasingly influenced by the use of computers and communication technologies (Chesley 2006; Hughes and Hans 2001). The American Community Survey (ACS), conducted by the U.S. Census Bureau, revealed that in 2018, 92% of all households in the United States had one type of computer and that 85% of households had a broadband internet subscription. The survey also highlighted the growth of smartphone ownership, claiming that 84% of households reported owning a smartphone, surpassing ownership of other computing devices, such as desktops, laptops, and tablets (Martin 2021). Although differences in computer ownership and internet connectivity vary for different groups of people in the United States—by age, race, socioeconomic status, geographic region, homeownership, English proficiency, and disabilities—the ACS survey findings suggest that ownership (84% to 92%) and connectivity (74% to 85%) have increased sharply over the last five years in the United States (Martin 2021).

As communication technologies evolve and become more accessible, the adoption and use of such technologies have become customary among family members of all ages (Hitlin 2018). Information and communication technologies allow family members the ability to communicate synchronously or asynchronously, spontaneously, more frequently, and at low cost (Lanigan 2009). Communication technologies serve as tools that have the potential to mobilize mass amounts of information and resources, which is particularly useful for decision-making. One way in which technology is used in family decision-making is through seeking health information. In fact, when asked to describe information seeking online, individuals from all over the world most commonly report looking up information about health and medicine (Silver and Huang 2019). As families become more "connected" and reliant on computer and communication technologies, it is important to understand how this "connectivity" influences family member's decision-making process regarding health decisions. The importance of having the ability to seek health information online became exceptionally evident with the coronavirus outbreaking in 2020.

In January 2020, the World Health Organization declared a global health emergency with the onset of the novel coronavirus and by March declared the COVID-19 outbreak a pandemic. To slow the spread of the virus, governments issued stay-at-home orders, closing businesses and schools, which forced families into their homes for their safety. Families were forced to consider how their daily needs, work, and commitments would be fulfilled with limited interaction with others outside their homes. Information and communication technologies became crucial to stay connected to others, to go to school, to satisfy work obligations, to find information, and to be entertained. While consistent connectivity was not reliable or accessible to all individuals, 90% of Americans reported that the internet was important or essential to them during the pandemic (McClain et al. 2021). In addition to completing daily tasks and communicating, information and communication technologies enabled family members to seek information about the novel coronavirus, its origin, symptoms, treatments, and prevention.

The COVID-19 pandemic highlights the importance of understanding how family members use information and communication technologies to find and validate health information. Families engage in health decision-making processes from the inception of each member until ultimately their death, and members within a family (e.g., children, parents, grandparents, etc.) may use different communication technologies and tools—email, websites, social media, and blogs—to seek information about health-related topics.

This chapter seeks to explore how family members use communication technologies in health decision-making for and among family members. While family members make health decisions regarding a multitude of conditions, diseases, and circumstances for each member, this chapter will use one topic—vaccinations—to consider how information and communication technologies are used in family decision-making regarding health decisions. Finally, the chapter will examine the role of trust in sources (impersonal and mediated information versus personal interactions with family members and physicians) and the complicated interaction effects that have been identified in relation to health-information-seeking behaviors (Yang, Chen, and Wendorf Muhamad 2017).

INFORMATION AND COMMUNICATION TECHNOLOGY FOR FAMILY HEALTH

As information and communication technologies have increased and have been commonly adopted within households, family members have additional tools to access informational resources, track health history, interact with physicians, and connect to broader social networks. Scholars and physicians have referred to the adoption of such tools as e-health. Eysenbach (2001) defines e-Health as:

> the intersection of medical informatics, public health and business, referring to health services and information delivered or enhanced through the Internet and related technologies. In a broader sense, the term characterizes not only a technical development, but also a state of mind, a way of thinking, an attitude, and a commitment for networked, global thinking to improve health care locally, regionally, and worldwide by using information and communication technology. (1)

Eysenbach argues that e-Health improves healthcare by making it more efficient, enhancing quality of care by sharing information between providers, empowering patients through access to personal health records, enabling individuals to gain services from areas that may have previously been unable to be reached geographically, and strengthening a partnership between providers and patients.

Access to personal health records through health portals has been a particularly useful benefit for families when making health decisions (Fiks et al. 2016; Kelly, Hoonakker, and Dean 2017; King et al. 2017). Electronic health records (EHRs) are secure digital health records that are recorded in real time and provide a "patient's medical history, diagnoses, medications, treatment plans, immunization dates, allergies, radiology images, and laboratory and test results" (Office of the National Coordinator for Health Information Technology 2019). In addition to providing EHRs, health portals allow patients to schedule appointments, request and attend virtual appointments, access articles and resources, and communicate with providers.

Family members are not limited, however, to using tools and resources offered by the providers (such as medical portals).

Another common use of e-Health in family decision making is the use of searching online for health information. The Pew Research Center reports that Americans indicate they most frequently use the internet for health-information-seeking purposes to find information for a specific health problems or conditions, medical treatments and procedures, diet and nutrition, exercise, prescriptions, and alternative medicines ("Internet Health

Resources" 2003). Family members search for health topics from mental health issues, diabetes, cancer, immunizations, to remedies for a common cold (Gage and Panagakis 2012; Fergie, Hilton, and Hunt 2016; Treadgold et al. 2020; Chi 2021; "Internet Health Resources" 2003). Searching for health information online is not limited to adults. Adolescents and young adults report using the internet as well to find relevant health information for topics such as sex, contraceptives, diet, and exercise (Borzekowski and Rickert 2001). Wang, Shi, and Kong (2021) conducted a meta-analysis of 44 research articles, which examined online health-information-seeking to identify the greatest factors of how individuals search for health information online. The researchers found that the perceived usefulness, quality, and trustworthiness of the information were the greatest determinants of online health-information-seeking behavior.

Magsamen-Conrad et al. (2019) explored the online health searching practices of middle-aged and older adults and found participants used online sources to seek information about a family member's condition and to seek supplemental information about a health condition for themselves or others. In some cases, participants sought health information online, rather than asking a family member (or someone in their social network) directly about their condition or diagnosis. The study highlights the importance of family members' "co-management" of health, information, and technology. Magsamen-Conrad et al. discovered "many middle-aged and older adults question their ability to effectively access needed information, even as they find themselves responsible for understanding and managing the role of technology in personal health management for themselves, their partners, and or other members of their families; [also] their efficacy is affected by those around them" (866–867). For example, participants reported that family members were both primary sources of assistance and of stigma when considering their media literacy and self-efficacy.

For some family members who are not media literate or perhaps do not have access to the internet, individuals must rely on "surrogates" in their social networks and family to access the wealth of health information online; if they do not choose to use a surrogate they may simply rely on printed materials and information from health professionals and family members (Massey 2016). It is important to recognize that as health information becomes more prevalent online, a digital divide continues to exist for certain sections of the population, typically those of lower income and education, elderly, disabled, and minorities (Feng and Xie 2015; Martin 2021; Jacobs, Amuta, and Jeon 2017).

While the scope of this chapter does not include an exhaustive overview of how family members use informational and communication technologies to address all health concerns and issues within their family, this work will use the topic of vaccinations to consider how family members rely on informational and communication technologies as tools to engage in decision-making.

VACCINATIONS

According to the World Health Organization vaccination "is a simple, safe, and effective way of protecting you against harmful diseases before you come into contact with them. It uses your body's natural defense to build resistance to specific infections and make your immune system stronger" ("Vaccines and Immunizations: What Is Vaccination?" 2020). Over a life span, family members are faced with making decisions about the uptake of different vaccinations (e.g., measles, mumps, rubella, polio, meningitis, HPV, pneumonia, pertussis, COVID-19, and others). While parents may make unilateral decisions regarding typical childhood vaccines (e.g., measles, mumps, rubella, rotavirus, hepatitis B, etc.), parents must often collaborate with teenagers to make decisions about vaccinations for cervical cancer or meningitis or with aging partners or parents about receiving vaccines, such as for pneumonia, pertussis, or COVID-19.

While vaccinations for many diseases have been widely accepted among families in the United States, previous research has identified a growing hesitancy within families to allow members to be vaccinated (Ashkenazi et al. 2020; Heiss, Carmack, and Chadwick 2015; Thaker 2021; Rhodes et al. 2020). Many scholars attribute the growing skepticism for childhood vaccines to Andrew Wakefield's erroneous research that was published in 1998 (and then redacted), reporting a link between the MMR vaccine and autism (Koslap-Petraco 2019). Although, Wakefield's research was discredited, the concern over a possible link between autism and vaccines continues to be discussed and debated throughout the world (Rao and Andrade 2011). Additionally, as "newer" vaccines have been developed over the last several decades, for HPV, H1N1, and COVID-19, concerns have been raised over the rapid development of vaccines and arguments have been made for the need for additional data to feel comfortable making such important decisions for family members (Thaker 2021; Rhodes et al. 2020; SteelFisher et al. 2010; Rodkey 2014).

Peretti-Watel et al. (2015) describe vaccine hesitancy as "a kind of decision-making process that depends on people's level of commitment to healthism/risk culture and on their level of confidence toward health authorities and mainstream medicine" (Conclusion, para. 1). They argue it is not as simple as separating individuals into pro- and anti-vaccine categories; but rather, to understand factors that influence individuals' vaccine hesitancy, researchers must examine how socioeconomic status, health-related cognition, attitudes, and beliefs affect an individual's hesitancy (Peretti-Watel et al. 2015). Also, interactions with physicians may play a role in family members' decision-making about vaccines. Peretti-Watel et al. (2015) explain:

> in some cases, health professionals may fuel patients' VH (directly, when homeopaths and naturopaths express convincingly their doubt regarding vaccination to their patients, or indirectly, when pro-vaccine physicians refuse to accept into their practices families who are reluctant to vaccinate their children), but sometimes vaccine-hesitant patients may raise doubts in their physician's mind. (Conclusion, para. 4)

Research has demonstrated the positive and negative impacts that physician communication and interaction have had on parents' choices regarding vaccinations (Heiss, Carmack, and Chadwick 2015; Lyons 2013; Jones et al. 2012; Fredrickson et al. 2004). Parents who are concerned about the safety of vaccinations and the accuracy of their physician's recommendation are sometimes confronted with a moral dilemma of doing what they perceive is best for their child versus what they perceive is best for a larger community. Clements and Ratzan (2003) argue that if an individual discovers that a medical professional has given incomplete information regarding vaccines, the individual may become resentful and suspicious, resulting in "a credibility gap between audience and source" (25). While it is evident that patient-physician interactions are influential, it is unclear how parents who choose not to vaccinate seek out and validate alternative sources regarding the safety and effectiveness of vaccinations.

When patients become dissatisfied with their physician, they may become searchers and view the internet as a more reliable source for information (Tustin 2010). Jones et al. (2012) found that "parents who did not view their child's healthcare provider as a reliable vaccine information source were more likely to obtain vaccine information using the Internet" (p. 1). Parents who do not vaccinate are not alone in their belief that the internet may serve as a credible source on vaccines. Surprisingly, one study found that physicians who do not recommend children get all routine vaccinations "reported the internet and magazine stories as one of the most trusted sources compared with physicians who did recommend all vaccines" (Gust et al. 2008, 578).

Individuals may turn to a variety of sources, other than their physician, when seeking health information. Smith (2011) argued that demographics influence how individuals seek alternative health sources. Smith (2011) reported:

> Older adults, Whites, those with more education and higher incomes are more likely than other populations to use and trust their health professional for information. Younger adults, those with more education and income were more likely to use and trust the Internet for health information than other populations.

> Younger adults, Hispanics, and those with less education and income were more likely to use and trust family and friends for health information than other populations. Finally, older adults, Blacks, and those with less education and income were more likely than other populations to use and trust TV for health information. (D. Smith 2011, 208)

In a study conducted in Austria, participants indicated they most commonly searched the internet for health information, followed by doctors, books, family, friends, newspapers, TV, and radio (Haluza et al. 2017). Heiss et al. (2015) found parents who chose not to vaccinate for pertussis used healthcare providers, personal values and beliefs, news media, public health campaigns, and nonpregnant family and friends as informational sources to make their decisions.

Several studies have specifically focused on different types of informational sources and their possible influence on individuals' choices to vaccinate (Head and Harsin 2016; Hofman et al. 2013). Cohen and Head (2014) conducted a qualitative study to explore the lack of vaccination practices among adolescents in rural Appalachian Kentucky. This area was selected because its vaccination rates were much lower than other populations. Cohen and Head (2014) conducted interviews with 21 parents and found three themes emerged: 1) "knowledge was not strongly related to a parent's behavior," 2) "parents with positive preventive health attitudes had the desire to protect their children's future through vaccination," and 3) "opinion leaders in the community served as important motivators for parents vaccinating their children" (295). Not only have community leaders served as influential sources for parents, but social capital within one's community has been determined to also "facilitate individual's decision-making through their participation in a variety of communication groups that exchange information, identify problems and solutions, manage conflicting information, and improve health" (Jung, Lin, and Viswanath 2013, 2).

Research over the past several decades has also examined the characteristics and motivations of the growing number of parents who are choosing not to vaccinate their children against preventable diseases. While socioeconomic status has, in the past, been associated with parents who choose not to vaccinate (Wooten, Luman, and Barker 2007), the United States has seen steady improvement in lessening the disparities of uptake in childhood vaccinations for those from lower socioeconomic households (Zhao and Smith 2013). Avery and Lariscy (2014) argued that socioeconomic status is not "as important as perceived vaccine safety and effectiveness when choosing whether or not to vaccinate" (834). Berezin and Eads' (2016) research suggests that it is children from households at each end of the socioeconomic spectrum—the affluent and the poverty stricken—that are most commonly found to be part of the unvaccinated community. Berezin and Eads (2016) posit that for affluent families "parental choice is the likely determinant of low vaccination rates" and that for poorer families "barriers to access are more likely the determinants of low vaccine rates" (240). Hesse and Rauscher (2016) found that family type also influenced parents' decisions to vaccinate. For example, participants who came from families with higher expectations of obedience and conversations with parents reported feeling more negatively about vaccinations (Hesse and Rauscher 2016).

In an examination of European countries, Lyons (2013) suggested that a combination of cultural factors—including political, economic and health systems—influence parental decision-making. Lyons (2013) suggest three emerging contradictions in vaccination research: "1) responsible citizen versus responsible individual, 2) scientific knowledge versus lay understand, 3) uncertainty and risk versus certainty and trust" (37). Unsurprisingly, the United States witnessed similar findings when the 2009 National Immunization Survey indicated parents who chose to delay or refuse vaccinations (compared to those who vaccinate) were less likely to believe in the effectiveness of the vaccinations, the safety of vaccinations, and that their child was susceptible to the diseases the vaccinations claimed to prevent (Smith et al. 2011).

Lee and Kim (2015) found that for mothers, in South Korea, salience and efficacy beliefs regarding vaccinations positively influenced mothers' "intentions to immunize their children, no matter what [information] sources they used" (293). Although a variety of sources are used in making vaccination decisions, parents and family caregivers are increasingly turning to online resources to collect data and information as they grapple with decisions regarding vaccinations.

Many "searchers" use the internet as a medium to collect health information. According to a survey by the Pew Research Center in 2000, over 80% of adults seek health information online, and over 52% find "almost all" or "most" health sites to be credible (Rainie and Fox 2000). In a more recent study in 2014, The Pew Research Center (2014) reported two-thirds of internet users (65%) believe they are "better informed about health and fitness today than they were five years" ago due to the ability to use the internet and their cell phones (p. 6). Socioeconomic status—income and education—and age both serve as indicators of those who are more likely to find health information online (Cotten and Gupta 2004). Also, individuals who seek health information online, compared to those who seek information solely offline, have been found to be happier and healthier (Cotten and Gupta 2004).

Not surprisingly, family members have different approaches when searching online for health information. Brunson (2013) argued that parents fall into three different categories regarding their health information seeking—acceptors, reliers, and searchers. Acceptors simply accept information that is given to them (for example by a health provider); reliers look to their social networks for information; and searchers conduct their own research "primarily through seeking information from published sources including government websites, books, and even the primary literature" (Brunson 2013, 5468). Although parents may look at primary and scholarly sources, they may not understand how the research "fit[s] into the broader body of knowledge" (Gullion, Henry, and Gullion 2008). Therefore, as family members are increasingly accessing health information online, it is important to understand what resources are available and how the materials are accessed and used to make health decisions.

When engaged in health information seeking, individuals may visit a variety of health-focused informational websites of governmental agencies (e.g., CDC and National Institute of Health), well known medical institutions (e.g., Mayo Clinic and Johns Hopkins), and health organization (e.g., WebMD), which commonly report or contain primary resources for health research. Alternatively, others may seek a more personal account through accessing blogs, personal webpages or social media platforms. As previously mentioned, individuals may also conduct online searches using popular search engines (i.e., Google, Yahoo!, DuckDuckGo, etc.).

If a family member turns to the internet to seek resources on the topic of vaccinations, he/she will find literature both in support and against vaccinations of all types (Macario et al. 2011; Grant et al. 2015). Although, it is important to note that when searching in general for information about vaccines, the availability of pro-vaccine sites have grown and outnumber those which are anti-vaccines (Elkin, Pullon, and Stubbe 2020). While searching "neutrally" for childhood vaccine information on Google, Facebook and YouTube, Elkin, Pullon, and Stubbe (2020) found that overall, most of the retrieved content took a positive stance toward vaccinations, but within the results for Facebook a nearly equal amount of positive and negative stance content existed concerning childhood vaccines. Although a large body of pro-vaccine information may exist online, it is also important to consider *how* family members may search for the information.

The search strategies that individuals employ when seeking information about vaccines will affect the results that are provided (Ruiz and Bell 2014; Wharton-Michael and Wharton-Clark 2020). If a parent is concerned about the risks of vaccinations and enters the search term "risks," assuredly results would present a more negative stance, compared to a parent who may search for "benefits" of vaccinations. Researchers have considered different theoretical frameworks—such as selective exposure and confirmation bias—to understand how preexisting beliefs influence seeking and validating health information (Chapman and Elstein 2000; Wharton-Michael and

Wharton-Clark 2020). For example, Wharton-Michael and Wharton-Clark, 2019) explored parents' online search strategies and identified three types of searchers: confirmation seekers (those who looked for information that aligned with what they believed), exhaustive seekers (those who sought all sources on the topic), and casual seekers (those who did not appear committed to their searches and relied more so on interpersonal interactions) (Wharton-Michael and Wharton-Clark 2020). Existing beliefs may also influence how individuals interact with others through social platforms.

With its exponential growth in use, increasing attention has been focused on the use of social media platforms and their role in users' decision-making processes regarding health decisions (Bradshaw et al. 2021; Elkin, Pullon, and Stubbe 2020; Giese et al. 2020). In 2020, there were over 3.6 billion users of social media, and that number is anticipated to increase to 4.4 billion by 2025 (Statista 2021). Social media, like all content on the internet, can be posted by a single user, who may or may not be credible on any given topic. In the past, health information was created, distributed, and discussed primarily by health professionals. With the introduction of the internet, however, healthcare professionals no longer serve as the sole or primary gatekeeper of health information. Individuals now have access to a wealth of primary and secondary health resources through online searches and can access their personal health records, containing lab and test results. While a wealth of credible online health information may be beneficial for individuals, the opportunity for misinformation could potentially harm family members' decision-making. Once again, as information and communication technologies are being utilized more commonly in the home, parents are more frequently relying on social media and the internet to access information about vaccines (Ashkenazi et al. 2020).

Conflicting results have oftentimes been presented when discussing the influence of social media on vaccine decision-making regarding choices for one's own (or other family member's) health. For example, Giese et al. (2019) conducted a study to explore if individuals' perceptions of flu vaccines (whether in support or against) would be influenced by information that they received from another communication message/link in either a homogenous group or a heterogenous group in an online environment. The study found that the communicated information did not impact participants' established beliefs regarding the efficacy or perceived risks of the flu vaccine. However, when asked to pass the information along to another, the participants did find messages to be more credible if the message aligned with their opinion of the flu vaccine and adjusted the communication to align more closely with their preexisting beliefs before passing the message along. These finding suggest that that the "echo-chamber" environment that social media platforms can host, do not necessarily have the persuasive power that some scholars suggest (Giese et al. 2020).

However, contradictory findings were reported by Bradshaw et al. (2021) in their examination of how online community members interacted with expectant, first-time, and new mothers in a closed Facebook group for parents who expressed concerns about the pros and cons of vaccinating children. A qualitative content analysis was conducted of online posts made in a closed Facebook group to understand how new moms were influenced by interactions with individuals who were against vaccinations. While the study was limited because it could not observe participants' actual behaviors, the results indicate new moms appeared to be influenced to delay or decline recommended childhood vaccinations after interacting with the anti-vaccine group members. Six themes were identified as tactics employed by anti-vaccine group members: "natural solutions, maternal empowerment, distrust of conventional medicine establishment, fear appeals, 'Russian Roulette' risk benefit analysis, and misinformation and misunderstandings." Bradshaw et al. (2021) reported,

> In cases of familial conflict about vaccination, spouses or partners turned to the group to generate 'evidence' to build a case around the dangers of vaccination to present to the pro-vaccine family member. In more than one case, these posters responded they were able to convince their partners not to vaccinate or to at least delay vaccinations based on viewings of these resources. (699)

The results of this study indicate a distinctly different result than Giese et al.'s study, suggesting echo chambers on Facebook, or any other social media platform, may be persuasive mechanisms that have the potential to influence family health-decision making.

In addition to taking part in groups on social media platforms, parents also can "follow" individuals or groups to stay abreast of current health topics and news. Many of the themes presented by anti-vaxxers found in Bradshaw et al. (2021) investigation of Facebook group posts can also be found in post made by social media influencers. For example, Leader et al. (2020) found that vaccine-hesitant influencers share their views on vaccines, the experiences of vaccine injured, concerns about the role of government and pharmaceutical companies, balancing risk verse benefit, and a parent's right or autonomy. Leader et al. discuss some social media influencers' reluctance, however, to post "strong" anti-vaccine claims and posit this may be due to their interest in not alienating followers to maintain a larger base of followers. Whereas membership in a closed group on social media platforms are typically comprised of like-minded individuals, resulting in an echo chamber, social media influencers may take a less polarized approach when discussing health topics to appeal to a larger audience.

Health information seekers can also use social media platforms to pose questions to a larger audience. Sharon, Yom-Tov, and Baram-Tsabari (2020) explored how individuals specifically used social Q&A platforms on Facebook and Yahoo! to acquire answers to their health questions. The researchers posited individuals would perceive a source to be credible if the source was viewed as competent, a person of integrity, and one who is benevolent toward others. Sharon, Yom-Tov, and Baram-Tsabari examined what type of questions were being asked about vaccines on the platforms and discovered the questions were primarily about risk, benefits, and time schedules. Most questions pertained to childhood and pregnancy vaccines. The researchers also found that both pro- and anti-vaccine responses were identified as "best answers." Although, the authors note that answers provided by healthcare professionals (in support and against recommending vaccines) were twice as likely to be identified as "best answer." The results lead the researchers to conclude, "that despite the proliferation of anti-vaccine messages, epistemic trust in mainstream science and medicine is robust" (Sharon, Yom-Tov, and Baram-Tsabari 2020, 1).

The issue of trust and credibility of information and informational sources has been extensively studied in health-information-seeking behaviors (HISB) (Hofman et al. 2013; Yang, Chen, and Wendorf Muhamad 2017; Sbaffi and Rowley 2017). When considering the perceived credibility of messages, credibility has been examined by source, medium, and message (Appelman and Sundar 2016). When specifically considering the credibility of source, three dimensions of source have been measured: competence/expertise, character/trustworthiness, and caring/goodwill (McCroskey and Teven 1999). More recently, Appelman and Sundar (2016) proposed that message credibility should and can be distinctly observed by measuring individual's perceptions of the accuracy, authenticity, and believability of a message.

Understanding the influence of notions of trust and perceived credibility on family members' health decision-making process is complicated given the numbers of factors that are associated with trust and credibility. As family members receive assorted messages, from multiple sources (e.g., health professionals, family members, and members within a social network) through a variety of mediums (e.g., television, apps on a smartphone, or internet search results, etc.), it can be difficult to isolate and identify the most salient factors. Yang, Chen, and Wendorf Muhamad (2017) explored the complex relationship between trust, social support (given by family members), and health-information-seeking behaviors (HISBs). The researchers found that social support from family members was extremely influential in that it predicted higher trust in health information that was provided by family members.

Yang, Chen, and Wendorf Muhamad (2017) report "trust is positively related to HISBs from all three sources [family, internet, and doctors], with the path linking trust to HISB from family being the strongest. The effect of social support on HISB from family is partially mediated by trust, while effect of social support on HISBs from the internet/doctors is fully mediated by trust" (Yang, Chen, and Wendorf Muhamad 2017, 1142). Even though family members have multiple sources and methods to collect health information, Yang, Chen, and Wendorf Muhamad's work suggest family support is instrumental in developing trust and that all sources should consider how to demonstrate social support in an attempt to build trust.

CONCLUSION

As information and communication technologies rapidly penetrate homes across the globe, it is essential to consider how the adoption of such technologies impacts family decision-making. Over 92% of households in the United States report owning at least one type of computer, and over 84% of Americans report owning a smartphone (Martin 2021); while over 80% of Americans indicate they seek health information online (Rainie and Fox 2000).

Advancements in technology have led to the development of e-Health—a transdisciplinary study of how communication technology is used to benefit and improve healthcare (Noar 2014). Information and communication technologies can mobilize informational resources so that individuals can access primary and secondary health sources, track personal health history, and view diagnoses, test results and treatment plans. The traditional gatekeepers of health information—healthcare professionals, health organizations, government institutions, and news media sources—are no longer the primary source and mediator of health information. As the gates to health information are dismantled by information and communication technology, family members are empowered as active agents in their own care and may take part in shared decision-making as they become more informed. Of course, this access introduces the potential for great benefit and perhaps harm.

Benefits

The introduction of the internet and e-Health enabled individuals across the world to become actively engaged in their healthcare and in the healthcare of their family members. The advancements and accessibility of information and communication technologies allows individuals to participate in new ways with health professionals, from the ability to be prepared for interactions with physicians (having prepared questions and information), to seeking supplemental information after receiving a diagnosis. Patients frequently use online portals to access health information, test results, provider information, and request medication refills or appointments.

The importance of health portals became particularly evident with the shutdowns during the COVID-19 pandemic. Access to health facilities was limited, and many individuals used health portals to interact with their physicians through email messaging and virtual visits. Since little was known about the novel coronavirus, individuals used social media, television broadcast and internet searchers to discover information about the virus, its symptoms, treatments, and the impact that the virus was having locally and globally. The COVID-19 pandemic highlights the essential function of information and communication technology in healthcare today.

In addition, the increase in mobile device use, among adults and adolescents, has literally placed an abundance of healthcare resources at our fingertips. Adolescents may search online for health topics they are hesitant to discuss with their family or friends. Individuals may search for supplemental information on a diagnosis that a partner or aging parent may have received. Or perhaps, an individual may seek natural remedies for a simple cold or ailment.

Family members have also used information and communication technologies to broaden their social networks with others to connect and form community with parents and families experiencing similar health issues or concerns (Bradshaw et al. 2021). Children have also been found to utilize social media to connect with others that share similar health conditions as well (Hausmann et al. 2017). The interactive tools provided by social media platforms, blogs, and chat rooms serve as ideal mediums for family members to expand their social networks to receive additional support for health concerns and issues.

This work explored the influence of information and communication technology on family's decision-making regarding issues of family health, with a particular focus on decisions about vaccines. Although family members can access a wealth of information online, members still rely on physicians as one of the most important sources to make health decisions, more specifically decisions regarding vaccinations (Heiss, Carmack, and Chadwick 2015; Fredrickson et al. 2004). Even though health professionals' roles as gatekeepers have been altered, family members still look to health experts when addressing health concerns. Rather than simply consuming information that is provided by a health expert, individuals are now able to be prepared with relevant questions, view test results and images, and seek additional information to become more knowledgeable on topics to take part in shared decision-making with health professionals. These actions are not limited to parents; adolescents and young adults may also seek information and be more knowledgeable about issues of health as they interact with their physicians and family members.

Intuitively, knowledge would appear to be beneficial for discussions and decision-making, however, knowledge without context or deep understanding may by problematic; therefore, introducing concerns about how family members may use technology to make decisions about their health. While information and communication technologies have the potential to revolutionize and improve healthcare for families, it is also important to consider the potential for harmful effects.

Harmful effects

Although e-Health provides opportunities for families to be better informed, engaged, and supported in their health, the infusion of information and communication technology into a household does pose potential risks. Perhaps the most frequently mentioned concern about accessing health information online is the potential for accessing misinformation (inaccurate information) or disinformation (inaccurate information provided to meet a specific agenda). This concern has received increased attention during recent health crisis that involve vaccinations. For example, in 2019 the United States experienced an outbreak in cases of the measles. The outbreak was credited in large part to unvaccinated communities in New York (Zucker et al. 2020). Also, during the current COVID-19 pandemic, many individuals are hesitant to vaccinate themselves or their children because they believe the new vaccine has been developed too quickly, may be risky, and may serve a political agenda (Thaker 2021). While multiple factors may influence an individual's level of vaccine hesitancy, many have questioned the influence of online messages that contain misinformation and question the impact of such communication on levels of vaccine hesitancy.

The work provided in this chapter shares findings that suggest online information—post on social media platforms, responses on Q & A social media platforms, websites, or YouTube—in some cases, appear to influence individuals' perceptions of health topics such as vaccinations (Bradshaw et al. 2021), and in other instances, appears to have no persuasive effect (Giese et al. 2020). For studies that suggest perceived influence, commonly, researchers point to evidence of selective attention, selective exposure, or confirmation bias effect (Giese et al. 2020; Wharton-Michael and Wharton-Clark 2020); suggesting that individuals look online for health information and interactions that align with preexisting beliefs, which brings into question the level of persuasion (if an individual has already established a particular attitude toward the topic). Individuals may seek online communities, to surround themselves with like-minded individuals, creating echo chambers that would isolate members from open dialogue that could potentially expose individuals to different experiences and opinions. The creation of echo chambers online remains a concern of media scholars as individuals would be benefited from exposure to diverse opinions and experiences. Although selective attention and exposure appear to be strong influences when dealing with information seeking online, Sharon, Yom-Tov, and Baram Tsabari (2020) offers some hope concluding, "that despite the proliferation of anti-vaccine messages, epistemic trust in mainstream science and medicine is robust" (Sharon, Yom-Tov, and Baram-Tsabari 2020, 1), as individuals continue to find health experts information/responses to be the most beneficial.

Additional concerns remain when considering how family members use information and communication technologies in family health decision-making. While all family members have access to a variety of health resources, members are not always capable of deciphering the information and placing the work into a larger body of research. Scholars are trained to understand research methodologies, including the limitations of methodological approaches and the need for valid and reliable results. Although a family member can access primary sources, it is unlikely that the member possesses the necessary skills to effectively evaluate the work, nor have the knowledge to situate the findings within a larger body of results. Similarly, family members typically do not possess a medical background and expertise that could provide a greater understanding when consuming online health information. Finally, individuals may not seek a medical experts' assistance, and rather, attempt to self-diagnose or treat symptoms given the information that is available to them online (Kuehn 2013).

Information and communication technologies have permeated family life across the world. This chapter explored technology's impact on family health decision-making by examining its impact on decisions regarding vaccinations. Technology has enabled family members to become active in their healthcare through accessing informational resources online, connecting with health professionals virtually, and creating broader social networks. While information and communication technology have become an integral part of healthcare, family members continue to rely on health experts, family members, and social networks when engaged in decision making. Additionally, perceptions of credibility and trust remain crucial elements of influence when considering a source, medium, or messages. Finally, it is extremely important for sources (any type) to establish a sense of social support to positively influence individuals' trust in the source. For families, decision-making about health matters can be a complicated process influenced by many factors. It is important to remember that information and communication technologies are powerful tools that can assist families in the decision-making process.

REFERENCES

Appelman, Alyssa, and S. Shyam Sundar. 2016. "Measuring Message Credibility." *Journalism & Mass Communication Quarterly* 93 (1): 59–79.

Ashkenazi, Shai, Gilat Livni, Adi Klein, Noa Kremer, Ariel Havlin, and Oren Berkowitz. 2020. "The Relationship between Parental Source of Information and Knowledge about Measles / Measles Vaccine and Vaccine Hesitancy." *Vaccine* 38 (46): 7292–98. https://doi.org/10.1016/j.vaccine.2020.09.044.

Avery, Elizabeth Johnson, and Ruthann Weaver Lariscy. 2014. "Preventable Disease Practices Among a Lower SES, Multicultural, Nonurban, U.S. Community: The Roles of Vaccination Efficacy and Personal Constraints." *Health Communication* 29 (8): 826–36. https://doi.org/10.1080/10410236.2013.804486.

Berezin, Mabel, and Alicia Eads. 2016. "Risk Is for the Rich? Childhood Vaccination Resistance and a Culture of Health." *Social Science & Medicine (1982)* 165: 233–45. https://doi.org/10.1016/j.socscimed.2016.07.009.

Borzekowski, Dina L. G, and Vaughn I Rickert. 2001. "Adolescent Cybersurfing for Health Information: A New Resource That Crosses Barriers." *Archives of Pediatrics & Adolescent Medicine* 155 (7): 813–17. https://doi.org/10.1001/archpedi.155.7.813.

Bradshaw, Amanda S., Summer S. Shelton, Easton Wollney, Debbie Treise, and Kendra Auguste. 2021. "Pro-Vaxxers Get Out: Anti-Vaccination Advocates Influence Undecided First-Time, Pregnant, and New Mothers on Facebook." *Health Communication* 36 (6): 693–702.

Brunson, Emily K. 2013. "How Parents Make Decisions about Their Children's Vaccinations." *Vaccine* 31 (46): 5466–70. https://doi.org/10.1016/j.vaccine.2013.08.104.

Chapman, G., and A. Elstein. 2000. "Cognitive Proesses and Biases in Medical Decision Making." In *Decision Making in Health Care: Theory. Psychology and Applications*, 183–210. New Work, NY: Cambridge University Press.

Chesley, Noelle. 2006. "Families in a High-Tech Age: Technology Usage Patterns, Work and Family Correlates, and Gender." *Journal of Family Issues* 27 (5): 587–608. https://doi.org/10.1177/0192513X05285187.

Chi, Yu. 2021. "Health Consumers' Knowledge Learning in Online Health Information Seeking."

Clements, C. J., and S. Ratzan. 2003. "Misled and Confused? Telling the Public about MMR Vaccine Safety." *Journal of Medical Ethics* 29 (1): 22–26. https://doi.org/10.1136/jme.29.1.22.

Cohen, Elisia L., and Katharine J. Head. 2014. "Identifying Knowledge-Attitude-Practice Gaps in Parental Acceptance of Adolescent Vaccinations in Appalachian Kentucky: Implications for Communication Interventions." *Journal of Communication in Healthcare* 7 (4): 295–302. https://doi.org/10.1179/1753807614Y.0000000069.

Cotten, Shelia R., and Sipi S. Gupta. 2004. "Characteristics of Online and Offline Health Information Seekers and Factors That Discriminate between Them." *Social*

Science & Medicine (1982), Social Science & Medicine, 59 (9): 1795–1806. https://doi.org/10.1016/j.socscimed.2004.02.020.

Elkin, Lucy E., Susan R. H. Pullon, and Maria H. Stubbe. 2020. "'Should I Vaccinate My Child?' Comparing the Displayed Stances of Vaccine Information Retrieved from Google, Facebook and YouTube." *Vaccine* 38 (13): 2771–78. https://doi.org/10.1016/j.vaccine.2020.02.041.

Eysenbach, G. 2001. "What Is e-Health?" *Journal of Medical Internet Research* 3 (2): E20–E20.

Feng, Yang, and Wenjing Xie. 2015. "Digital Divide 2.0: The Role of Social Networking Sites in Seeking Health Information Online From a Longitudinal Perspective." *Journal of Health Communication* 20 (1): 60–68.

Fergie, Gillian, Shona Hilton, and Kate Hunt. 2016. "Young Adults' Experiences of Seeking Online Information about Diabetes and Mental Health in the Age of Social Media." *Health Expectations: An International Journal of Public Participation in Health Care and Health Policy* 19 (6): 1324–35. https://doi.org/10.1111/hex.12430.

Fiks, Alexander G., Nathalie DuRivage, Stephanie L. Mayne, Stacia Finch, Michelle E. Ross, Kelli Giacomini, Andrew Suh, et al. 2016. "Adoption of a Portal for the Primary Care Management of Pediatric Asthma: A Mixed-Methods Implementation Study." *Journal of Medical Internet Research* 18 (6): e172. https://doi.org/10.2196/jmir.5610.

Fredrickson, Doren D., Terry C. Davis, Connie L. Arnould, Estela M. Kennen, Sharon G. Hurniston, J. Thomas Cross, and Joseph A. Bocchini Jr. 2004. "Childhood Immunization Refusal: Provider and Parent Perceptions." *Family Medicine* 36 (6): 431–39.

Gage, Elizabeth A, and Christina Panagakis. 2012. "The Devil You Know: Parents Seeking Information Online for Paediatric Cancer." *Sociology of Health & Illness* 34 (3): 444–58. https://doi.org/10.1111/j.1467-9566.2011.01386.x.

Giese, Helge, Hansjörg Neth, Mehdi Moussaïd, Cornelia Betsch, and Wolfgang Gaissmaier. 2020. "The Echo in Flu-Vaccination Echo Chambers: Selective Attention Trumps Social Influence." *Vaccine* 38 (8): 2070–76. https://doi.org/10.1016/j.vaccine.2019.11.038.

Grant, Lenny, Bernice L Hausman, Margaret Cashion, Nicholas Lucchesi, Kelsey Patel, and Jonathan Roberts. 2015. "Vaccination Persuasion Online: A Qualitative Study of Two Provaccine and Two Vaccine-Skeptical Websites." *Journal of Medical Internet Research* 17 (5): e133–e133. https://doi.org/10.2196/jmir.4153.

Gullion, Jessica Smartt, Lisa Henry, and Greg Gullion. 2008. "Deciding to Opt Out of Childhood Vaccination Mandates." *Public Health Nursing* (Boston, Mass.) 25 (5): 401–8. https://doi.org/10.1111/j.1525-1446.2008.00724.x.

Gust, Deborah, Deanne Weber, Eric Weintraub, Allison Kennedy, Fatma Soud, and Adam Burns. 2008. "Physicians Who Do and Do Not Recommend Children Get All Vaccinations." *Journal of Health Communication* 13 (6): 573–82. https://doi.org/10.1080/10810730802281726.

Haluza, Daniela, Marlene Naszay, Andreas Stockinger, and David Jungwirth. 2017. "Digital Natives Versus Digital Immigrants: Influence of Online Health

Information Seeking on the Doctor-Patient Relationship." *Health Communication* 32 (11): 1342–49. https://doi.org/10.1080/10410236.2016.1220044.

Hausmann, Jonathan S., MD, Currie Touloumtzis MPH, Matthew T. White PhD, James A. Colbert MD, and Holly C. Gooding MD, MSc. 2017. "Adolescent and Young Adult Use of Social Media for Health and Its Implications." *Journal of Adolescent Health* 60 (6): 714–19. https://doi.org/10.1016/j.jadohealth.2016.12.025.

Head, Katherine J., and Amanda Harsin. 2016. "Mother Knows Best: Valenced Subjective Normative Influences on Young Women's HPV Vaccination Intentions." *Florida Communication Journal* 44 (1): 15–24.

Heiss, Sarah N., Heather J. Carmack, and Amy E. Chadwick. 2015. "Effects of Interpersonal Communication, Knowledge, and Attitudes on Pertussis Vaccination in Vermont." *Journal of Communication in Healthcare* 8 (3): 207–19.

Hesse, Colin, and Emily A Rauscher. 2016. "The Relationship Between Family Communication Patterns and Child Vaccination Intentions." *Communication Research Reports* 33 (1): 61–67. https://doi.org/10.1080/08824096.2015.1117444.

Hitlin, Paul. 2018. "Internet, Social Media Use, and Device Ownership in the U.S. Have Plateaued after Years of Growth." Pew Research Center. https://www.pewresearch.org/fact-tank/2018/09/28/internet-social-media-use-and-device-ownership-in-u-s-have-plateaued-after-years-of-growth/.

Hofman, Robine, Pepijn van Empelen, Ineke Vogel, Hein Raat, Marjolein van Ballegooijen, and Ida J. Korfage. 2013. "Parental Decisional Strategies Regarding HPV Vaccination Before Media Debates: A Focus Group Study." *Journal of Health Communication* 18 (7): 866–80.

Hughes, Robert, and Jason D. Hans. 2001. "Computers, the Internet, and Families: A Review of the Role New Technology Plays in Family Life." *Journal of Family Issues* 22 (6): 776–90. https://doi.org/10.1177/019251301022006006.

"Internet Health Resources." 2003. Pew Research Center. https://www.pewresearch.org/internet/2003/07/16/internet-health-resources/.

Jacobs, Wura, Ann O. Amuta, and Kwon Chan Jeon. 2017. "Health Information Seeking in the Digital Age: An Analysis of Health Information Seeking Behavior among US Adults." *Cogent Social Sciences* 3 (1): 1302785. https://doi.org/10.1080/23311886.2017.1302785.

Jones, Abbey M., Saad B. Omer, Robert A. Bednarczyk, Neal A. Halsey, Lawrence H. Moulton, and Daniel A. Salmon. 2012. "Parents' Source of Vaccine Information and Impact on Vaccine Attitudes, Beliefs, and Nonmedical Exemptions." *Advances in Preventive Medicine* 2012: 932741–48. https://doi.org/10.1155/2012/932741.

Jung, Minsoo, Leesa Lin, and K. Viswanath. 2013. "Associations between Health Communication Behaviors, Neighborhood Social Capital, Vaccine Knowledge, and Parents' H1N1 Vaccination of Their Children." *Vaccine* 31 (42): 4860–66. https://doi.org/10.1016/j.vaccine.2013.07.068.

Kelly, Michelle M., Peter L. T. Hoonakker, and Shannon M. Dean. 2017. "Using an Inpatient Portal to Engage Families in Pediatric Hospital Care." *Journal of the American Medical Informatics Association: JAMIA* 24 (1): 153–61. https://doi.org/10.1093/jamia/ocw070.

King, Gillian, Joanne Maxwell, Amir Karmali, Simon Hagens, Madhu Pinto, Laura Williams, and Keith Adamson. 2017. "Connecting Families to Their Health Record and Care Team: The Use, Utility, and Impact of a Client/Family Health Portal at a Children's Rehabilitation Hospital." *Journal of Medical Internet Research* 19 (4): e97–e97. https://doi.org/10.2196/jmir.6811.

Koslap-Petraco, Mary. 2019. "Vaccine Hesitancy: Not a New Phenomenon, but a New Threat." *Journal of the American Association of Nurse Practitioners* 31 (11): 624–26. https://doi.org/10.1097/JXX.0000000000000342.

Kuehn, Bridget M. 2013. "More Than One-Third of US Individuals Use the Internet to Self-Diagnose." *JAMA: The Journal of the American Medical Association* 309 (8): 756–57. https://doi.org/10.1001/jama.2013.629.

Lanigan, Jane. 2009. "A Sociotechnological Model for Family Research and Intervention: How Information and Communication Technologies Affect Family Life." *Marriage & Family Review* 45 (6–8): 587–609. https://doi.org/10.1080/01494920903224194.

Leader, Amy E., Amelia Burke-Garcia, Philip M. Massey, and Jill B. Roark. 2021. "Understanding the Messages and Motivation of Vaccine Hesitant or Refusing Social Media Influencers." *Vaccine* 39 (2): 350–56. https://doi.org/10.1016/j.vaccine.2020.11.058.

Lee, Hyun Ou, and Soyoon Kim. 2015. "Linking Health Information Seeking to Behavioral Outcomes: Antecedents and Outcomes of Childhood Vaccination Information Seeking in South Korea." *Journal of Health Communication* 20 (3): 285–96. https://doi.org/10.1080/10810730.2014.927035.

Lyons, Antonia C. 2013. "Morality, Responsibility and Risk: The Importance of Alternative Perspectives in Vaccination Research." *International Journal of Behavioral Medicine* 21 (1): 37–41. https://doi.org/10.1007/s12529-013-9346-6.

Macario, Everly, Edgar Morales Ednacot, Lars Ullberg, and John Reichel. 2011. "The Changing Face and Rapid Pace of Public Health Communication." *Journal of Communication in Healthcare* 4 (2): 145–50. https://doi.org/10.1179/175380611X13022552566254.

Magsamen-Conrad, Kate, Jeanette M. Dillon, China Billotte Verhoff, and Sandra L. Faulkner. 2019. "Online Health-Information Seeking Among Older Populations: Family Influences and the Role of the Medical Professional." *Health Communication* 34 (8): 859–71.

Martin, Michael. 2021. "Computer and Internet Use in the United States: 2018." American Community Survey Reports. https://www.census.gov/content/dam/Census/library/publications/2021/acs/acs-49.pdf.

Massey, Philip M. 2016. "Where Do U.S. Adults Who Do Not Use the Internet Get Health Information? Examining Digital Health Information Disparities From 2008 to 2013." *Journal of Health Communication* 21 (1): 118–24.

McClain, Colleen, Emily Vogels, Andrew Perrin, Sechopoulos Stella, and Lee Rainie. 2021. "The Internet and the Pandemic." Pew Research Center. https://www.pewresearch.org/internet/2021/09/01/the-internet-and-the-pandemic/.

McCroskey, James C., and Jason J. Teven. 1999. "Goodwill: A Reexamination of the Construct and Its Measurement." *Communication Monographs* 66 (1): 90–103. https://doi.org/10.1080/03637759909376464.

Noar, Seth M. 2014. "Internet and E-Health." In *Health Communication Theory, Method, and Application*, 1st edition, 428–53. Routledge.

Office of the National Coordinator for Health Information Technology. 2019. "What Is an Electronic Health Record (EHR)?" HealthIT.Gov. September 2019. https://www.healthit.gov/faq/what-electronic-health-record-ehr.

Perett-Watel, Patrick, Heidi Larson, Jeremy Ward, William Schulz, and Pierre Verger. 2015. "Vaccine Hesitancy: Clarifying a Theoretical Framework for an Ambiguous Notion." *PLoS Currents* 7 (February).

Rainie, Lee, and Susannah Fox. 2000. "The Online Health Care Revolution: How the Web Helps Americans Take Better Care of Themselves." Pew Research Center. https://www.pewresearch.org/internet/2000/11/26/the-online-health-care-revolution/.

Rao, T. S. Sathyanarayana, and Chittaranjan Andrade. 2011. "The MMR Vaccine and Autism: Sensation, Refutation, Retraction, and Fraud." *Indian Journal of Psychiatry* 53 (2): 95–96. https://doi.org/10.4103/0019-5545.82529.

Rhodes, Matthew E., Beth Sundstrom, Emily Ritter, Brooke W. McKeever, and Robert McKeever. 2020. "Preparing for A COVID-19 Vaccine: A Mixed Methods Study of Vaccine Hesitant Parents." *Journal of Health Communication* 25 (10): 831–37. https://doi.org/10.1080/10810730.2021.1871986.

Rodkey, Johanna. 2014. "Factors Contributing to the Low Completion Rate of the HPV Vaccine Series and Potential Strategies to Increase Uptake among Adolescents in the United States."

Ruiz, Jeanette B., and Robert A. Bell. 2014. "Understanding Vaccination Resistance: Vaccine Search Term Selection Bias and the Valence of Retrieved Information." *Vaccine* 32 (44): 5776–80. https://doi.org/10.1016/j.vaccine.2014.08.042.

Sbaffi, Laura, and Jennifer Rowley. 2017. "Trust and Credibility in Web-Based Health Information: A Review and Agenda for Future Research." *Journal of Medical Internet Research* 19 (6): e218–e218. https://doi.org/10.2196/jmir.7579.

Sharon, Aviv J., Elad Yom-Tov, and Ayelet Baram-Tsabari. 2020. "Vaccine Information Seeking on Social Q&A Services." *Vaccine* 38 (12): 2691–99. https://doi.org/10.1016/j.vaccine.2020.02.010.

Silver, Laura, and Christine Huang. 2019. "In Emerging Economies, Smartphone and Social Media Users Have Broader Social Networks." The Pew Research Center. https://www.pewresearch.org/internet/2019/08/22/in-emerging-economies-smartphone-and-social-media-users-have-broader-social-networks/.

Smith, Diane. 2011. "Health Care Consumer's Use and Trust of Health Information Sources." *Journal of Communication in Healthcare* 4 (3): 200–210. https://doi.org/10.1179/1753807611Y.0000000010.

Smith, Philip J., Sharon G. Humiston, Edgar K. Marcuse, Zhen Zhao, Christina G. Dorell, Cynthia Howes, and Beth Hibbs. 2011. "Parental Delay or Refusal of Vaccine Doses, Childhood Vaccination Coverage at 24 Months of Age, and the

Health Belief Model." *Public Health Reports (1974)* 126 (2_suppl): 135–46. https://doi.org/10.1177/00333549111260S215.

Statista. 2021. "Number of Social Network Users Worldwide from 2017 to 2025." September 10, 2021. https://www.statista.com/statistics/278414/number-of-worldwide-social-network-users/.

SteelFisher, Gillian K., Robert J. Blendon, Mark M. Bekheit, and Keri Lubell. 2010. "The Public's Response to the 2009 H1N1 Influenza Pandemic." *New England Journal of Medicine* 362 (22): e65–e65. https://doi.org/10.1056/NEJMp1005102.

Thaker, Jagadish. 2021. "The Persistence of Vaccine Hesitancy: COVID-19 Vaccination Intention in New Zealand." *Journal of Health Communication* 26 (2): 104–11.

Treadgold, Bethan Mair, Emma Teasdale, Ingrid Muller, Amanda Roberts, Neil Coulson, and Miriam Santer. 2020. "Parents and Carers' Experiences of Seeking Health Information and Support Online for Long-Term Physical Childhood Conditions: A Systematic Review and Thematic Synthesis of Qualitative Research." *BMJ Open* 10 (12): e042139. http://doi,org/10.1136bmjopen-2020042139.

Tustin, Nupur. 2010. "The Role of Patient Satisfaction in Online Health Information Seeking." *Journal of Health Communication* 15 (1): 3–17. https://doi.org/10.1080/10810730903465491.

"Vaccines and Immunizations:What Is Vaccination?" 2020. World Health Organization. December 2020. https://www.who.int/news-room/q-a-detail/vaccines-and-immunization-what-is-vaccination.

Wang, Xiaohui, Jingyuan Shi, and Hanxiao Kong. 2021. "Online Health Information Seeking: A Review and Meta-Analysis." *Health Communication* 36 (10): 1163–75.

Wang, Xiaomin, Xudong Zhou, Lin Leesa, and Sarah Mantwill. 2018. "The Effect of Vaccine Literacy on Parental Trust and Intention to Vaccinate after a Major Vaccine Scandal." *Journal of Health Communication* 23 (5): 413–21. https://doi-org.pitt.idm.oclc.org/10.1080/10810730.2018.1455771.

Wharton-Michael, Patty, and Alyssa Wharton-Clark. 2020. "What Is in a Google Search? A Qualitative Examination of Non-Vaxxers' Online Search Practices." *Qualitative Research Reports in Communication* 21 (1): 10–20.

Wooten, Karen G., Elizabeth T. Luman, and Lawrence E. Barker. 2007. "Socioeconomic Factors and Persistent Racial Disparities in Childhood Vaccination." *American Journal of Health Behavior* 31 (4): 434–45. https://doi.org/10.5993/AJHB.31.4.10.

Yang, Qinghua, Yixin Chen, and Jessica Wendorf Muhamad. 2017. "Social Support, Trust in Health Information, and Health Information-Seeking Behaviors (HISBs): A Study Using the 2012 Annenberg National Health Communication Survey (ANHCS)." *Health Communication* 32 (9): 1142–50.

Zhao, Zhen, and Philip J. Smith. 2013. "Trends in Vaccination Coverage Disparities among Children, United States, 2001–2010." *Vaccine* 31 (19): 2324–27. https://doi.org/10.1016/j.vaccine.2013.03.018.

Zucker, Jane R., Jennifer B. Rosen, Martha Iwamoto, Robert J. Arciuolo, Marisa Langdon-Embry, Neil M. Vora, Jennifer L. Rakeman, et al. 2020. "Consequences of Undervaccination—Measles Outbreak, New York City, 2018–2019." *New England Journal of Medicine* 382 (11): 1009–17. https://doi.org/10.1056/NEJMoa1912514.

Chapter Five

With Great Power Comes Ethical Communication

Technology, Superheroes, and Family Conversations in Communication Ethics

Christina L. McDowell Marinchak
and Tyrell J. Stewart-Harris

In today's historical moment people face competing goods that often make difficult decisions even more challenging. While conventional wisdom tells us that there is a moral right and wrong, that people should be good, teachings about moral issues to children have changed. In a long-term study, Smith et al. concluded many emerging adults are adrift in their moral thinking, telling us that the adult world into which they are emerging is also adrift (2011, 61). Conversations about ethics are only happening occasionally and/or at a cursory level for many young adults, leaving a void in the understanding of everyday communication ethics. As communication ethicists note, when a person is not taught to think about or practices ethics, the ability to recognize ethical issues and act ethically may jeopardize their professional and personal relationships (Tompkins 2016). According to a recent Pew Research study, 85% of Americans go online on a daily basis (Perrin and Atske 2021). On average children are spending four to six hours a day watching or using a screen (American Academy of Child & Adolescent Psychiatry 2021). To be clear, we are not advocating that six hours of screen time is healthy, rather, calling attention to the influx of technologies in our lives, in our families. Types of conversations around ethical communication are lacking, and one way that technology can facilitate these conversations in families is through television/movies and some of the most influential American pop culture icons—superheroes.

This chapter explores the facilitation of communication ethics with technology in family communication through the superhero. First, we discuss gaining practical wisdom (*phronesis*) through human interactions. Second, we explore praxis as a way to understand practical wisdom in action. Praxis has a reflective component and is an action that has a contemplative or theoretical framework that grounds an experience. Working from this viewpoint, family communication provides children opportunities to discover meaning through family interactions. Third, we address family communication and technology, and focus on memorable moral messages. With memorable moral messages, we are specifically attentive to the communication ethics implications in human interactions. Lastly, we conclude with an application section of family conversations in communication ethics through the use of technology and superheroes.

Life lessons from superheroes remind us about the power of good, the need for compassion, and the benefits of collaboration. Watching superhero media as a family creates an opportunity for discussions on morals with children who will want to explore what is happening on screen. By creating space for conversations about the actions and behaviors of the characters on screen, families can build a framework for understanding what it means to be "good" and how one ought to act in different situations. We are talking about superheroes because they are one example of technology, specifically television and movies, used by families to discuss ethical communication—to nurture memorable moral messages in family conversations with children.

PRACTICAL WISDOM: WITH GREAT ABILITY COMES GREAT ACCOUNTABILITY

Our everyday communication interactions provide an opening for gaining *phronesis* or practical wisdom. *Phronesis* can then serve as a hermeneutic entrance into understanding how children gain practical wisdom through family communication. According to Aristotle, *phronesis* is a form of practical wisdom and is applied to the virtue of practical prudence. Aristotle states, "prudence . . . is about human concerns, about things open to deliberation. For we say that deliberating well is the function of the prudent person more than anyone else" (Irwin 1999, 91). The actions taken by the prudent person then are not only deliberate, but also reflective. From this standpoint, *phronesis* is wisdom gained through reflective actions.

Aristotle states, "no one deliberates about things that cannot be otherwise, or about things lacking any goal that is a good achievable in action. The unqualifiedly good deliberator is the one whose aim accords with rational calculation in pursuit of the best goods for human being that is achievable in action" (Irwin 1999, 92). *Phronesis* is not only having knowledge, but putting that knowledge into action. For example, when a child first learns to write, the child is very carefully tracing along in his or her writing book, trying his or her best to get each line perfect. Yet, once the child learns the forms and stops thinking about each line, his or her handwriting becomes looser (sometimes worse), but the child begins to develop his or her own style that does not require him or her to think about each line and dot. Thinking of the letter is enough to make it appear. With this, there is also a responsiveness component involved in gaining *phronesis*.

How human beings respond in a situation is tied to gaining *phronesis*. In this way, practical wisdom asks a person to engage what is before them. As such, a person's response matters and how the problem in a situation is addressed makes all the difference in the outcome. Therefore, the prudent person faces the problem straight on and responds after reflecting on the situation at hand. Moreover, the prudent person obtains *phronesis* because *phronesis* is making wise choices in action for others, community, in addition to the self.

Making wise choices yields active engagement for others, the community, and the self. In the ancient or classical historical period in which Aristotle lives, people are dependent on the polis (the place of civic engagement). Through the polis, Aristotle, allowed people to engage in *phronesis*. In today's society, the polis is not present; however, there is still the need for an active engagement in society by people. Personal narrative structures determine a person's view toward life, therefore, in order to engage *phronesis* the human being first engages reason or logos—the rational component. For example, as children grow up a need emerges to recognize how human will equates with practical wisdom, or reason applied to our daily conduct.

The family unit and superheroes offer an opportunity for children and parents to explore practical wisdom, prudence, and phronesis in general. Families are often held together by a strong sense of community. Even when imperfect, family is about a kind of harmony and practical wisdom for guiding life. Children, as they grow up, use their family interactions to develop phronesis and learn appropriate, balanced, behavior. Superhero stories, in a similar manner, are set in the polis-like communities. For the chapter, we are talking about superhero stories because they are prevalent in our historical moment. Similar stories from the past serve as a parallel to superhero stories today. For example, stories in the Bible like David and Goliath (i.e., the underdog prevails), the oral traditions of which Aesop's fables emerge (e.g., teachings of great truths and morals), or the tales told by indigenous cultures such as the Alaska native folklore (e.g., lessons in heritage). Many of these stories exists to protect the polis—the community—and illustrate how the characters use their own phronesis to do so. Superheroes are similar. Like family interactions, the causes, and results, of human behavior in the stories told (or, viewed media) are a space for parents and children to discuss choices, effects, and balance.

Furthermore, it can be argued that superheroes exist in a world of hyper-phronesis. If a problem exists, it can usually be solved by directly practical and moral behavior. For example, Superman's greatest superpower is not his heat vision, invulnerability, or flight, it is that he always makes the right decision, that he has perfect knowledge of moral behavior and the practical actions that will lead to the best outcome. Superman is phronesis incarnate. In contrast, Spider-Man lacks Superman's perfect knowledge and often tries to do the right thing, but his attempts backfire, and he often ends up hurting himself or his community. A good example of this is demonstrated in Peter B. Parker's[1] introductory scene in *Spider-Man: Into the Spider-Verse* where his choice to help his community and act in a moral way were often out of step with the needs of his personal and family life, which led to his failed marriage and depressed state. The choices and actions of characters like Superman and Spider-Man offer a way for parents to create a discussion of ethical family communication and provide opportunities for their children to develop and reflect on the components of phronesis and move toward an understanding of praxis.

PRAXIS: SUPER HEROICS IN ACTION

Families of origin provide the foundation for children to develop personal meaning within their own life. One way this is revealed is through communication within the family, for family is a context in which "interdependence and connecting with others" can be fostered (Schwab 2019,114). This exemplifies the interconnectedness of phronesis and praxis (Holba 2021, 196). A philosophical praxis approach illustrates this claim. Calvin Schrag introduced communicative praxis claiming that discourse, both written and spoken, is not only "about" something, but also "for" someone or "by" someone (1986, 34). Using this textured approach, which is comprised of "communication" and "praxis," Schrag emphasizes the importance in answering the questions of 'what,' and 'who' or 'who is speaking' in a communicative encounter (1986, 34). In doing so, Schrag reveals the mechanics of communicative praxis or the factors involved with a communicative commitment between the encounters and the participants.

Calling attention to the relations between thought, language, and actions held within the communicative space these mechanics are the embedded coordinates of both "discourse" and "action" (1986, 41). Moreover, these coordinates provide a foundation for communicative praxis as an expression (1986, 41). In turn, if communicative praxis is textured through the gathering of the display of meaning within speech, and also encompasses the display of meaning through action, then the mechanics of communicative praxis, 'discourse' and 'action' are essential features in the unfolding of meaning in any communicative encounter (1986, 30).

The communicative encounter is also a public account. As Arnett points out, "Schrag defines rhetoric of prepositions, 'by,' 'about,' and 'for,' offering basic coordinates for a rhetoric of public accounting" (1986, 6). From this viewpoint, Schrag's understanding of the rhetoric of prepositions is a public account of family communication between a parent and child, exemplifying "by" the parent, "about" the child's experience, and "for" the purposes of learning about appropriate conduct through family communication. Family communication can then serve as a way in which the transition from the learning that takes place as a child fosters the communicative practices applied as an adult.

Praxis has a reflective component and is an action that has a contemplative or theoretical framework that grounds an experience. Family communication provides children opportunities to think about different concepts and principles essential to their development. Children can begin to recognize their own values, which allow them to make the "right" decisions as adults. For instance, family storytelling can be used to communicate morals and values to illustrate what it means to live a good life. As Schwab discusses, "stories are made available to us through the communities we live in that offer ways of making sense of our world and whether we are cultivating a 'good' place within the world" (2019, 108). Thus, "stories serve the function of explaining and justifying one's conception of the good life (2019, 109). These conclusions, which Schwab discusses in a study of morals and values in American emerging adults, adds weight to the argument that when a child is able to take what they learn in their youth and apply it later as an adult, the pedagogical praxis approach to learning is played out; by applying theory to actions.

While applying theory to a practical situation is not always discussed, it is present. During the younger years, a child is given multiple tasks to complete, and thus action is taken; however, the action, at the same time, is grounded by theory. There is a 'why' behind every 'how'—an interpretive and reflective approach of doing things. Moreover, praxis is the act of real people making real choices that have consequences to their own lives and the lives of those around them; theory-informed action. Thus, through family communication, children are given the opportunity to publicly put what they have learned in the home into action.

TECHNOLOGY AND FAMILY COMMUNICATION: EVEN SUPERHEROES USE CELL PHONES

When we focus on human communication, it is important to note that the ways in which we choose to communicate reflects something about ourselves. Our communication style, our preferences for platforms, our expectations about immediacy all announce certain things about who we are as a person. Since families are one of the communication-zones we all spent the most time interacting with as children, our communication styles are also a reflection of our family background and understanding of ethical communication. Often children carry some burden from their parents' choices about appropriate communication styles.

A simple example of this would be the way that some people value face-to-face communication over digital or asynchronous forms of communication. For instance, one of the authors grew up in a family that valued direct, face-to-face, communication. Phone calls and letters were not considered valuable ways to handle important information. In the family it was understood that you would not leave a note to someone about eventful information. You would find the person and tell them the news, good or bad, and handle the response in the moment. If the author had a disagreement with his father, for instance, the two had to discuss the problem in person standing a few feet away from each other. Attempting to communicate in any other way was used as evidence the problem was not that important. To this day, the author cannot imagine leaving a letter for his father about anything. This has foundationally impacted the way that the author handles positive and negative communication as an emerged adult. The author's communicative preference is to handle important messages (joyous or conflictive) in person.

The communication style preferred in this example is directly related to McLuhan's idea that "the medium is the message" (1994, 7). The medium chosen to communicate directly shaped the message. If the communication happened in person, the message carried more weight. If the message was written or left on an answering machine (pre-voicemail), it was shaped into and viewed as something that was not as important or relevant. In this instance, the family's style of communication also created a situation where as an emerged adult the author does not use social media and texting is limited to unimportant information because the author struggles to view those types of communication as valuable.

A weakness of this approach was that it was generally awkward for the author, as an emerging adult, to speak with his parents, looking into their eyes, about issues and concerns, but it forced the author to confront the morality of his own and his parents' actions and words daily. According to a long-term study on emerging adults by Smith et al., young adults are not learning early on how to "constructively engage moral issues" (2011, 62). One probable cause is that there are now so many ways to communicate that seem to have conflicting moralities. Even among social media platforms, the ethos can entirely change (i.e., Twitter fosters aggression, Instagram fosters cynicism) what is considered moral behavior. How can parents, who have not spent much more time than their children in the new world of communication show them what is right? Parents cannot, but they can open a dialogue to help their children to begin thinking about the struggles of modern communication and develop a phronesis and praxis of their own.

Technology is difficult to manage and maintaining ethical communication on platforms that exist outside the family and spaces that extend beyond the home is difficult, but these challenges are the perfect opportunity for a deeper discussion on the role of ethical communication in the family. Robert Putnam in *Bowling Alone* discusses the breakdown of the traditional family unit over the last several decades. He states, "the effects of electronic entertainment—above all, television—in privatizing our leisure time has been substantial" (2020, 283). That privatization of leisure can be a negative unless parents intervene and use television, videogames, and other forms of "electronic entertainment" as a way of connecting with their children.

For instance, there are numerous examples in television and movies showing how children fail to use a cell phone (technology) to reach out to their parents when they need help and these moments can be powerful tools for talking with children about the choices and how they might react in a similar situation. These media scenes not only demonstrate the integration of technology into our work, but also provide an opening to talk about, for example, being responsible. Using the television or movies as a tool to discuss communication choices can avoid the situation where parents provide blanket statements about the harms of screen time, without mentioning that "all technological change is a trade-off" (Postman 1998, 1), and figuring out those tradeoffs with their children.

This viewpoint provides an opening for a discussion of change with how technology and screen time is viewed by emerged adults. We can always talk about the implementation of new technologies and every time a new technology is developed there is a concern (i.e., radio in cars leading to accidents). There is a nuanced difference in screen time in respect to communication and communicating with other people and why this approach can be used to build family relationships. As Postman argues, "the ways in which the interaction between media and human beings give a culture its character and, one might say, help a culture to maintain symbolic balance" (1998, 11). As parents, we are trying to balance the benefits of screen time with its negatives, but we can also approach this conflict through a discussion with our children about imbuing moral choices and demonstrating visual rhetoric through the ways we communicate and the tools that we choose to use.

Memorable Moral Messages

Unfortunately, speaking with children about their communication choices is not enough if the children cannot remember the messages we are trying to impart or the ideas we are trying to help them develop. Therefore, successful communication will look for ways to cut through the noise of global media sources to make memorable, moral messages with our emerging adults. As Smith et al. explain, "with the advent of globalization, the Internet, digital video, and cable and satellite television, this cohort of young people has exponentially more information, narratives, and political, ideological, and moral claims at its fingertips than any generation before" (2011, 64). As parents, we are responsible for teaching our children how to cut through the information, narratives, and moral claims so that they can find a communication and moral style that allows them to live ethical lives.

One way to make our messages stand out is to attach them to the messages of popular media by framing family interactions around shared screen experiences, specifically superhero films because the fictional portrayals of the larger-than-life stories and bright colors are attractive to emerging adults (and emerged adults). The philosopher and novelist Umberto Eco in *Confessions of a Young Novelist* points to such a value in exploring how fiction is important for moral cultivation because it does not offer any solutions but asks readers to create and imagine solutions (2011, 5). In discussing the difference between creative and scientific writing, Eco writes:

> in a poem or a novel, one wants to represents life with all its inconsistency. One wants to state a series of contradictions, making them evident and poignant. Creative writers ask their readers to try a solution; they do not offer a definite formula (except for kitschy and sentimental writers, who are aiming to offer cheap consolation). (2011, 5)

Eco advocates for the reader to have their own interpretation of the messages within the fiction, much like we are advocating for film to be used to in family interactions with emerging adults to make our messages memorable. Like Eco, we agree that creative writers (or producers) build worlds which model the human condition (2011, 12). For many emerging adults, it is hard to understand the messages parents provide, but it is much easier to remember and engage with shared experiences. Our hope is that by focusing on superhero films and engaging with our emerging adults about what they think and see during the film, we will be able to engage in memorable messaging that will not feel like parenting or lecturing. The objective is that these conversations will become memorable because they are part of a shared experience.

Memorable messages are powerful because they offer a kind of centering experience that emerging adults can return to in adulthood. Waldon et al., explain that, "memorable messages have been defined as brief statements received at a relatively early age, readily recalled for a long period afterwards, and perceived to have influenced a person's life" (2014, 377; Knapp et al. 1981). For instance, for Spider-Man, "with great power comes great responsibility" is the memorable message, and the character returns to it during times of stress or confusion to re-center himself ethically.

The example of Spider-Man is very similar to how children interact with memorable messages and the character can be used as a discussion point for engaging with why and how children understand their parents' messages. For instance, "research suggests that young adults recall "memorable messages" from their parents when evaluating their own moral conduct (Waldon, Kloeber, Goman, Piemonte, and Danaher 2014, 374; Smith and Ellis 2010). With this, if parents can use superheroes, like Spider-Man, to engage with their children about ethical communication and behavior, those children will be more likely to internalize the messages of their parents and return to them as a source of strength and guidance in later life.

Another reason to turn to superheroes is that they offer an understandable example of children's struggles in their daily lives. Superheroes' actions offer an entry point for discussing communications and behaviors without focusing on the specific positive or negative actions of a child, which can lead to them shutting down. "Children are curious about moral matters from a young age" and combining that curiosity with a kind of safe space for conversation will potentially create deeper engagement and lead to the creation of more memorable moral messages (Waldon, Kloeber, Goman, Piemonte, and Danaher 2014, 374; Coles 1986; Turiel 2008). Essentially, superheroes can be used as a Trojan horse to foster curiosity and moral memorability in the minds of children so that they can have genuine communication with their parents.

MILES MORALES: A MULTIVERSAL CASE STUDY OF EMERGING SUPER HEROICS

Spider-Man: Into the Spider-Verse is a 2018 animated superhero film that follows the exploits of Miles Morales as he becomes his universe's Spider-Man.

The film is rated PG and has grossed over $375 million worldwide (www.imdb.com). Over the course of the film, Miles witnesses the loss of a potential mentor, gains a new mentor, struggles with family communication, resists change, suffers from imposter syndrome, learns about friendship, and ultimately begins to believe in himself.

We chose this film over the other superhero films of the last 15 years because it is a stand-alone story, focuses on a teenager and his family dynamics and friendships, and approaches his emergence in to super heroics in what feels like a realistic manner. In many ways, the super heroics are just there to give the viewer a reason to follow Miles's story and to move the plot along, but the film is actually a rich character study of an emerging adult in a seemingly impossible situation. In the film Miles's power is not so much that he is Spider-Man, but that he is a spider-person with a deeper connection to his friends, family, and community.

This section will focus on three themes from the film that might lead to memorable moral conversations with emerging adults: 1) the need for compassion, 2) the benefits of collaboration, and 3) the super-power of good.

The Need for Compassion (Heroes Have Compassion)

In the first real scene with Miles and his father, Jefferson, the audience gets a glimpse at the film's message for compassion. This scene serves as a good starting point for a conversation about compassion because it is Jefferson, not Miles, who is more in the wrong. The scene opens with Miles and Jefferson discussing Miles's first day at Visions Academy, a high-end charter school.

> Miles: I'm only here 'cause I won that stupid lottery.
>
> Jefferson: No way. You passed the entry test just like everybody else, okay? You have an opportunity here, you wanna blow that, huh? You want to end up like your uncle?
>
> Miles: What's wrong with Uncle Aaron? He's a good guy.
>
> Jefferson: . . . We all make choices in life.
>
> Miles: It doesn't feel like I have a choice right now
>
> Jefferson: YOU DON'T!
>
> (*Into the Spider-Verse* 2018)

In this scene, it is clear that Miles is upset about attending the school, and may even feel like he is an imposter or that he does not belong. Jefferson is thinking about Miles's promising future, gets upset about being questioned, instead of trying to understand Miles's perspective.

As parents, we have all faced situations where we have reacted too suddenly and immediately felt bad about the things we have said or done. For example, one of the authors prepared a dinner for her toddler (who was in the beginning stages of learning how to communicate verbally). After getting up from the table a couple of times, the child was asked to please sit down and eat their dinner. The child replied with what the parents thought was "shut up." The child's father immediately reacted because that phrase is not said in their household. The child broke out in tears and the father proceeded to explain that we do not tell people to shut-up in an attempt to resolve the impolite behavior. The father asked the child, "do you understand" and the child replied, "yes, shut up." The father paused and said, "what did you say?" The child replied with the same words, however, this time also used a hand gesture of thumbs-up. In that moment, the father realized the child had responded to the request to sit down and eat their dinner with saying "thumbs-up." Caught in the moment, both parents missed the child using the thumbs-up gesture and only heard the unclear verbal part of the interaction. In the scene described above, we see this relatable anguish on Jefferson's face.

Jefferson's behavior is a good family conversation starter because he is more at fault than Miles and it is more interesting and engaging to talk with emerging adults about how emerged adults mess up than it is to look at how people their age make mistakes and hurt others. Also, as viewers we get to see how the lack of compassion from Jefferson is what leads to later scenes in the film where Miles, when scared or in need of help, refuses to call his father or answer calls from his father. In those moments, Miles needed compassion and support, and he mistakenly believed that his father would be unable to offer those things because of their earlier interactions. This scene of Miles speaking with his father offers a chance to explore how missed opportunities for compassion can negatively impact present and future family communication.

Feeling compassion and support from his father is so important that Miles's full powers do not awaken until the scene where his father is finally honest, open, and compassionate with him and explains:

> Look sometimes, people drift apart, Miles. And I don't want that to happen to us, okay? Look, I know I don't always do what you need me to do or say what you need me to say, but I'm . . . I see this . . . this spark in you. It's amazing, it's why I push you. But it's yours and whatever you choose to do with it, you'll be great. Look call me when you can, okay? I love you. You don't have to say it back though.
>
> (*Into the Spider-Verse* 2018)

This is the first time that Jefferson is fully open with Miles and tries to connect with him on a more compassionate level. Gone is the directive, frustrated father, and instead we have a person simply trying to understand and be understood by another person. Even the final line, "You don't have to say it back," highlights that Jefferson is finally able to understand Miles's discomfort. This compassion from and connection to his father is the final spark that Miles needs to gain control of his powers and help his friends save the city.

In today's historical moment, there is an increased need for people to act in an ethical manner and demonstrate genuine care (compassion) for other people. Ethical engagement makes caring for other people possible in both good and bad times. Care in ethical engagement opens up the opportunity for genuine concern for the other person in a given moment. It is a concern and challenge to comprehend the way things are, the way things have been, and the direction things are going in order to take ethical action. According to Arnett, Fritz, and Bell (2009), care is a "human answer to call the other, a willingness to meet and attend to someone other than oneself" (192). People develop an ethical orientation of caring through the communication interaction that calls a person to be attentive to the needs of others. Care then is ever present in a person's life, including family communication.

Family communication has the potential to open up a person's eyes to the goodness in others, and limit judgment. These communications hold the opportunities as well as the risks that accompany caring. Caring is a way to be in relation with other people (Arnett and Arneson 1999, 243). Engaging in family communication with a child, the adult is demonstrating a genuine concern for the needs of the other person (the child), announcing a commitment to upholding an "ethic of care" (Noddings 1984, 79). It is important to approach every family communication in life with care and compassion, knowing that for better or worse caring is central to the ethical response. Care binds the self to another person and calls attention to a person's willingness to meet every situation with an open heart toward the other.

Let us return to Spider-Man. If Jefferson had shown more care when speaking with Miles during the opening scenes of the film, Miles might have had a safer transition into becoming Spider-Man. At the very least, Miles would have gone through the moments of fear and aloneness knowing that he had the support of his father and moved through his transition with more confidence and power. Scenes like this one illustrate that superheroes have and have a need for compassion and can serve as an example in family conversations about care and support (e.g., showing up for other people).

The Benefits of Collaboration (Spiders Assemble)

One of the major conflicts in the film is the difference between Miles's father (Jefferson) and his Uncle Aaron. While Jefferson is always honest with Miles, he does not become fully compassionate until the end of the film. On the other hand, Uncle Aaron is always compassionate and understanding, but is not as honest as Jefferson, and doesn't truly open up until he passes away in Miles's arms.

The compassion Aaron shows Miles allows the two to collaborate and create art that becomes a part of Miles's character arc throughout the film.

> Uncle Aaron: Whoa, slow down a little . . . that's better . . . that's perfect. The real Miles, comin' out of hiding. Now you can cut that line with another color. That's it . . .
>
> Miles: Little help? (Miles climbs on Aaron's shoulders)
>
> Uncle Aaron: You want drips? 'Cause if you do, that's cool, but if you don't you gotta keep it moving . . .
>
> Miles: That's intentional!
>
> Uncle Aaron: Wow.
>
> Miles: Is it too crazy?
>
> Uncle Aaron: No man. Miles I see exactly what you're doing here, man.
>
> (*Into the Spider-Verse* 2018)

This scene works as a family conversation starter because the viewer gets to see the result of Miles and Aaron's collaboration. As the scene progresses Aaron watches, provides feedback, allows Miles to stand on his shoulders, and even paints an outline of Miles, so that Miles can complete his mural. Without their trust and collaboration, it would have been impossible for the image to exist. In this way collaboration is shown to be generative. Collaboration is working with others to create new things.

Another scene that highlights the power of collaboration is when Miles and Peter B. Parker work together to infiltrate the Alchemax lab to find out what the Kingpin's (the bad guy's) plan is, so they can prevent him from harming the community, and Peter learns that he does not need to do everything alone.

> Peter: Go back outside!
>
> Miles: No, I can't sit there and just let Spider-Man die without doing anything about it. I'm not doing that again.

Peter: (Visibly reacts. Softens.)

Miles: What?

Peter: (Thinks it over) Most people I meet in the workplace try to kill me, so, you're a nice change of pace.

(*Into the Spider-Verse* 2018)

Traditionally, Spider-Man's adventures have mostly focused on the difficulties of being Spider-Man alone, Miles's adventures have shown that he needs to work with others. He needs Peter to teach him, he needs the support of his family, the resources of Aunt May, and the friendship and compassion of Gwen and the other Spider-People. The above scene is shown as the first time that Peter realizes how nice collaboration can feel. Peter's enjoyment of collaboration comes up again at the end of the film when Miles is able to show he's learned from Peter, and Peter realizes the he might want children, and is able to rekindle his relationship with Mary Jane (his ex-wife).

Throughout the film, collaboration is shown in a positive light and the examples in the film create opportunities to speak with emerging adults about collaboration in their lives. While clichéd, the idea that two heads are better than one is a reminder of the benefits of collaborating with other people (even when we do not necessarily want to collaborate). For example, in the workplace collaboration (teamwork) is needed to support the organization, or, interpersonally, people have to enter into collaboration to fulfill certain roles (like parenting). Family conversations around collaboration help children learn to respect others, recognize strengths of people in a given situation, even how to control emotions—to embrace an ethic of collaboration.

Maintaining an ethic of collaboration asks a person to behave appropriately and respectfully; to be civil with others. Being civil with others is about more than having good manners; it is about how we behave in given situations (Holba 2021; Fritz 2013). In our communicative interactions, "all verbal and nonverbal communication shapes how [people] engage civilly" (Holba 2021, 272; Fritz 2013). Civility "protects and promotes respect for human beings and supports various social contexts within which human lives find meaning and significance" (Fritz 2013, 3). From this viewpoint, public commitment is announced. Public commitment toward other people becomes significant in everyday ways when a person thinks about moving out into the world for the good of the family, friends, or colleagues. In practical terms, people enact this when they think about how they can help a given group. Family communication not only gives children the opportunities to obtain the interactions skills for collaboration and the expected skills to participate, but also opens up the opportunity to teach children to engage civilly.

In the film, we see an example of this collaboration when the different Spider-People attempt to train Miles, but end up chasing him off because their unproductive style of training does not work well. However, when the Spider-People change their approach and meet Miles where he is by acknowledging his fear, loss, and pain, they are all able to work in harmony during the final battle. If we look at the characters in the film as a Spider-Family, we can see that they are demonstrating a good way for emerging adults to explore different collaborative styles and how to adapt to the needs of different collaborators.

The Super-Power of Good

Into the Spider-Verse is about superheroes, so it is mostly a film about the power of good and helping others, but the scenes that focus on the choices of the Kingpin, the main antagonist, seem to exemplify the power of good the most. For instance, when we are first introduced to how the Kingpin lost his family, we are shown a scene of him fighting Spider-Man:

> Kingpin: You're dead, Spider-Man.
>
> Vanessa, Kingpin's wife, walks in with their 13-year-old son, Richard just as KINGPIN is about to deliver the death blow to Spider-Man. They can't believe the level of violence they're seeing.
>
> Vanessa: Wilson, what are you doing?
>
> Kingpin TURNS AROUND with BLOOD SPLATTER on his face. He realizes what they've seen.
>
> Kingpin: Vanessa.
>
> Vanessa: Richard, c'mon . . .
>
> Vanessa takes Richard's hand and FLEES.
>
> Kingpin: Vanessa! Richard! No!
>
> She gets into her car and PEELS OUT. Richard turns around in his seat and looks back at Kingpin as they DRIVE AWAY.
>
> Vanessa: Don't look back, honey. It's okay. It's okay.
>
> (*Into the Spider-Verse* 2018)

This scene is important because it explains the film's understanding of good by demonstrating what the film views as bad or negative behavior.

As we learn in this scene, the Kingpin is hiding his true nature from his family. The Spider-Man who the Kingpin does away with early in the film does not hide his true nature from his family. Both his aunt and his wife know that he is Spider-Man, and he accepts their support as he tries to help his community. The Kingpin, on the other hand, knowingly does wrong and hides it to such an extent that his wife immediately tries to get away from him when she realizes his true nature (this scene is echoed again at the end of the film when an alternate-universe version of Vanessa sees the Kingpin attacking Miles and runs away).

Here the Kingpin is not just bad because he does bad things, but because he is not honest with his family and community. He, as shown again when he hosts a dinner for the Spider-Man he did away with, is out for himself and does not actually care about others. It is this lack of care that keeps him from accomplishing his goals and doing good things.

In contrast, we can look at the example of Peter Parker, the Spider-Man the Kingpin got rid of, when he is eulogized by his wife, Mary Jane Parker:

> My husband Peter Parker was an ordinary person. He always said it could have been anyone behind the mask. He was just the kid who happened to get bit. He didn't ask for his powers. But he chose to be Spider-Man. My favorite thing about Peter is that he made us each feel powerful. We all have powers of one kind or another. But in our own way, we are all Spider-Man. And we're all counting on you.
>
> (*Into the Spider-Verse* 2018)

As Mary Jane speaks, we learn that the goodness of Spider-Man comes from the choice to help others and the compassion to help others feel powerful as well. Spider-Man is not focused on personal gain; instead, he is focused on communal good and using his strength to improve his community. This is the exact opposite of what we see the Kingpin doing as he rushes to build and use the collider even as he is warned it could destroy the city by both Spider-Man and Dr. Octavius (the Kingpin's collaborator).

The last example of the power of good occurs during the final battle between the Kingpin and Miles, during which the Kingpin argues that Miles took his family when it was the Kingpin's poor choices that caused his family to leave:

> Kingpin: You took my family, and now I'm gonna make sure you never see yours again.
>
> Jefferson: Get up, Spider-Man!

Miles: I'll always have my family. You ever hear of the shoulder touch?

(*Into the Spider-Verse* 2018)

This scene closes out the film's understanding of good because we have the Kingpin, who ignored his family and community, being punished by having his dreams dashed and being sent to prison. While Miles is rewarded with his father supporting him as Spider-Man, stopping the Kingpin, saving the city, being able to finally call his father on the phone, and adoration from the community he saved. The positive response from Miles's actions shows us that the film believes that community, family, compassion, and collaboration are key to being a good person and doing good things for the world.

Lessons in what it means to be a good person are commonplace in family communication. For example, teaching children about kindness, generosity, gratitude, acceptance, empathy to name a few. These family communication teachings ultimately provide children with the foundation to understand the importance of living a virtuous life. In a previous section, we discussed gaining practical wisdom, or *phronesis*, through family communication. In doing so, the virtue of prudence was illustrated. The Aristotelian virtue of prudence refers to "the virtues of choosing and acting upon what is good according to right reason in a specific situation amid all the complexities and competing claims of daily existence" (Keating 2007, 61). For Aristotle, practical wisdom, then, requires learning how to live well (Irwin 1999). An attribute of practical wisdom is having the capacity of seeing what is good for the self and for others. From this viewpoint, practical wisdom demands deliberate action. The basis comes from the interaction that people have with other people and an understanding that such wisdom equals deliberation, care and discernment in pivotal moments (i.e., making ethical choices or decision making).

In this historical moment, people are faced with competing goods that often make difficult decisions even more challenging. As Arnett, Fritz, and Bell suggest, "one of the defining givens of communication today is that there is little consensus, or public agreement, about what is right and wrong. Such a moment propels communication ethics to the forefront of communicative importance as we negotiate difference together" (2009, 1). In an such an "era of narrative and virtue contention" a "universal sense of the 'good' is no longer normative, no longer the accepted reality" (2009, 1). The metaphor of "the good" is central to this discussion and provides a way for families to discuss what it means to be a good person—to live a virtuous life. The good "describes a central value or set of values manifested in communicative practices that we seek to protect and promote in our discourse together" (2009, 2). Furthermore, "goods are often associated with what is right and proper for humans to be and to do" (2009, 3). However, the importance rests in recognizing differences in views of "goods or views of what should be 'ethical' in this historical moment (2009, 2). As Arnett, Fritz, and Bell call attention to, "the multiplicity of goods requires us to show up and to take the time and energy to learn and reflect upon the goods at hand" (2009, 10). When it comes to the topic of being a good person, most people will readily agree that the basis of being a good person is doing the right thing and saying the right thing. Where this agreement usually ends, however, is on the question of what is "right." Whereas some are convinced that what is right is morally driven, others maintain that what is right is in the eyes of the beholder.

Practically speaking, the possibilities for family communication about being a good person are twofold: 1. to talk about what is right and wrong; and, 2. to talk about how a person cannot assume that what they hold as good (e.g., right and wrong) will be the same for another person. The hope is that children learn to be attentive and reflective in their decision-making, learning not only to engage in the right actions but also to engage in the right actions for the right reasons as well as acknowledge difference. Again, we find that superheroes are a valuable tool for family communication because they are often going through the same struggles as emerging adults. Through his journey, Miles has to decide what is good and what kind of person he wants to be. He needs to learn not only to act, but when and how to act, and learn to reflect on his actions so that he can improve. Emerging adults can relate to Miles's journey because it is their own.

CONCLUSION: ANYONE CAN WEAR THE MASK

In sum, the quote Spider-Man is most associated with, "With great power comes great responsibility," serves as an example of how discourse and action, grounded in practical wisdom, feed into each other to form praxis. When Peter Parker became Spider-Man, he was only concerned with self-interest and wealth. After a series of life-changing events, Spider-Man sheds the self-interest seeing his powers as being held under the power of responsibility. Spider-Man's stories all focus on how he attempts to put his discourse into action as a part of his personal and superhero lives. The discourse in action aspect is so important to the character that a large part of his appeal is watching him try to live out his understanding of responsibility and the fallout from holding oneself to such an impossible standard. In addition to the entertainment value, Spider-Man's stories work as small lessons on the limits of discourse and action. Just because great power comes with great responsibility does not mean that it's always possible to achieve, and there are times when it might be better not to act. These are fruitful discussions that parents can and should take up with their children. Subsequently, the use of technology and superheroes can serve as an important place to go for value and communication ethics in family communication, fostering memorable moral messages in emerging adults.

REFERENCES

American Academy of Child & Adolescent Psychiatry. "Screen Time and Children." Accessed October 21, 2021. https://www.aacap.org/AACAP/Families_and_Youth/Facts_for_Families/FFF-Guide/Children-And-Watching-TV-054.aspx.

Aristotle. (1999). *Nicomachean Ethics.* Translated by Terence Irwin. Hackett Publishing Company, Inc.

Arnett, Ronald C. (1986). *Communication and Community: Implications of Martin Buber's Dialogue.* Southern Illinois University Press.

Arnett, Ronald, and Pat Arneson. (1999). *Dialogic Civility in a Cynical Age: Community, Hope, and Interpersonal Relationships.* State University of New York Press.

Arnett, Ronald, Janie Harden-Fritz, and Leeanne M. Bell. (2009). *Communication Ethics Literacy: Dialogue and Difference.* Sage.

Coles, Robert. (1986). "Our Moral Lives." *Society,* no. 23 (4): 38–41.

Eco, Umberto. (2011). *Confessions of a Young Novelist.* Harvard University Press.

Fritz, Janie H. M. (2013). *Professional Civility: Communicative Virtue at Work.* Peter Lang.

Holba, Annette M. (2021). *Philosophy of Communication Inquiry: An Introduction.* Cognella.

Keating, Michael. (2007). "The Strange Case of the Self-Dwarfing Man: Modernity, Magnanimity, and Thomas Aquinas," *Logos: A Journal of Catholic Thought and Culture,* no. 4: 61.

Knapp, Mark L. Cynthia Stohl, and Kathleen K. Reardon. (1981). "'Memorable' Messages." *Journal of Communication,* no. 31 (40); 27–41.

Lord, Phil, and Rodney Rothman. (2018). Screenplay of *Spider-Man: Into the Spider-Verse*. *Sony Pictures*, https://origin-flash.sonypictures.com/ist/awards_screenplays/SV_screenplay.pdf.

McLuhan, Marshall. (1994). *Understanding Media. The Extensions of Man.* The MIT Press.

Noddings, Nel. (1984). *Caring: A Feminine Approach to Ethics and Moral Education.* University of California Press.

Perrin, Andrew, and Sara Atske. (2021). "Almost Three in Ten US Adults say They are Almost Constantly Online." Pew Research. Accessed October 21, 2021. https://www.pewresearch.org/fact-tank/2021/03/26/about-three-in-ten-u-s-adults-say-they-are-almost-constantly-online/.

Postman, Neil. (1998). *Five Things We Need to Know About Technological Change.* (Talk delivered in Denver, Colorado. March 28, 1998).

Putnam, Robert. (2020). *Bowling Alone: The Collapse and Revival of American Community.* Simon & Schuster.

Schrag, Calvin. (1986). *Communicative Praxis and the Space of Subjectivity.* Indiana University Press.

Schwab, Joseph R. (2019). "What is the Good Life? A Master Narrative Approach to the Study of Morals and Values in American Emerging Adults." *Journal of Adult Development*, no. 27: 108–17.

Smith, Sandi W., and Jennifer Butler Ellis. (2010). "Memorable Messages as Guides to Self-Assessment of Behavior: An Initial Investigation." *Communication Monographs,* no. 68(2): 154–68.

Smith, Christian, with Kari Christofferson, Hilary Davidson, and Patricia Snell Herzog. (2011). *Lost in Translation: The Dark Side of Emerging Adulthood.* Oxford University Press.

Tompkins, Paula. (2016). *Practicing Communication Ethics: Development, Discernment, and Decision-making.* Routledge.

Turiel, Elliot. (2008). "The Development of Children's Orientations Toward Moral, Social, and Personal Orders: More Than a Sequence in Development." *Human Development,* no. 51 (1): 21–39.

Waldon, Vincent R., Dayna Kloeber, Carmen Goman, Nicole Piemonte, and Joshua Danaher. (2014). "How Parents Communicate Right and Wrong: A Study of Memorable Moral Messages Recalled by Emerging Adults." *Journal of Family Communication,* no. 14: 374–97.

NOTE

1. In the film, there are two Peter Parkers. Peter Parker is younger and blond, and he dies early in the film. Peter B. Parker is an older version of the Peter Parker most would recognize from the films and comics of the early 2000s.

SECTION II

Interruption

Chapter Six

Cellular Television and the Reallocation of Familiar Attention

Joel S. Ward

It could be said, without exaggeration, that family relations rely in large part upon the quality of our attention, attention not only to the matters of each family member, but to the members themselves. The kind of attention given to another person that transcends simple matters of concern like injury or basic needs occurs in ordinary talk, conversation between members addressing the person, not simply their problems. What characterizes this attention, how it benefits families, and the cellular television as a likely distraction is the substance of the argument I make here. If attention is so valuable, what consequence could we expect from a general loss of attention within families? This matter I find to be particularly important as a father of multiple children. My intent is to enhance the case for attention in families. I am keenly aware that many families suffer under the burden of new communication technologies generating upheaval and distress for both parents and children. My concern is less about a specific point argued and more about how we as members of families respond to that obligation of giving our attention to our parents, our partners, and our progeny.

A CALL TO ATTENTION

Michael Hyde, in *The Call of Conscience* (2001) argues that attentiveness defines human communication ethics proposing that "people's whose lives are uniformed by conscience are known as psychopaths" (Hyde 2001, 255). While Hyde's remark may sound severe, we know that what he says bears true. In Hyde's terms, attentiveness to the call of conscience reverts to renewed attention given to those around us. Such a call often comes from the genuine gaze of a person upon another's face, and a recognition that what is seen is more than what appears. To be able to see beyond appearances to the spirit of someone requires keen attentiveness, since hearing the call of conscience requires a carefully tuned inner ear. As Hyde remarks, such a call is "an eloquent rhetorical interruption" that supports hard conversation about noteworthy and familiar events (Hyde 2001, 255). This interruption calls our attention to someone with whom we are genuinely familiar and often face-to-face. Hyde situates his own discussion of conscience within the debate surrounding voluntary euthanasia, asking how a loved one might counsel a family member who may, because of illness or impairment, want to end their life. Difficult conversations like these call our attention to an important feature of family communication. These conversations require careful attention since the quality of such conversations often influences our most important and weighty decisions.

Not surprisingly, a myriad of interruptions vie for our attention and prevent us from hearing such a call. For a long time, communication media technologies have interfered with the interruption of the call of conscience, primarily because the call is quiet. New media present questionable odds regarding our ability to resist having our attention directed away from our homes and toward anything else. Some may fairly say that before cell phones it was television, before television it was the radio, and before radio it was the book. This is in part true. However, while inert medias have always sustained our attention, they have never overwhelmingly replaced the genuine gift of attention that Hyde so carefully articulates. What we observe in modern families is the genuine displacement of this gift by what we might call the active or electronic media of television.

Neil Postman noted this change in the power of electronic media by its ability to continually move (Postman 1988, 73). Since electronic media once transferred via electricity, and now digitally via light, movement characterizes all modern media displayed on a screen. The tendency toward movement incurs a variety of problems but the most obvious in our case is the question of attention. In new media, this characteristic is not mitigated by production techniques, it is leveraged. For example, since movement readily captures the eye as it scans a scene, introducing movement into a scene induces our eyes to travel and fixate on the object that is moving (Ware 2022, 43). Even if we wanted to give our attention to something in front of us, the designers of new media are employing all sorts of proven methods to draw our attention away from our immediate context back to its continuous offering of visual imagery (Crawford 2015, 92). As Richard Lanham noted as early as 2006, our modern information economies are built around the ability to attract and sustain our attention (Lanham 2001, xi). As the means of attracting our attention proliferate, our ability to give attention to each other atrophies (McLuhan 1964, 6) and those who suffer most are those closest to us physically and relationally. This closeness encourages a necessary vulnerability that often results in suffering because the vulnerable cannot contend with the stronger more adept companion.

I suggest that the vulnerable are those who suffer most since they are the least likely to command attention, even when it is not given. Sherry Turkle has noted in her bestselling study *Alone Together,* that modern technologies seem to be aimed directly at children and the elderly, the most vulnerable people in any population or family (Turkle 2011, 106). Quite obviously, these problems of attention deficit are well documented, and are not only from the twenty-first century. A 1972 study by the surgeon general of the United States found that the same was true for the advent of television as a new media technology introduced little more than twenty years prior. That study's author notes "Infants as young as 6 months gaze at it; little children sit in front of it for hours at a time; millions of elderly, sick and, institutionalized people keep contact with the world mainly through television" (Television & Behavior 1982, 1). In this instance, the comment made refers to traditional television sets. The case to be made for viewing our new cellular media technology as if cell phones were small televisions requires little effort.

Increasing use of cell phones and other digitally networked devices is often explained as a convenient response to the need for information and or desire to stay connected to people. Yet general observation (Carr 2011, 5–6) shows that the proliferation of digitally connected devices only minimally enhance our ability to show sustained attention to a single topic or subject, and an increase in feelings of loneliness and isolation felt by people using social media is well documented (Marttila, Koivula, and Rasanen 2021, 59). Loneliness may be viewed primarily as psychological condition, but for our purposes it is easy to see that loneliness occurs from inattention. People who do not receive sufficient attention, who aren't visited or spoken to, become lonely. In fact, the earliest studies of internet usage (Kraut, Patterson, Lundmark, Keisler, Mukhopadyay, and Scherlis 1998, 1017–1031) by computer scientists studying human computer interaction note that the claims of technologists appear paradoxical. As digital information technologies have advanced, instead of increasing the opportunity for conversation we observe a decline in human interactions. In parallel, as bandwidth limitations decrease, digital media expands the reach of televiewing, not just text for reading but often photographic, and video images drive information network expansion. YouTube, a digital television distribution platform, was the most downloaded mobile application in both the years 2020 and 2021. Up to five hundred hours (about three weeks) of video are uploaded to the YouTube platform every *minute* worldwide. Rather than considering our cellular devices phones, they are better understood as small televisions. The increasing use of visually oriented applications such as SnapChat, Instagram, and TikTok providing both video and still images, offer a preponderance of evidence for a shift away from tele-talk and toward television. The irony of this expansion manifests in the continuing growth of televiewing technologies that feature content developers seeking to build an audience, in other words, vying for more and more attention.

The proliferation of visual social media content supports the case that cell phones would be better seen as pocket-size televisions. Even the design of the device supports such an idea. Cell phones now primarily have no obvious buttons and are primarily navigable via a screen interface. The screen interface, much like a television, is dark unless turned on, when an image chosen by the owner is immediately displayed. Photographic technology has followed this display-oriented design, continually enhancing lens and light sensor technology, even integrating slight movement into photographic images. The newest social media applications primarily feature photographic and video content, often mixing the two. When social media applications feature photographic content, the simulation of active vision still occurs via the horizontal pan of the photos as viewers browse through them. Video content in more popular social media apps have followed the standard viewing aspect ratio, vertical rather than horizontal, indicating that much of the content viewing occurs when the cell phone is held in the hand. Video applications still retain a horizontal bias for displaying full screen videos without interface ornaments, but much of the visual content favors the device held in the hand. Alongside the applications development, the cell phone has acquired a variety of attachable stands that help viewers use them more for television than for talking.

Cellular communication devices are now made for television rather than telephony. Historically, telephones never acquired the same sort of attention that television has, perhaps because the technology of television, with its ability to transfix the viewer, has surpassed the telephone as a worldwide audiovisual technological phenomenon. Prior to digital communication networks, the phone offered a simple means of distant conversation. Cell phones built around screen technology quickly abandoned the call function. Cell phones, like the introduction of television in the early 1940s and 1950s, have since produced a similar kind of absorption, completely reorganizing leisure time in the United States. "Screen time" as a leisure activity has had less effect on workplace culture while its impact on domestic life is more notable. Television changes family's leisure time inducing since its beginning a series of lengthy and in-depth studies of how television as a technology reorganized family life in the United States. Every decade since television became a fixture in American homes, book length studies have attempted to understand its influence on family communication. Its influence was even recognized by government consultants who encouraged its use for "world leadership" (Dizard 1966, vii). Scholarship in the latter half of the twentieth century doesn't share the optimism expressed after television's broad expansion into every country in the world. Quite early in television's adoption into homes, concerns were expressed about the division of attention and its influence on children's development including increased passivity (Schramm, Lyle, and Parker 1961, 159), loss of creative imagination (Anderson, Huston, Schmitt, Linebarger, and Wright 2001, 69), a measurable change in consciousness, (Winn 1977, 17), and its function as the primary model for a child's social development (Newcomb 1976, 139). The debate regarding television's effect is broad and scientifically imprecise, but prevailing sentiment runs through all the literature. Television exacts a significant influence on human interactions within the family. Most notable is a comment made by Margaret Andreasen in the edited volume *Television and the American Family*. She remarks, "perhaps the change in television models that had the greatest impact on families, however, was the one that appeared in the mid-1950s: the handle" (Andreasen 1990, 27). As television became more available inside the home, the move toward a second set was quick. Today, the cellular telephone/vision weighing in at less than 200 grams, can be found in the hand of even the youngest child. This extension of the medium into every area of life places an important emphasis on the question of human attention. Any important and difficult task requires sustained and undivided attention. For the youngest child, this important and difficult task is the development of attention itself, the ability to respond appropriately to a phenomenon emphasized by their caregiver. This ability serves as the foundation for a child's ability to learn what they are being taught. An inability to attend to what receives emphasis by a parent or teacher promises to bar any child from acquiring necessary and important lessons. This situation appears even more pointed when a child begins organized schooling.

The relationship between the time a child's attention taken by television and doing school is worthy of note because schoolwork, although now considered to be the primary occupation of a child, was originally considered a leisurely activity (Pieper 1998, 4). Observation of children after having learned to read demonstrates that given the choice, children readily choose to read over more difficult mundane manual labor. Television proves to be a powerful replacement of reading as a leisure activity significantly reorganizing children's leisure time. This reorganization remains a major concern for those who are responsible for rearing and educating children, both parents and teachers. In a 1961 book-length study of television use by children, the authors note that "the average child spends on television as much time as he spends on school, more time than he spends on all the rest of media" (Freedman 1961, 170). These reports from sixty years ago show that soon after its adoption, television offered a significant diversion for children in American households, completely reorganizing their leisure time with a reduction in reading time, playing outdoors as well as the number of hours slept in a week (Schramm, Lyle and Parker 1961, 14). In a summary comment from the same study, Lawrence Freedman, a child psychiatrist, likens television to public fantasy, differentiating it from the private daydreams of children suggesting that television tames the creativity of children's minds. The most significant comment for our discussion of cell phones conceived as pocket-size televisions has to do with this remark. He suggests by quoting Orwell's critique of television that mass media produces the "surrender of personal, physical and intellectual activity" (Freedman 1961, 190). However, his primary point relies not on seeing television as a primary inflection of influence on the child but rather, "we need to learn whether the child has been reared in a relatively harmonious and loving atmosphere so that his own capacity to emphasize-to feel with other human beings-has flourished" (Freedman 1961, 191). Freedman's comment points to two important features of a child's upbringing and education that are worthy of note. First, the technology in Freedman's view clearly intersects with a child's ability to emphasize. In other words, the ability to give attention. Second, that the intervention of a technology that reorganizes a child's leisure time has a distinct influence on a child's ability to "feel with other human beings" (Freedman 1961, 191). This attention to a child's ability to empathize, to recognize the necessary attention one must give to others, to share their sense of what requires emphasis leads to an important conclusion about inattentiveness as a mental habit. This suggestion highlights Sherry Turkle's more recent notice of a developing inattentiveness between children in middle schools. Called by a private preparatory school to consult on cell phone use among adolescents Turkle interviewed teachers who were terribly concerned about their students' friendships (Turkle 2016, 68). School, instead of a place in which to learn and make friends, had, according to the adults, become a parasitic environment in which the weak and vulnerable suffered. An inability to attend, to emphasize, suggests a much larger problem than what some would call simple attention deficit.[1] Inattentiveness leads to a lack of empathy, a reduction in general concern for others in one's immediate surroundings.

Freedman's comment corresponds well with Ivan Illich's thoughtful study of *askesis* in his essay *Guarding the Eye in the Age of Show*. The title of his essay gives way his concern about the inattentiveness encouraged by continuous and noisy imagery playing before the eyes. Askesis, the ability to discipline the senses to properly assign attention, is the quality necessary to well organize all sense perception (Illich 2001, 5). Illich, views *askesis,* or the ability to properly emphasize, as essential for developing an ethical perspective in human relations. Illich traces the emphasis of *askesis* to the Greek term *emphainein*, which we understand via Aristotle's definition of *emphainein* meaning "to appear." The appearance of a thing presents itself to a discerning eye because of the appropriate allocation of attention. Allocated attention generates the perceptive gaze of a human, directing the eye as an organ with visual taste (Ware 2022, 12). An eye directed by the proper emphasis, attends to a structure or anticipated framework which gives order to the pieces of sense data received by the eye. Although eyes attend to standard types of stimuli, such as movement, they can also be trained like any other sense. For example, the ability of the jeweler to trace careful and minute details in metalwork or recognize a flaw in a gemstone requires a kind of attentiveness frequently found in a variety of crafts. This kind of fixation *enables* the coordinated movement of hands and feet along with our ability to follow a series of signifying episodes. The simple action of receiving a cup of hot tea requires a tremendous amount of working memory and coordinated movement in order avoid injuring those involved. These physiological conditions of allocated attention simultaneously produce "a kind of dance of meaning" (Ware 2022, 118).

Television works against this kind of allocated attention first by directing the eye with its own prescribed conceptual framework since representational imagery presents the attentiveness of another eye and purposefully directs attention toward the desired subject of an image. Second, television segments seeing from our other senses. Televised imagery aims to attract attention since the commercial enterprise and artistic intention supporting its creation orchestrate the process of gaining and retaining viewers. Instead of attention ordered by willful action, visual attention is segmented, captured, and directed by the visual framework of televised imagery. Those objects that appear in the immediate context of the seeing person compete poorly. Antoine Picon finds this element of televiewing in the very architecture of digital information networks beginning with the distribution of processes and effects away from their execution and into a system via the electronic switch.[2] The electronic switch separates the actor from action because the same action, switched electronically, can be accomplished via a control room. This "control room" view subtly orients the seeing eye toward television since the action of the switch far away from the actor must then be captured and sent back to the control room to confirm the switch performed the desired action (Picon 2010, 20). Actions and their reactions are recorded via a system of dials and displays that provide the control room operator the necessary feedback for subsequent directions. Picon's architectural observation sounds eerily like the increasingly complex operation of social media feeds converting our friends and families into social networks engaged through control rooms. In the control room, messages sent to friends and family can be observed and tracked registering degrees of engagement and interest. Feedback is essential.[3] The subliminal question posed: how long can I sustain my family's attention?

Illich's discussion of *askesis* and his concern for a well-trained eye extends beyond that initial idea that an eye might carefully attend to an object requiring skillful manipulation. Because the eyes are such an important guide for action, revealing the world where one can go and what subjects and objects lay before me, the ethics of the gaze, as Illich puts it, requires textured training (Illich 2001, 5). *Askesis* is concerned not just with a single sense but with what Marshall McLuhan calls the *human sensorium*, the interplay of the senses as they work together to illuminate and coordinate the reality of the world that lays before me (McLuhan 1995, 41). This coordination of the senses bears the ethical burden of attention since it is the discipline of my senses which develops the necessary awareness of others around me, their conditions of joy and suffering of which I take note. Illich finds this ascetic training delivers a different understanding of what it means to see, and how my friend appears to me when I look at him. He writes "The freedom to walk is conditioned by my willingness to engage in *askesis* of the feet. In a similar way, an imageless gaze at my friend's face can be cultivated only through a continual guard of the eyes; it has become a fought-for ideal that I can pursue only by constant training" (Illich 2001, 20).

This gaze, the careful attention to a person that rests not on his appearance but on him arises not from a scrutiny of that which lies on the surface. Instead, it is a looking that sees more than what light can reveal. This kind of revelation occurs when the attentiveness of my eyes lies within what might immediately attract the eye and looks more intently for character in the eye, in the gesture, in a posture. This kind of look discovers a person, under, around, and within the person who is with me immediately. Gaston Bachelard describes a similar gaze in his warm descriptions of fire as a light and heat that clarifies depth different than raw light (Bachelard 1938/64, 40). Light plays across surfaces, the light of fire with its warmth penetrates, evoking the sense of desire observed in the affectionate look or the telling gaze. Such an attentiveness represents more than the clinical observation of surface and instead wants a knowledge unknown by the quick glance of television. The view of television is the "farther shore of objective reality" (Illich 2001, 21), the control room viewpoint that scans a series of dials and meters to test for points of manipulation but never moves to genuinely look, to see what really happens, and to touch. While control room action appears attentive, the quality of this attention eludes the nature of genuinely looking, to see a person and not an appearance. The scrutiny of the control room operator retains the distance of operation, all the senses suffer the reduction of mechanism. On the receiving end of this attentiveness a person probed, not held, and touched.

The stimulating capture of attention generated by distant activity resonates with Freedman's concern for the relationship between privacy in imagination and our ability to appropriately emphasize. As we attempt to get a bird's-eye view, we also become the object of scrutiny by others, higher observers who carefully track and graph a digital image generated by social media interactions. What we feel as intimate connection becomes a catalog of private events generating a digital persona. In digital information networks, attention isn't just captured, it responds to calculated direction. According to Freedman, the inability to willfully allocate attention and make proper emphasis relates directly to several clinically labeled social pathologies (Freedman 1961, 192), which, in Freedman's view, make sustaining human relationships difficult or nearly impossible. The ability to differentiate between fantasy and reality and the capacity to endure the ordinary conditions of reality are the marks of a child who can properly emphasize, direct attention, and gently interpret simple appearances. Emphasis corresponds with the ability to contemplate, to offer the necessary gaze that produces a genuine grasp of what is being seen. Illich differentiates genuine subjects of attention from what he calls, "the show." For Illich the proper assignment of gaze offers "a foundation for the art of grasping reality" and the eye remains "a haptic organ that can finger and fondle, poke and paw: the criteria for the existence of visibilia (Illich 2001, 13). Disoriented emphasis results in a reversal of what is important and a loss of common situation.

Disoriented emphasis requires little explanation. Too many families suffer from inattentiveness produced by the hypnotic gaze of television. The difference in our current time lies not in television's dominating presence within the home, but rather its dispersal into every situation, we find families together. Televisions now are carried in pockets and in hands. Families eating dinner at home might have competed for attention with an old television set, but now children must outdo portable televisions to garner parental interest. Parents waiting with children for the bus, sitting with them on the playground, watching their children compete in sports, attending a musical performance or play, or even simply standing with their child in the kitchen, are increasingly attentive to televisions and refrain from looking at their children. The mistake would be to consider television as programming, rather than to realize that television is simply the allure of seeing something at a distance. Combined with Picon's "control room affect" television now responds to the viewer by providing a control panel with which to manipulate what is seen. The imagery on the screen is often provided not by TV or film producers but by our relationships with friends and family. We are the program (Galloway 2012, 135). Children, while vulnerable, learn quickly, and the easiest solution to the inattentiveness of family life is to teach inattention.

While studies vary, the consensus appears to show that most children in the United States receive their first cell phone at the age of 10. However, the point to be made here is not children receiving cell phones but that televisions can now be carried around by any small child. In tandem with the increase in the number of television devices, even video game devices offer the screen resolution and internet connectivity to allow children to watch video media on major distribution platforms like Youtube. If you suffer the indignity of not receiving attention from members of your own family, you can find shelter in the attractiveness of images designed and coordinated to sustain even a child's untrained eye and wandering attention. The tendency to blame children for their inattention to their surroundings falls flat when casual observation reveals that children are being given the tools of inattention and then accused of their inability to properly attend and identify what ought to receive emphasis.

WANDERING ATTENTION AND PURPOSEFUL ACKNOWLEDGMENT

Why does attention wander? The truth is, our eyes are continuously wandering, moving across the landscape to capture the large image required for careful navigation. At the very base, studies in eye physiology reveal that the eye is constantly moving to generate the larger scene that appears before us (Ware 2022, 4). In other words, the problem of attention lies with our ability to fixate rather than attracting the eye and it is only with careful attention can an eye develop the ability to fix upon a subject in view and remain oriented. Implicit in the case I have tried to make is the suggestion that we ought to attend to people in our immediate surroundings, those who Turkle has named our "nearest neighbors" (Turkle 2011, 23). These "nearest neighbors," the members of our family and our children, are those who are being taught what they should pay attention to in this new economy of attention. That Lanham calls this an economy is apt, since the origin of economy derives from the Greek *okionomikê*, or law of the household (Meikle 1997, 44). Our modern use of the word suggests a system in which things are traded and exchanged that have value to a person in the market. What should strike us as odd is how we have so easily exchanged this valuable, life-sustaining quality of attention for very little except conflict and loneliness. As Jill Burk and Maryl McGinley point out, social media connectedness in the modern age hasn't improved households; instead, it results in mothers who are lonely (McGinley and Burke 2022). Michael Hyde's case for attentiveness to the call of conscience as an orientating obligation for giving our attention to our near and dear loved ones cannot be easily brushed away.

Two occasions of parenthood clearly illustrate the need for attentive parenting both as a purposeful acknowledgment of children and a pedagogical focus for raising them. Every event attended by a parent involves the moment when a child, disconcerted by the public attention of the crowd, scans the group for the face of their parent. The look is quick and brief yet poignant. The child seeks the attention of their parent, even at a distance, to find reassurance in a moment of performance or even being lost in a group of their peers. At an even younger age, the desire for attention finds its expression in the common utterance, "Dad, look at me!" These instances ought not to be dismissed as narcissistic attempts to be the center of attention. Instead, they are what Max Van Manen calls pedagogy, for pedagogy is the "activity of teaching, parenting, educating or generally living with children that requires practical acting in concrete situations and relations" (Van Manen 2015, 4). The pedagogic orientation serves as a reminder that paying attention to families, and especially to children in families, requires careful attention and emphasis. Van Manen couples his discussion of pedagogy with an emphasis on tact, suggesting that tactfulness typifies the pedagogic moment because it requires a responsiveness to a new and unique encounter and characterizes parenting as "knowing what to do when one does not know what to do" (Van Manen 2015, 15). The responsiveness required to tactfully engage a child requires careful attention. The pedagogic moment, in Van Manen's view, is easily missed for a variety of reasons but much of what he says can be distilled into a matter of attention and emphasis. For the pedagogic moment, much like a child's scan of the crowd for her parent, can be easily missed. Van Manen's emphasis on pedagogy resonates with Illich's discussion of *askesis,* since tactfulness requires a careful coordination of all the senses and acknowledges that when operating in concert, the eye can touch just as the fingers can see. To know how to gently apply one's gaze or carefully to look at a vulnerable face requires remarkably careful attention. This careful attention cannot be immediately apprehended but as in the case of any skillful or tactful exercise requires years of development and practice. Just as an excelling athlete learns to coordinate the activity of hands, feet, eyes, and ears, so even the daily activity of living together as families requires a habitual attention to the ways we look, step, turn and touch.

Television as a media in the life of a child shifts her ability to properly attend to real things and people since her gaze has absorbed the attentional qualities of televised images. Television as a curated and crafted form of attention replaces the willful and ordered allocation of attention demonstrated and cultivated by pedagogically oriented parents and caregivers. Neil Postman's extensive survey and subsequent critique of telecommunication technologies arose from this very reorientation of attention away from a viewer's immediate context and the abstract amplification of visual stimuli resulting in disorientation. This disorientation manifests emotionally as ambivalence, a lack of care, since allocating attention in the televised scenario generates a peculiar kind of stress.[4] Barely able to apprehend and organize such rapid visual stimuli, viewers develop a numbness to cope with the rapid and random reorganization of attention (Postman 1985, 8). Instead of a viewer giving attention, attention tiredly follows what it is fed.

A pedagogical perspective reorients and revitalizes our severed and numbed visual sensibilities. A pedagogical understanding of attention recognizes that we must give our attention to identify what genuinely requires emphasis. We both learn and teach via this ordinary means of looking and seeing what and who it is that requires care. Hyde's call to conscience offers a demanding but devoted view of what living in a family offers, especially to those who are the most vulnerable. In fact, its origination announces that we ought to be concerned about vulnerable people, the aged and the young. Home education theorist Charlotte Mason recommends cultivating a child's attention so that she can continue to learn and take delight in her surroundings and relationships (Mason 1954, 56). Careful observation opens the world to the child's imagination, drawing her into rich relationships with objects, animals, and people. Such careful attention serves as the foundation for a useful education that permits the child to develop into an attention-giving person, who understands the nature of giving and receiving attention, recognizing its genuine character and the deceit of "the show." Hannah Arendt, in *The Human Condition*, proposed that the modern age suffered from a reversal of the *vita activa* and the *vita contemplativa* invisible action displaces careful contemplation as the true character of humanity. Yet the ordinary occasion of a newborn child easily dispels this reversal. For unlike many other things, a newborn child, while quite little, motionless, and meek, easily becomes the singular subject of a new mother's attention. The new mother contemplates the life of this child whose appearance means so much more than the rosy glow of her new skin. Such attentiveness reveals in part the tender touch of the eye as it contemplates the life hidden within the quietly resting child. Tiny handheld televisions bid to rob the child of this gaze and rob parents of that visible admiration found in the eye of every upward look. Resistance to the absorbent and inviting condition of television recalls attentiveness to families, promising much more than views and seeing much more than moments lost in the endless movement of televised media.

REFERENCES

Anderson, D. R., A. C. Huston, K. L. Schmitt, D. L. Linebarger, and J. C. Wright. 2001. "Early Childhood Television Viewing and Adolescent Behavior," *Monograph of the Society for Research in Child Development*, 66 (1).

Andreasen, Margaret. 1990. "Evolution in Family's Use of TV" in *Television in the American Family*, edited by B. Jennings. Lawrence Earlbaum.

Arendt, Hannah. 2018. *The Human Condition*. 2nd ed. University of Chicago Press.

Bachelard, Gaston. 1938/1964. *Psychoanalysis of Fire*. Beacon Press.

Carr, Nicholas. 2011. *The Shallows*. W.W. Norton & Co.

Crawford, Matthew. 2015. *The World Beyond your Head: On Becoming an Individual in an Age of Distraction*. Farrar, Straus and Giroux.

De Zengotita, Thomas. 2006. *Mediated.* Bloomsbury USA.

Dizard, Wilson P. 1966. *Television: A World View*. Syracuse University Press.

Freedman, L. Z. 1961. "Daydream in a Vacuum Tube" in *Television in the Lives of our Children*, edited by W. Schramm, J. Lyle, E. B. Parker. Stanford University Press.

Galloway, Alexander. 2012. *The Interface Effect*. Polity Press.

Hyde, Michael. 2001. *The Call of Conscience*. University of South Carolina Press.

Illich, Ivan. 1995. "Guarding the Eye in the Age of Show" *RES: Anthropology and Aesthetics* 28, 46–61.

Kraut, R., M. Patterson, V. Lundmark, S. Keisler, T. Mukhopadhyay, and W. Scherlis. 1998. "Internet paradox: A social technology that reduces social involvement and psychological wellbeing?" *American Psychologist* 53 (9), 1017–31.

Lanham, Richard. *The Economics of Attention: Style and Attention in the Age of Information*. University of Chicago Press, 2006.

Marttila, E., A. Koivula, and P. Rasanen. 2021. "Does excessive social media use decrease subjective wellbeing? A longitudinal analysis of the relationship between problematic use, loneliness, and life satisfaction," *Telematics & Informatics* 59.

Mason, Charlotte. 1954. *Home Education: Training and Educating Children under Nine*. Vol. 1. Charlotte Mason Research & Supply.

McGinley, M., and J. Burk. 2022. "Motherhood and Loneliness: The Social Media Dilemma" in *Family Communication and Technology: Continuity, Interruption, and Transformation*. Lexington Books.

McLuhan, Marshall. 1964. *Understanding Media*. MIT Press.

———. 1962/2011. *Gutenberg Galaxy*. University of Toronto Press.

Meikle, Scott. 1997. *Aristotle's Economic Thought*. Clarendon Press.

Newcomb, Horace. 1976. *The Critical View of Television*. Oxford University Press.

Picon, Antoine. 2010. *Digital Culture in Architecture*. Birkhäuser Architecture.

Pieper, Josef. 1998. *Leisure the Basis of Culture*. St. Augustine's Press.

Postman, Neil. 1985/2005. *Amusing Ourselves to Death*. Penguin Books.

———. 1988. *Conscientious Objections: Stirring Up Trouble about Language, Technology and Education*. Vintage Books.

Schramm W., J. Lyle, and E. B. Parker. 1961. *Television in the Lives of our Children*. Stanford University Press.

Television and Behavior: Ten Years of Scientific Progress and Implications for the Eighties. National Institute of Mental Health. 1982. U.S. Department of Health and Human Services.

Turkle, Sherry. 2011. *Alone Together*. Basic Books.

———. 2016. *Reclaiming Conversation*. Penguin Books.

Van Manen, Max. 2015. *Research Lived Experiences*. Routledge.

———. 2017. *Pedagogical Tact*. Routledge.

Ware, Colin. 2022. *Visual Thinking for Information Design*. Elsevier.

Winn, Marie. 1977/1985. *The Plug-In Drug: Television, Computers and Family Life*. Penguin Books.

NOTES

1. Sherry Turkle's work in *Alone Together* discusses the odd dynamic between robot companions and humans who desire their attention. In one eerie encounter, she details a study in which a lonely child tries to elicit the attention of a robot, only to realize that the simulation of attention is simply a show. The result: a child angry and betrayed acts violently toward the robot. More recent work by Kathleen Jameson, *Challenging Sociality* (2020), outlines a disturbing convergence between the language used by roboticists about robots and clinical therapists' descriptions of autistic children. The resulting proposal by researchers: gives autistic children robots since they behave more mechanically than other humans. Of course, noting Turkle's comment regarding robotic companions for the most vulnerable suggests that even more vulnerable than cognitively average children are those children with communication and cognitive traits that require careful attention.

2. This difference is amplified in the new digital interface. Buttons and switches that previously could be touched and adjusted are now all simply a feature of the interface. Everything can be seen; nothing can be touched except on the glassy surface that separates the finger from the image.

3. The problem of feedback, and how cybernetic systems are command and control networks can be found in the work of Norbert Weiner, an original theorist of cybernetic computation. Weiner assumed that information networks would facilitate command and control communication as a feature of their design. See his book *The Human Use of Human Beings* (1950) and *Cybernetics: Or Control and Communication in the Animal and the Machine* (1948).

4. See Marshall McLuhan, *Understanding Media* (1994), and Thomas De Zengotita, *Mediated* (2006, 24–25).

Chapter Seven

Formative Media Consumption

Utilizing Media as Grammatical Foundations of Families

Anthony M. Wachs

Parenting in the twenty-first century has become increasingly difficult because parents not only have to deal with the perennial issues that arise in raising children, they also have to manage raising children within an increasingly technological society. Smartphones and the internet were universally adopted so rapidly that little thought and contemplation of the effects of integrating these technologies into virtually all aspects of human existence was able to take place. A simple but difficult question discerning parents must ask is not if they should get their child a cell phone, but when. All too often the issue is forced through the social pressure experienced by other children being given these devices at early ages—the problems of which are ubiquitous at this point. In providing a portal for instantaneous access to the entire globe, new media have broken down the barriers of family, home, and the rest of the world. Indeed, the breaking down of this barrier has had the effect of dissolving many of the traditional components of family relationships and identity. The family as a social institution is being obsolesced because it has been reduced to a collection of atomized individuals living under the same roof, but in radically different symbolic and mediated worlds. Thankfully a tradition of scholarly reflection concerning the effects of media exists that can be helpful for navigating issues of family communication in a technological age.

Marshall McLuhan wrote extensively on the effects of media on human life. He notoriously noted that "the medium is the message." By uttering this one small, potent hyperbole he brought the field of communication's focus of attention upon the medium or channel of communication in a manner that was previously unknown. Specifically, he brought attention to the effects that media have upon messages and how media are environments that change how human beings interact with one another. Many within communication have erroneously taken this to mean that content or messages are irrelevant in analyzing communication. In numerous places, but especially *Classroom Without Walls*, McLuhan explained that children are educated by the information environment of the culture found within new media. New media made information highly accessible, whereas in the past it had been sparse. He challenged educators and parents to evaluate the information environment found within the culture itself as a source of education and formation. Along these lines, in his dissertation on the classical and medieval trivium, McLuhan noted that grammatical education, far from being simply concerned with the mechanical makeup of sentence structure, was actually moral education found within poetry and literature. With the development of modern media, the "grammar" of our cultural worldview, i.e., the moral foundation, shifted from being founded upon literature to artifacts found within popular culture. This chapter analyzes how media consumption can become a focal point of family identity. Specifically, parents can constructively engage movies, television shows, video games, YouTube videos, and even social networking platforms as "grammatical" resources for the formation of their children. It provides practical applications for parents for forming and educating their children through engaging these artifacts.

METHODOLOGICAL AND THEORETICAL INTRODUCTION

For those that are at least vaguely familiar with media ecology, it often comes tarnished with the reputation of being a form of technological determinism. In this chapter I work to transcend this largely inappropriate, but sometimes warranted, concern.[1] The media ecological approach advanced in this chapter is an alternative anthropology to the modern dichotomy that postulates human beings either as being determined—whether it be through genetic, sociohistorical, or technological forces—or as rationally autonomous. Taking up this line of inquiry is of central importance for the conclusions made in this chapter with regards to family communication, for the position one takes concerning these matters has deep implications for how one approaches the family as a whole, the individuals that make up the family, and the nature of the relationships within the family.

Technological determinism, like all other forms of determinism, postulates a theory of human beings as having no individual or collective agency and that the history of the species is determined by technological developments. Though it sounds extreme, the position that humans are determined by external forces is increasingly common. This line of reasoning often comes in the form of blaming technological developments for being the source of the main problems in the world, including those within families. Here one only need to think of the many instances of people blaming violent video games, movies, and music for acts of violence committed by teenage males. In terms of media consumption and family communication, technological determinism would run along the lines of committing oneself to forbid one's children to watch television, go to the movies, or play video games. Indeed, if the medium is truly the message, then would not television, internet, and our cell phones be the root of all our problems? Technological determinism, like other forms of determinism, implies a horrifyingly absurd anthropology that would deny the existence of any form of free will, which is the foundation for attributing any dignity to the human person.

In recognizing the problem with technological determinism, a tendency exists to deny that media consumption has real affects upon users. This position is an equally extreme vision that can be called technological pragmatism. This position denies the real effects and influence that media have upon us. This position is akin to those that would deny that "advertising has any effect upon them." Indicative of this position was a former colleague's mockery of technological effects in his argument that sarcastically posited that the invention of the ballpoint pen significantly harmed society on account of it eradicating the reflective moments found between writing and dipping a quill pen in ink. This position is equally extreme for it would equivocate the phenomenological and sociological effects of the ballpoint pen with those of the smartphone or printing press. In terms of family communication, this position would maintain that a family having a television, computer, and cell phone within every single person's bedroom has no effect upon the communicative environment of families. This position is equally absurd, but rather than being horrifying, it is downright naive.[2] Even though these two positions are extreme, we cannot simply exist on a spectrum between these poles because they logically pull us in one direction or the other. Without an alternative coherently advanced, we will be stuck within the polarity of this dualism of modern thinking derivative of Descartes's mind-body split.

Media ecology can be considered an alternative or third way to exploring the relationship between our environment—including the media environment—and our ability to make free moral and practical choices. The will need not be understood as boundless to be free, and environmental, genetic, and technological influences need to be deterministic causes. With this in mind, Neil Postman described this third way of understanding ourselves and the effects of technology use through a story contained in Plato's *Phaedrus* in a way that helps put media effects under a critical lens. In this dialogue, Plato described a discussion between the Egyptian god Theuth and king Thamus about the value of Theuth's invention of writing. Theuth believed it would benefit society while Thamus believed it would harm society; each had one eye open to the various effects of technology. Postman utilized this story to say that media ecology attempts to train people to be "two-eyed prophets" concerning the effects of media on humans.[3] The result of this education and training is inherently pragmatic because it allows for knowledgeable decisions to be made with regards to practical technological use.

Beyond the media ecology principle of being a two-eyed prophet concerning the effects of technology, this chapter brings together two major elements of media ecological scholarship that are not often handled together, but the connection is fruitful especially when applied within family communication. The first element is typical of media ecology analysis. Media ecology is frequently posited as form studying a) how media influence both how individuals experience the world and b) how media create environments. The second element, a lesser studied aspect of media ecology, is Marshall McLuhan's analysis of the classical and medieval trivium, most specifically the study of grammar, as described above.[4] As such, in this chapter I explore and show how we can simultaneously be attentive to the importance of both medium and message. This dual attentiveness becomes apparent through practical application of prudent parenting with regards to media consumption. In the final analysis, we could rephrase McLuhan's famous and hyperbolic aphorism "the medium is the message" to more accurately say "the mediated message is the message."[5]

The first aspect of media ecology that is applicable to family communication is understanding of media as environments. Media understood as environments is a basic principle of media ecology that states that media influence, not determine, the way that people perceive and act. Just as the physical environment conditions the action and perception of a population, media function as environments that influence human action and perception. So, the first step in analyzing media is to understand how different media change how individuals perceive the world. As such, the next section will overview the ways in which different types of media alter the way we perceive reality, and by extension create communicative environments to which prudent parenting must be responsive.

The second line of media ecological analysis that will be developed is the way in which content functions as the "grammar" of worldviews. This stage of analysis is unique in the media ecology paradigm for it focuses on the content, or message, contained in media. This focus is particular to the thought of McLuhan and is a largely ignored element of his thought.[6] One benefit of this line of thinking is that it helps the media ecological paradigm from falling into technological determinism. Highlighting the content with its form allows a twofold awareness that awakens us from our mediated slumber that McLuhan argued was the cause of technological determinism.[7] This awareness is particularly important for family communication, because engaging the mediated environment within which the family now lives has become an essential aspect of modern parenting.

FAMILY COMMUNICATION AND MEDIA ENVIRONMENTS

Throughout his corpus, but most notably for this study in *Amusing Ourselves to Death* and *The Disappearance of Childhood*, Postman showed how literacy creates a linear, logical, and abstract orientation toward perceiving reality.[8] In the latter work, he showed how literacy was fundamental in socially constructing adolescence as an extended period of maturation between childhood and adulthood. Many of the distinctions traditionally made between adults in children are derived from the modern environment that assumes universal literacy and standards derived from the practice of reading. Postman noted this in his emphatic statement that "the printing press created a new definition of adulthood *based on reading competence*, and, correspondingly, a new conception of childhood *based on reading incompetence*."[9] In fact, both McLuhan and Postman, associate our modern notions of autonomous individualism and rationality as by-products of the printing press. Maturity in this sense was postulated as development of an individual that was a self-governing, rational optimizer. This individual was derivative of having a fixed perspective that developed with increased reading competency and breadth of knowledge. However, television fundamentally deconstructs this period of development, dissolves the difference between children and adults, and consequently alters our notion of mature individualism.

In *The Disappearance of Childhood*, Postman showed that television breaks down the boundaries between childhood and adulthood. In contrast to print, television's content is inherently accessible to audiences of all ages. For example, in terms of sexuality, print is largely inaccessible because of its utilization of vocabulary that is unfamiliar to children. Additionally, this sort of material is frequently put on shelves out of reach of children. However, with regards to television, little is left to the imagination of a child flipping through channels and stumbling upon Lil Nas X on the VMAs simulating oral sex in a hypothetical prison shower. Additionally in this work Postman shows that the distinction between adulthood and childhood is increasingly broken down by the sexualization of children and the infantilization of adults.[10] Furthermore, the distinction is dissolved through the infantilization of adults on television programming. This is easily seen in the ubiquitous instances of immature adults, admittedly for comedic effect, in shows such as *Brooklyn Nine-Nine*. The point is this just one of an innumerable instances of examples that could be provided. Whereas examples of this can be provided in literature, television is more mimetic in nature and form, and viewers identify with characters and repeat lines ad nauseum with ease.

Additionally, in *Amusing Ourselves to Death*, Postman details how television is a medium that turns everything on it into entertainment. Whether it be educational content, religious content, or political content, the television turns it into entertainment that keeps one watching for the sake of television's real content, i.e., the selling of consumer goods through commercials. Postman's analysis here is notably puritanical, especially in contrast to the media ecology of Marshall McLuhan, for it would reject utilizing television as a medium of serious content including educational and political programming.

Ultimately, electronic and digital technologies have created a new environment of individualism, or better labeled hyper-individualism. In the past, one of the responsibilities of parenthood was the education and formation of the child into a mature adult. This form of maturity was based upon acceptance of responsibilities in the world and finding one's unique place in contributing to a community. However, according to Postman families have failed in their function as a defense against information glut. Postman argues that television and the internet created a world of instantaneous information. Information was sent from all parts of the world to nobody and with the vast amount of information at our hands created what he called "information glut." He likened this to a form of intellectual AIDS in that our immunity to bad information had broken down. We no longer had the ability to detect BS. He wrote about this in his book *Technopoly* long before we entered into the acclaimed post-truth era, i.e., a world in which we can no longer tell the difference between news and fake news. Without a coherent vision of our place in the world, we are left feeling nauseously anxious seeking forms of escape. As such, the model of individualism that has developed is defined by a condition of isolated immaturity. Families, traditionally, were a primary defense of information vetting, but have largely been made irrelevant in the contemporary media environment.

In his book *The World Beyond Your Head,* Matthew Crawford shows how brain-hacking techniques are utilized in casinos to program people into addicts.[11] The real problem is not with the techniques of manipulation, but rather within the user themselves. This is not to "victim-shame" but to recognize the disease or the root cause of the symptoms. Essentially modern "Western educated industrialized rich democratic" (W.E.I.R.D.) life has conditioned us into an illusory understanding of individualism that is toxic. The idea is that the self is an autonomous nomad that is able to construct a meaningful life according to its own terms. In effect the individual is deracinated from the social fabric of existence. Being told that meaning is subjective, the individual is left on their own to figure out the meaningfulness of their existence. The effects of this W.E.I.R.D. experience have been documented somewhat extensively but can be summarized in a few key points. Essentially, the effect of this pseudo-individualism programmed into us is that individuals suffer from a solipsistic isolation. We live in an age that privileges social connection, but we in fact live in "tragic isolation," which Dietrich and Alice von Hildebrand poignantly describe as the essence of that hell.[12]

As such we seek to numb ourselves in a mediated slumber and we seek to annihilate the source: the responsibilities of subjectivity. In other words, we desire de-subjectification or the annihilation of the self. Byung-Chul Han has extensively documented the effects and causes of this state of existence both in terms of our dominant philosophy, i.e., the grammatical foundation of our culture, and technology's role in the problem.[13] The point here is that this deracination leaves individuals suffering from an unbearable anxiety—or to use Camus's terminology, nausea—such that individuals utilize a variety of techniques to fade away out of subjective consciousness. This fading away is de-subjectification or the annihilation of the self.

De-subjectification, or annihilating the self, is complex and somewhat macabre terminology for the increasingly common experience of finding ways to melt away one's concerns and anxiety through the consumption of technologies of passivity. The experience of de-subjectification can be understood by the experience of going down a 'YouTube hole' or getting stuck in a series of TikTok videos in which one's normal experience of consciousness begins to fade into the technology itself. The result of this hole within one's conscious experience is a complete sense or a complete loss of sense of time. When one's subjectivity returns across each of these experiences the user is left asking where the time went. This loss of one's normal orientation that distracts one from the concerns of life to focus upon something like a video clip is accurately labeled the annihilation of the self or de-subjectification. It is a common experience phenomenologically whether one fades away through the use of recreational drugs, a slot machine, a television program, or losing oneself scrolling through social media and or TikTok. When parents are clueless about this environment and give children the newest gadgets of the day, kids easily slip into this form of programming.

Here one might say that we have failed in acting as two-eyed prophets, for it would seem that we have focused on merely the problems of our technologies. The reason for this is partially, as Postman notes, that the advantages are so self-evident in our world today. It is obvious that the internet provides a needed function in society in making news from around the world accessible, in making knowledge accessible through a simple Google search. Cell phones connect us to our children in such a way that we rarely ever have to fear about their location when they are away, for they are a phone call or text away, and their location can even be known through tracking apps. Most important though, there must be a principle of moderation instilled in children and modeled by parents in the use of our technologies, and we must institute in children a love of reading. Literacy is one of the surest forms of media that can work against the ill effects of digital and electronic media.[14] What the next section will develop through McLuhan is how we can engage constructively with our technologies through the content on them.

MEDIATED GRAMMARS

In the previous section, we focused upon the effects of media primarily through the thought of Neil Postman. This section, however, will turn to the thought of McLuhan. In particular, we will discuss the importance of understanding content, or the messages transmitted via media. Though only the most hardened and puritanical media ecologist would absolutely maintain that content is irrelevant, content is often a matter of discussion left for others. However, McLuhan's analysis of the classical and medieval trivium is ripe for study not only in media ecology, but also in the applied form of family communication. His analysis of content through the medium of the trivium is directly applicable for understanding communication choices in the context of family. Most importantly, we will discuss how this analysis is fruitful for parents in discussing what the family should watch and how to communicate about its content.

The classical and medieval trivium was the basis of Western education from ancient to medieval times. The arts of the trivium, or tri-via, means the three ways or roads, were the ways in which speech, the human mind, and even the natural world was studied. Most important for family communication is its understanding of grammar as the basis of one's worldview and the foundation of culture.[15] This understanding of grammar can be perplexing in contemporary society, for our modern understanding of grammar is the tedious mechanical construction and dissection of sentences. A major source of confusion in modern times concerning the study of grammar has its source in how we learned grammar in school, which means the "proper" construction of sentences that follow conventional rules. Grammar is so often times hated because it truly is the memorization of skills and rules grounded largely in mere convention.[16] In his dissertation on the trivium and within *The Laws of Media*, McLuhan explains why this is such a problematic understanding of grammar. The teacher of letters and literature in Ancient Greece was called a grammarian, or teacher of grammar. They would have taught what we understand as grammar in its mechanical form, but they understood that grammar in teaching literature was far more than learning letters. This reduction seems absurd when translated into modern times, as if a professor of English is nothing more than a composition teacher. Literature, or more helpfully, stories and narratives, contain values and morals. The teacher of grammar through the teaching of a culture's stories, in many senses, was a gatekeeper of the moral foundation of the culture and society. The nomenclature of "stories" and "narratives" is more useful than "literature" in our current historical moment, for literature would seem to only be referencing what is taught in books. Rather, the stories that inform our society are found throughout the new media whether it be movies, television, the internet, YouTube, or even TikTok.

According to the media ecological analysis above, one might state that the association of grammar to the medium of literature renders it meaningless for our time, but McLuhan makes clear that beyond the study of technologies that change cultures from one period to the next, the trivium is the foundation that unites all of us as human beings. We all have minds, we all use reasoning, and we all speak. Consequently, there is a formal foundation that allows us to translate language interculturally. This is not to throw the Sapir-Whorf hypothesis out the window for Chomsky's structural theory of generative grammar, but it is to say that there is truth in both theories, the point being that grammar as a pedagogical tool of culture uses media to found the morals of children. Literature affects us differently than television, but common to both media is that they function to inform the worldviews of those who consume the stories told on that medium. This is to say emphatically that yes, content indeed matters. The lesson that can be easily deduced from this is that families ought to be attentive to both the types of media they consume and how much of each, but also attentive to what is said through each medium.

In his *Classroom Without Walls*, McLuhan attempted to draw attention to how the new media function in this pedagogical fashion. In this work, he wrote to educators to help them understand why the modern classroom seems so irrelevant to the modern student. Indeed, the analysis is even more fundamental for parents and family communication, for parents are the first educators of the young. Beyond understanding how media effects the family environment, parents ought to be cognizant of the pedagogical and formative grammar of messages, in particular the stories we attend to. What is at stake is clearly developed within the media ecology tradition.

Douglas Rushkoff has clearly laid out the history and effects of narrative decline in society through the deconstruction of narrative form on television, movies, and new media. The postmodern deconstruction of that way of understanding and patterning particular experiences in life and information one comes across is to render the individual helpless.[17] On an individual level, we are left helpless in terms of making sense of reality, for the strong pattern of understanding contained within traditional plotlines that helped us to make sense out of reality have been fundamentally deconstructed. On a corporate level, the deconstruction of narratives has left society fragmented and equally at risk of destruction. Indeed, Rushkoff explains that the rise of conspiracy theory is the direct result of our inability to corporately make sense of reality.[18] On a sociological level, we are fragmented and are no longer on the same page of the same book, but rather invested in entirely different stories and realities, which has given rise to the toxic phenomenon of identity politics. Thomas de Zengotita has clearly analyzed this situation as a form of corporate solipsism directly related to media consumption.[19]

Along these lines, Neil Postman in his book *Technopoly* noted that an effect of information glut and our new mediated environment is that the traditional social defenses that protected the individual and society's ability to function in the world and make sense of reality no longer have social relevance.[20] The traditional defenses included the family, schools, and institutions of government, just to name a few. This chapter specifically is designed to understand how family communication about media consumption can help to rebuild a defense system against a disease that is destroying our society. The understanding of the environmental effects of technology is merely one step toward doing this, but just as important is this understanding of our stories being a medium of a culture's morality. The next section demonstrates how this is so.

My goal in this section is to analyze different stories that ought to be thought about deliberately when introducing them to children. The truth or falsity of any story is not found within its literal connection to material reality but rather within the moral contained in it. For instance, our modern temptation would be to say that the story of King Midas is false, which is true only in the literal sense. No king existed that was given the gift of making things gold by mere touch. The greater truth of the story is found within its explanation of how greed corrupts our appreciation of the good things that we have. Only the most nihilistic and absurd of stories would have no moral contained within them, but even this is a "grammatical" or moral message. So let us examine two examples of stories that any parent or educator ought to treat carefully, no matter what medium the story is found upon.

In order to investigate the moral or lesson of a story, one needs to utilize a limited form of literary criticism. This statement is not to assume that one has specialized knowledge or training in literary theory, criticism, or composition, but rather assumes a generalist education. At minimum one simply needs an ability to look at the characters, the setting, and the plot to ask oneself what is the real message of this story. Even if one cannot figure out the moral message of a story, one can utilize elements of the story as the basis of conversation among family members consuming the same material.

Again, I am not attempting to enter into any commentary on what makes good literature or how one ought to properly criticize a text, but rather to explore how a family can utilize the stories they consume in any form as a focal point of conversation. The only prerequisite to doing this is the simple ability to ask the question what was this story about beyond a literal summary of the characters and events. For instance, if one were to remain at the level of literal analysis in examining the story of the Three Little Pigs, one would merely say that it is about three little pigs that leave their mothers home to build their own lives but are forced to overcome attacks by a big bad wolf. On a deeper level, the story can be interpreted in a multiplicity of ways, but most obviously it informs the reader of the importance of getting one's work done well especially when one does not want to do it.

At this point I will provide two examples of stories that one ought to be cautious with when giving to children, though that would obviously depend on the grammatical structure of one's worldview. The first is that of Thomas the Tank Engine. If one were to ask what the grammatical foundation of morality is of show Thomas the Tank Engine, or for that matter any children's book featuring the land of Sodor, one would see that the consistent message provided concerning Thomas's value, or any train for that matter, is that of being "a really useful engine." The message of the series propagandizes a message of finding one's value in being a really useful tool. Now obviously simply watching an episode or two, or for that matter the series will not necessarily turn a child into a modern-day wage slave and corporate cog in the machine, but if the other material that is persistently consumed through various media conform to this message, or, dare I say, if this is held with deepest regard on a child's part, a major portion of one's worldview will be that of evaluating one's self simply in terms of their usefulness to society. This cautionary tale may seem silly but in reality, it is an extension of Postman's disdain for *Sesame Street* and other 'educational programming' for kids. Though he was concerned with the medium or form of the message, we can be cautious of the moral of the story no matter its medium.

On a slightly more complex scale is the Jack London novel *The Call of the Wild*. This story is more complex to understand because it is more deeply tied to the historical and philosophical moment of London's time than Thomas the Tank Engine and it does not browbeat its message into the reader as is done in every turn. *The Call of the Wild* describes the journey of Buck the domesticated farm dog and his journey from the social conventions of the farm to the wild wilderness. As Buck makes his way from the farm to the wilderness, he finds himself persistently violating the norms and conventions that would define him as a good, potentially moral, dog. Eventually Buck finds himself willing to follow the call of the wild, which really just means to follow his instincts and his desires. In this sense, *The Call of the*

Wild supports a Nietzschean transvaluation of values and speaks of the ways in which morality is merely a social convention that prevents one from being happy, i.e., doing whatever one desires. In summary, these are examples of the grammatical foundations contained within stories that inform the worldviews of consumers. Again, any story on its own is benign, but parents ought to be aware of the wholistic foundation provided by the stories with which families engage across platforms. The idea here is that parent can cognizantly consume stories with children and make these stories a focal point of conversation. In fact, the internet contains numerous resources, such as Common Sense Media, that provide thematic questions that families can address before and after consuming these narratives.

MEDIATED MESSAGES AND THE FAMILY

The unique element of this chapter is that it brought media ecology analysis into the context of family communication. Media ecology is frequently studied in terms of its broad sociological implications. From there media ecology easily lends itself to the individual level in terms of understanding the effects of media on first-person experience. Between the sociological and individual, media ecology can be used to study how, for example, texting effects interpersonal communication or how businesses can make choices with regards to the proper medium for communication with clients and potential customers. However, little has been done with regards to family communication. This is regrettable because family communication is inherently and arguably more media ecological than these other situations. One could potentially reduce family communication into an intimate form of small group communicative environments, but it is inherently so much more than that. These small group interactions are informed by the medium of family identity. The work done in family communication, especially from a symbolic interactionist approach, lends itself clearly to media ecology analysis. The reason for this is because media ecology has maintained a focus on being mindful of the whole that is greater than the parts and also the danger of reducing this material to a mere technique to produce an effect.[21]

Without this rhetorical, symbolic interactionist, background, media ecology analysis lends itself far too much to technological determinism. In teaching how media effect environments and individuals, one could erroneously think that, for example, ensuring that one's child reads will create a mature individual. Rather, this chapter advocates for a media ecology grounded in the understanding that teaches or utilizes this media ecological analysis as principles for strong family communication. In other words, one cannot simply socially engineer one's family around these principles, but rather must understand the communal elements that must be a part of the family identity. For example, a love of learning and reading is engrained in children by family read alouds; reading together whether as a group or individually (just as you would watch a movie together) becomes a part of family identity. As such a child is able to say, family read alouds are just what we do on Wednesday evenings.

Social learning theory in family communication shows that one's communication habits are formed less so by what one is taught and more so by what is modeled by parents.[22] So, if you see your parents argue poorly, you end up being a poor arguer, especially in the family situation. Just as social learning theory shows that communication habits are learned from one's parents, children learn their media consumption habits from their parents. In terms of media consumption, children will learn basic and largely unhealthy media consumption habits, let alone simply bad manners, when parents model behaviors such as texting while driving or using one's phone during dinner (assuming that the family actually eats dinner together). It is a myth to think that it is merely "kids these days" that have a technology problem. Our technology does not care what your age is when using an app that has been specifically designed to create addiction in one's users. For some the idea that corporations would weaponize brain-hacking for profit sounds conspiratorial, but the evidence at this point is so ubiquitous it's not worth citing.[23] One need only watch the popular Netflix documentary *The Social Dilemma*, to understand the deep-reaching ways that we willingly become the tools of large corporations that in no way shape or form have our or our children's best interest in mind. Brain hacking techniques make it such that our attention is not only commanded by notifications that distract us, but rather attention at this point calls for, demands, and desires distraction. One should begin to truly fear the environment that we are creating when one considers the fact that the generation raised upon unregulated consumption of this type of media has yet to come into the public sphere.

The reason this is so pertinent for this chapter is that the family is the first line of embeddedness and situatedness within communities of meaning-making. The family, then, in a natural non-W.E.I.R.D. environment is likewise situated and embedded in a greater culture's meaning-making system. Han details this in his analysis of the importance of rituals.[24] Indeed, he notes that ritual, not simply routine but culturally grounded communal practices, are to time as home is to space. Along these lines, especially with regards to social learning theory, the rituals of a family matter: will children learn passive engagement with reality in the technological routines that they implicitly learn from their parents or will they learn healthy ways of existing in being in the world? This would naturally include rituals surrounding family media consumption, e.g., reading books, watching movies, playing games (board, card, and virtual) together as a family.

Carl Whitaker, father of family therapy, famously stated that "there are no individuals in the world only fragments of families." This idea within family communication can be intimately connected to the study of media ecology. What is most important about it for this study though is that it recognizes implicitly our culture's perverted anthropology of autonomy. The rejection of modern autonomy is quite ubiquitous in higher education. So much so that we have swung to the opposite direction maintaining the self as a fragmented illusion.[25] Though this is the case on a broad theoretical level, in terms of the pragmatics of how most people conduct their lives, they assume to have autonomy and control over their choices. Indeed, this is equally conditioned by the environment in that our whole political system, and frequently the education system as well, is modeled by the enlightenment rationality that gave rise to modern Western democracy. The position that I maintain in this chapter is that strong family communication, especially around media consumption, can be the most sure-fire way to resituate ourselves as fundamentally social creatures. The family is the first society that we encounter, and if it breaks down as a sociological structure then inevitably society will equally break down. Family communication in this sense serves as the ultimate remedy for the disease of enlightened scientific rationality the symptom of which is the longing for de-subjectification, annihilation of the self, or acquiescing to being socially engineered and programmed into a society run by algorithms.

Some of the family communication rituals that embed non-W.E.I.R.D. people into culture and family include doing chores with one another, playing games, eating meals together, and holiday celebrations. For the purpose of this chapter though we are less concerned with those forms of rituals and more so with how media consumption can healthily teach us how to exist in the world and manage our anxiety. Most important, some technologies are so overwhelmingly addictive that it may be best not to use them. For instance, TikTok and other social networking programs are specifically designed by multinational corporations to create addiction for the sake of selling products, i.e., advertising. It may be best not to use these but there is a multiplicity of other new media that not only have to be used in modern existence but should be used. On a broader communication scale, one can think of the media and technology they and their children consume as drugs.[26] When one looks at the problem through this lens, we who are interested in family communication can begin to explore the phenomenon in a unique way. The question no longer is exclusively about technology, but rather within the nature of being human itself. We can begin to ask questions concerning why it is that people prefer any form of distraction that numbs them from the concerns that are phenomenologically present to them.

To the degree that our technologies have the unintended effect of driving a toxic form of individualism while concomitantly making us into more programmable, simplified beings,[27] the family can be considered to be the first medium, not of the artificial realm of technology but of the natural world, for situating the self into healthy social relationships. However, this can only be done if we are deliberate about the role of this medium in creating healthy situated individualism, i.e., personness. Effectively, the study of family communication through the lens of media ecology could indeed be a first line of philosophical defense for those that are concerned with the push toward posthumanism, which postulates that our new "nature" is that of the cyborg and is essentially any merging of the artificial and natural.[28] This line of analysis can bear fruit in future research in analyzing how different forms of family yield different effects upon society. For instance, if the family is not a neutral container of relationships but a medium or environment, then changes to it would yield environmental effects. Specifically, how one understands the monogamous parents versus the polyamorous parents would indeed have environmental effects upon the parents and children individually but also as the family considered as a whole. In the final analysis, media are environments that inform our worldviews. To provide a form of stability in our chaotic times, intentional media consumption can be utilized as a focal point of family communication that combat the chaos created by unreflective use of technology.

WORKS CITED

Bandura, Albert. 1977. *Social Learning Theory*. Englewood Cliffs, NJ: Prentice Hall.

Crawford, Matthew. 2015. *The World Beyond Your Head: On Becoming an Individual in an Age of Distraction.* New York: Farrar, Straus and Giroux

———. 2021. *Why We Drive: Toward a Philosophy of the Open Road.* New York: Custom House.

Harari, Noah Yuval. 2017. *Homo Deus: A Brief History of Tomorrow.* New York: Harper Collins.

Hildebrand, Dietrich von and Alice von Hildebrand. 2017. *Art of Living.* Steubenville, OH: Hildebrand Press.

Logan, Robert K.. 2013. *McLuhan Misunderstood: Setting the Record Straight.* Toronto: Key Publishing House.

McLuhan, Marshall. 1962. *Gutenberg Galaxy: The Making of Typographic Man.* Toronto: University of Toronto Press.

———. 1989. *Global Village: Transformations in World Life and Media in the 21st Century.* New York: Oxford University Press.

———. 2003. *Understanding Media: The Extensions of Man.* Corte Madera, CA: Gingko Press.

McLuhan, Marshall, Kathryn Hutchon, and Eric McLuhan. 1977. *City as Classroom: Understanding Language and Media*. Agincourt, Ontario: The Book Society of Canada.

McLuhan, Marshall, and Eric McLuhan. 1988. *Laws of Media: The New Science*. Toronto: University of Toronto Press.

Postman, Neil. 1986. *Amusing Ourselves to Death: Public Discourse in the Age of Show Business*. London: Penguin Books.

———. 1993. *Technopoly: The Surrender of Culture to Technology*. New York: Vintage Books.

———. 1994. *The Disappearance of Childhood*. Random House.

Rushkoff, Douglas. 2013. *Present Shock: When Everything Happens Now*. New York: Current Hardcover, 2013.

Rushkoff, Douglas. 2017. *Throwing Rocks at the Google Bus: How Growth Became the Enemy of Prosperity*. New York: Portfolio.

Strate, Lance. 2017. *Media Ecology: An Approach to Understanding the Human Condition*. New York: Peter Lang.

Wachs, Anthony M. 2020. "Inhabiting the Digital: Habituating Humanness into Digital Ecologies." In *Communication and Learning in an Age of Digital Transformation*, edited by Birte Heidkamp, David Kergel, Ronald C. Arnett, and Susan Mancino, 101–16. London: Routledge.

Wachs, Anthony M. 2015. *The New Science of Communication: Reconsidering McLuhan's Message for Our Modern Moment*. Pittsburgh, PA: Duquesne University Press.

NOTES

1. Logan, Robert K., *McLuhan Misunderstood: Setting the Record Straight* (Toronto: Key Publishing House, 2013), 103–113; Strate, Lance, *Media Ecology: An Approach to Understanding the Human Condition* (New York: Peter Lang, 2017), 34–37.

2. Crawford, Matthew. 2015. *The World Beyond Your Head: On Becoming an Individual in an Age of Distraction.* New York: Farrar, Straus and Giroux; Crawford, Matthew. 2021. *Why We Drive: Toward a Philosophy of the Open Road.* New York: Custom House.

3. Postman, Neil, *Technopoly: The Surrender of Culture to Technology* (New York: Vintage, 1992), 3–5.

4. Lance Strate has recently explicitly included the connection to the trivium and semiotics in the discipline of media ecology in his recent book *Media Ecology: An Approach to Understanding the Human Condition*. Strate, 17–19.

5. McLuhan became (in)famous for his penchant to "probe" ideas and speak in hyperbole. Taken literally, "the medium is the message" means that content does not matter, but only its form. McLuhan playfully brought attention to the effects of media and dismissed the content of messages in his famous writings, but with

broader reading of his corpus, it becomes clear that he is not dismissive of messages themselves.

6. Wachs, Anthony M. 2015. *The New Science of Communication: Reconsidering McLuhan's Message for Our Modern Moment.* Pittsburgh, PA: Duquesne University Press.

7. McLuhan, Marshall. 1989. *Global Village: Transformations in World Life and Media in the 21st Century.* New York: Oxford University Press. 11–12; McLuhan, Marshall. 1962. *Gutenberg Galaxy: The Making of Typographic Man* Toronto: University of Toronto Press. 247–248; McLuhan, Marshall. 2003. *Understanding Media: The Extensions of Man.* Corte Madera, CA: Gingko Press. 15, 23, 31, 63–70; Wachs, 83.

8. Postman, Neil. 1986. *Amusing Ourselves to Death: Public Discourse in the Age of Show Business.* London: Penguin Books.; Postman, Neil. 1994. *The Disappearance of Childhood.* New York: Vintage. 30–32.

9. Postman, *Disappearance*, 18.

10. Ibid., 91–92.

11. Crawford, *World Beyond*, 89–112.

12. Hildebrand, Dietrich von and Alice von Hildebrand. 2017. *Art of Living.* Steubenville, OH: Hildebrand Press. 45, 49.

13. Han, Byung-Chul, and Erik Butler. 2015. *The Burnout Society.* Stanford, CA: Stanford Briefs, an Imprint of Stanford University Press.

14. Wachs, Anthony M. 2020 "Inhabiting the Digital: Habituating Humanness into Digital Ecologies." *Communication and Learning in an Age of Digital Transformation.* Eds. Birte Heidkamp, David Kergel, Ronald C. Arnett, and Susan Mancino. London: Routledge. 101–116.

15. Wachs, Anthony M. 2015. *The New Science of Communication: Reconsidering McLuhan's Message for Our Modern Moment.* Pittsburgh, PA: Duquesne University Press. 108–112.

16. The media ecology tradition can easily explain this in that speaking and writing follow completely different rules. Not only does spoken language not contain notations like commas, but spelling does not exist in nature. One of the joys of watching a young child learn to read and write phonetically is found within their incorrectly spelt words that are phonetically appropriate. Their phonetically correct spelling is "incorrect" because spelling conventions are largely the product of historical and cultural changes to spoken language.

17. Crawford, *World Beyond*, 3–8; Rushkoff, Douglas. 2013. *Present Shock: When Everything Happens Now.* New York: Current. 15–58.

18. Rushkoff, Douglas. 2013. *Present Shock: When Everything Happens Now*. New York: Current Hardcover. 197–250.

19. Ibid., 77, 129–173.

20. Postman, *Technopoly*, 71–91.

21. Logan, 123–134.

22. Bandura, Albert. 1977. *Social Learning Theory*. Englewood Cliffs, NJ: Prentice Hall.

23. Crawford shows that the programming of our modern technologies is oriented toward creating a society of "pliable choosers." Crawford, *World Beyond*, 70–78.

24. Han and Butler; *The Disappearance of Rituals: A Topology of the Present*. Cambridge, UK: Polity Press.

25. Harari, Noah Yuval. 2017. *Homo Deus: A Brief History of Tomorrow.* New York: Harper Collins.104–111.

26. Wachs, *Inhabiting the Digital*.

27. Crawford, Matthew, *Why We Drive: Toward a Philosophy of the Open Road* (New York: Custom House, 2021), 181–206; Rushkoff, Douglas, *Throwing Rocks at the Google Bus: How Growth Became the Enemy of Prosperity*. (New York: Portfolio, 2017), 30–44.

28. Harari; Wachs *New Science of Communication*, 161–189.

Chapter Eight

Motherhood and Loneliness

The Social Media Dilemma

Maryl R. McGinley and Jill K. Burk

INTRODUCTION

In *Mom Genes: Inside the New Science of our Ancient Maternal Instincts,* Abigail Tucker argues that motherhood is not simply another hat one wears, but instead a cellular event that rebuilds the female brain (2021). Tucker looks at maternal aggression, depression, the declining birth rate, the maternal instinct, maternal stress, and the fact that remaining fetal cells impact a woman for the rest of her life—in ways both good and bad. Her book is a scientific reminder that motherhood is complex and often underexamined. Our scholarship examines some philosophical and communicative implications of twenty-first century motherhood by surveying uses and implications of novel communication technologies; more specifically focusing on the navigation and integration of social media communities.

Tucker notes in her book that the world of science has largely ignored women, specifically mothers (2021, 3–4). We see the same gaps in family communication scholarship. For example, recent searches utilizing a recognized and relevant communication scholarship database reveal fewer than 35 articles discussing motherhood, loneliness, and social isolation. Interpersonal communication textbooks often address communication with romantic partners or within families, but rarely focus on motherhood. Furthermore, according to the Census Bureau (2017), there are 43.5 million mothers in the United States between the ages of 15 and 50, a group that ought not be ignored. We are both mothers who came into motherhood as technological social spaces developed around us and became part of the landscape of family life. We struggled to navigate these novel communication technologies—as our children and the technology were in their infancy.

As many of us continue to rely on social media to "stay connected," especially with our families considering the COVID-19 pandemic, we feel it is meaningful to explore the relationship between social media use and isolation, looking at mothers in particular. We hope to illuminate the significance of combining social media with embodied communities to strengthen relationships and to combat feelings of loneliness in mothers. Leaning solely on social media communities for support during motherhood may intensify feelings of isolation and loneliness due to a lack of social capital and its disembodied nature. Fostering embodied relationships and joining communities that move beyond social media can enrich support and feelings of belonging, and therefore, work to diminish feelings of loneliness and isolation.

This chapter examines the connection between loneliness and social media use, focusing specifically on motherhood and isolation. The first section addresses a rise in loneliness among new mothers. The second section examines social media platforms with an eye toward the dark side of disembodied communication as well as the potential richness of extended networks. Finally, we turn to Robert Putnam's (2000) work on community and his use of alloys as a constructive framework to examine the potentiality to enrich belonging through online communities.

MOTHERHOOD AND LONELINESS

For the purposes of this chapter, when using the term *mothers*, we are paying particular attention to women who have become new mothers either by way of giving birth or through adoption, and/or mothers who have children young children. While the postpartum period (six weeks after childbirth) of motherhood is often studied, we are extending that time period for the purposes of this work. Women with young children tend to feel that they have fewer opportunities to engage, communicate, and interact with others due to the all-encompassing nature of caring for young children, especially if they do not work outside the home (Lee, Vasileiou, and Barnett 2015, 13–15). Anecdotally, we have found that mothers' social connections tend to increase if and when children enter a day care environment or school environment. Therefore, although certainly not exclusive, we are focusing this discussion on mothers with young children who may not be in a school or day care setting. First time mothers find themselves navigating a shift in identities and social roles, which can lead to feelings of loneliness and isolation (Lee, Vasileiou, and Barnett 2015). As an antidote to combat loneliness, many mothers turn to social media in search of communication, connection, and community.

In the last 10 years, there has been a reemergence of "community" as online forums and groups pop up in social communities, seemingly taking the place, or serving a similar role as traditional communities. Many mothers turn to these communities for support postpartum. In fact, Edison Research (2019) reported mothers are the one group of people not slowing down when it comes to social media. The same report also showed 92% of mothers use social media compared to 79% of the population 12+. These high numbers are significant when it comes to motherhood and mental health as a 2017 study from Brigham Young University reported mothers who compared themselves to other mothers on social media platforms felt more depressed, more overwhelmed in their parental role, and less competent as parents. Other research supports this detrimental side of comparison, reporting that mothers often experience feelings of guilt, higher levels of stress and anxiety, and lower self-efficacy when they compare themselves to other mothers on social media (Henderson, Harmon, and Newman 2016). One of the authors of this chapter remembers feeling inadequate as she saw other moms on social media documenting each month of their newborn's life with a full photo shoot. Why hadn't she been doing that? Was she not a good mom? It made us wonder: in such a vulnerable population, can social media create the illusion of deficiency? On the surface, social media and online communities seemingly connect new moms with family, friends, and other parents, but does the medium produce interpersonal support similar to the support traditional interpersonal communication and communities can generate?

We write this chapter in the wake of the coronavirus pandemic, which adds urgency to the question of the connection between motherhood and mental health. Recent scholarship examines mothers who worked/are working from home during the COVID-19 pandemic and found this working environment had a negative impact on the mental well-being of mothers (Guy and Arthur 2020). Earlier research points to the connection of idealized motherhood and the pressure to be a perfect mother adding to increasing anxiety and loneliness (Henderson, Harmon, and Newman 2016). Contemporary conversations about community, technology, and well-being often acknowledge the role of social media. Suzanne Venker from the *Washington Examiner* sees the breakdown of community and family bonds in general as a larger cultural issue. She points to endless work hours and the pursuit of material success and perfection as foundational issues. Venker believes people numb their loneliness with all kinds of things (alcohol, TV)—but she highlights social media as a major player in this notion of collective isolation. She goes on to say, "the shallow interactions of social media do not fulfill our yearning for connection" (Venker 2018). While her research looks at the trend in general, this chapter looks specifically at how turning to social media communities impact mothers and their mental health. We believe, as Turkle observes in *Alone Together: Why We Expect More from Technology and Less from Each Other*, "People are lonely. The network is seductive" (2011, 3).

Beniamini et al. (2019) referenced a 2018 study by the British Red Cross that found 82% of moms under 30 feel lonely sometimes and 43% are lonely often or always. These statistics are staggering and remind us of the renewed discussion of loneliness in healthcare settings and public conversation. Holt-Lunstad and co-authors advocate for loneliness and social isolation to be added to the list of public health concerns (2015, 235). Moreover, Cacioippo and Cacioippo (2018) describe loneliness as a "public health problem." In a 2018 edition of *The Lancet,* an international weekly medical journal, they petition the medical community to take notice and begin addressing this problem within their patient population. Marso (2021) in an article written for the medical community, specifically primary care physicians, discusses a 2019 survey distributed and disseminated by YouGov where "despite all their digital connectedness, one in five millennials . . . reported having no true friends." Marso continues by discussing another 2020 survey conducted by a primary care physicians advisory board, which "found that if primary care clinics offered help with loneliness ('help finding friends and social activities'), millennials would be more likely than any other generation to take them up on it" (30). Thus, digital association is not translating into meaningful connection.

Cacioppo and Cacioppo (2018) define loneliness as a "condition that makes a person irritable, depressed, and self-centered and is associated with a 26% increase in the risk of premature mortality" (2018, 428). Loneliness "is the perception of social isolation, or the subjective experience of being lonely" (Holt-Lunstad et al., 237, 2015). Loneliness, where individuals lack social connections, puts people at risk for premature mortality (Holt-Lunstad et al., 235, 2015). According to Weis (1985), there are two "forms of loneliness. One form is experienced typically, as an aching emptiness and is a response to the absence of an attachment figure. The other form is experienced, typically, as feeling of marginality, of exclusion, and is a response to the absence of a place in an accepting community" (3). We'll refer to Weis's first form of loneliness as attachment loneliness and his second form of loneliness as community loneliness. While new mothers may feel loneliness because of the loss of an attachment figure, we suspect that the form of loneliness most new mothers feel is community loneliness. Many new mothers experience an abrupt shift in and loss of community, or perception of loss, upon the birth or adoption of an infant, especially first-time new mothers. Women who previously worked in a community, socialized in a community, and, perhaps, exercised in a community now find themselves spending many more hours away from community due to the care of their newborns. One of the authors of this chapter who lives in a rural area found the isolation of motherhood to be profound while living in a remote setting. In addition, the other author of this chapter, who lives in a more suburban setting, found herself desperately trying to "make friends" with any new mom who might be home during the day in the neighborhood she lived in, just so she could have a conversation with someone. The community loneliness that many mothers may be feeling has them turning to social media communities for connection and support.

Computer-Mediated Communication and Social Media Communities

While *connecting* with people in online communities may seem like an antidote to loneliness, Dreyfus, Putnam, and Turkle's research tells us that people who spend more time online tend to feel lonelier (2001; 2000; 2011). It is worth noting that Putnam (2000) and Dreyfus (2001) were writing before the expansion and explosion of social media—around 2008. The computer-mediated communication we are focusing on in this chapter is social media platforms and the communities formed in those spaces. Early scholarship referred to these communities under the broad umbrella of computer-mediated communication; therefore, we interchange that term with social media communities in this work.

We acknowledge that there are instances of mothers using large online communities as a lifeline. These communities can be full of resources and information on areas such breastfeeding, formula, diapers, colic, allergies, and sleep, to name a few. When used as information-seeking platforms, social media platforms may offer answers. If your child is refusing to nurse or drink from a bottle, an inquiry in a social media space may elicit dozens of responses—and maybe even the ultimate solution to your problem. But the full context of a child who isn't eating well or struggling to latch goes beyond a brand of bottle or lip tie, with it can come exhaustion and doubt. Those pieces are not necessarily addressed in the online messages about feeding, because that kind of communication can feel one-dimensional.

In general, the research discussed in this section points us to the claim that relying solely on social media for community contact and connection can be detrimental to our health, increase our feelings of loneliness, and can create a false sense of belonging. Putnam (2000) makes a strong case for this by outlining the ways in which computer-mediated communities are often lacking in social capital. For Putnam, the more integrated we are within our communities, the healthier we are, both mentally and physically. He says, "of all the domains in which I have traced the consequences of social capital, in none is the importance of social connectedness so well established as in the case of health and well-being" (2000, 326). We believe that many computer-mediated spaces may create the illusion of community, but without social capital and embodied connections, online communities cannot replace a physical shoulder to lean on when we feel lonely. One of the authors was following a thread in a group about sleep schedules for a young child. For the author, the interaction among group members about sleep was a conversation, but the original person who posted about getting her daughter to sleep eventually stopped updating the group. The author was left wondering what happened, where did my "friend" go, while also contemplating the asymmetry in the relationship. She felt like she was part of a conversation and a relationship, but the other member of the group was perhaps just venting and then moved on without explanation. This scenario frequently occurs in online communities but occurs less in physical communities. Friends do not often disappear without advance communication and knowledge.

To further explore computer-mediated communication, we now look specifically at its disembodied nature as well as its assembly of communities online. Hubert Dreyfus (2001) examines the significance of the lack of 'body' in online communication; for Dreyfus, the body is a source of our sense of our grip on reality. In his work, he makes a case for a connection between the anonymity of the internet and social media platforms and feelings of skepticism and distrust (2001). The anonymity online communities offer can create a disconnect when it comes to the potential depth of a relationship. One can invest less, care less, trust less, and disengage without much effort, as we see in the above example with a person leaving what another felt to be an ongoing conversation without an explanation.

Developing Putnam's notion of social capital along with Dreyfus's notion of anonymity illuminates the fissures in online social media communities further. Putnam believes that "networks of community engagement foster sturdy norms of reciprocity: I'll do this for you now, in the expectation that you (or perhaps someone else) will return the favor" (Putnam 2000, 20). In the large virtual networks that many mothers rely on for advice postpartum that sense of social capital can often be lacking, as the community is so large. Putnam sees great potential in computer-mediated communication, as opportunity for civic engagement and social connectedness are impressive. The internet obviously offers an opportunity for people who share similar interests, but not space and time to connect and communicate.

Human communication consists of both nonverbal and verbal communication. There is a wholeness that occurs when we communicate using both our verbal and nonverbal capacities. Amy Cuddy (2015) discusses William James's 1884 work titled "What is an Emotion." In this work, James asserts "that bodily experiences cause emotions, not the other way around" (Cuddy 2015, 174). James states "Common sense says, we lose our fortune, are sorry and weep; we meet a bear are frightened and run; we are insulted by a rival, are angry and strike" (174). To think of this in another way, social media only allows for verbal communication; it provides even less nonverbal cues than a conversation using a telephone. We try to provide nonverbal-type cues when using social media, by using emojis and stylistic devices such as capital letters. But writing is not communication, it is often called correspondence. Communication consists of both verbal and nonverbal communication. If we are missing either the verbal or nonverbal component, are we fully communicating? If we are not fully communicating, then perhaps that's one reason we may feel lonely when we are in online communities. We are sending information and receiving information, but something is missing. If as James states and Cuddy's work supports, the body causes emotions, then we are left feeling fragmented, as if something is missing when we are not communicating with our bodies, too. In a practical application, one of the authors had a baby who wouldn't nurse. She wrote a post asking for help in her mom group, she called and described the issue to a lactation consultant, and she eventually had one come into her home. Having the lactation consultant in her home was the only way she eventually came to understand and address the issue.

Putnam (2020) also discusses that the lack of nonverbal communication cues while navigating social media communities in comparison to face-to-face communication presents a challenge. Humans are savvy at decoding nonverbal cues (as Putnam notes, particularly when it comes to emotions, trustworthiness, and cooperation). What are the implications of communication without those cues, especially when looking at a group of tired, sometimes desperate new moms who really just need compassion? Organization theorists Robert G. Eccles and Nitin Nohria (1992) "point out face-to-face encounters provide a depth and speed of feedback that is impossible in computer mediated communication" (75). What Putnam calls the "poverty of social cues" in online communities prohibits depth in connection and can inhibit trust. He notes that this can lead to dehumanization, misrepresentation and misunderstanding. In *Bowling Alone*, Putnam (2000) writes, "all these problems are less serious in dealing with clear, practical issues but more serious in situations of uncertainty and ambiguity" (2000, 177). There are few things more ambiguous and uncertain than having and raising children. There is a clear comparison here to online schooling too, and why so many people have struggled with the switch to virtual classrooms during COVID-19. There is a disconnect; and while it may necessary in some cases, when we can have embodied communication, we benefit.

Dreyfus (2001) believes that "our body, including our emotions, play a crucial role in our being able to make sense of things, our sense of reality of things, our trust in other people . . . and our capacity for making the unconditional commitments that give meaning to our lives" (90). Social media communities allow us to become detached and disembodied—unsituated. Dreyfus relies on a Carnegie-Melon study from 1998 called "Internet Paradox: A Social Technology that Reduces Social Involvement and Psychological Well-being?" Kraut et al. (1998) sum up their findings:

> This research examined the social and psychological impact of the internet on 169 people in seventy-three households during the first one to two years on-line. . . . Greater use of the internet was associated with declines in participants' communication with family members in the household, declines in the size of their social circle, and increases in their depression and loneliness. (3)

As noted in the first section of this chapter, these findings were just reinforced by a study out of Brigham Young, almost 20 years later. For Dreyfus (2001), the problem lies in missing people's actual embodied presence to one another. The parallel to an online 'mom group' is clear. What many of these moms' need is someone who is 'there for them.' The disembodiment and lack of context can create anxiety in mothers.

Putnam (2020) notes that social capital improves when we recognize the ways in which our fates are linked. He notes, "People who have active and trusting connections to others . . . develop and maintain character traits that are good for the rest of society" (288). That sense of connection, which can make us more empathetic and less cynical, can be hard to develop in a large community online. Putnam believes the size of the community has an impact on that feeling of disconnection. In larger communities, there can be less participation. Many online mom groups are very large. In combing through Facebook groups "for moms," we found groups as large as 150,000 members (interestingly this is a group for moms and technology). Putnam notes that many online communities are grouped around very specific commonalities. In groups this large, many "members" do not participate because they don't need to. While we tend to feel that social media allows for more participation, the same voices are often heard. The most vocal and the most active group members participate and their comments are moved to the forefront due to the algorithmic nature of social media. Therefore, authentic conversation rarely happens. Community connectedness is integral to richness in social capital. Putnam (2000) connects social capital to happier, healthier, smarter, more stable communities. Deficiencies in reciprocity and mutual concern are threads present in social media platforms that we want to address and enrich by combining those communities with embodied ones.

Constructive Framework to Enrich Belonging to Online Communities

In our current historical moment, it would be unwise or even perhaps nearly impossible to completely shun and turn away from all forms of social media or personal technology devices. The many ways in which we use these devices are staggering. Therefore, to that end, we hope to provide a constructive approach to thinking about and utilizing social media to increase communicative support and decrease maternal loneliness. The scholarship conducted by Turkle (2015) and Putnam's (2020) "Afterword" rounds our thinking and direction. Through integrating Putnam's concept of alloys with Turkle's focus on mindfulness and solitude, we hope to provide a philosophically grounded communicative approach to thinking about maternal loneliness and social media and technology use.

However, perhaps even before initiating, creating, and engaging in social media platforms, we feel conscious reflection and mental preparation are needed and crucial. While we want to advocate for the importance of mindfulness when using and communicating via social media, we acknowledge the concept of mindfulness feels trendy. Pick up any popular press piece on stress or motherhood and you will see this term being used. While we recognize the omnipresence of the idea, we feel the ontological state of mindfulness is truly what many mothers need. True mindfulness takes energy and effort. Being mindful calls us to be present to the moment that is in front of us, while acting with an intentionality toward that moment. Mindfulness can be understood as our phenomenological engagement with our present moment, our personal technological devices, and our social media platforms. The intent to act and engage seems to be "a given"; we think . . . yes, of course, I make conscious decisions and actions regarding my social media usage; however, the research states otherwise. For example, Turkle (2015) discusses the *circuit of apps* we often sequence through. Turkle describes this as phenomena where at a moment of boredom, we pick up our phones and circuit through all of our social apps, "just to check to them." Turkle interviews a college junior who states that she does this because she "likes the feeling of 'rapid-fired switching' and thinks that no [college] class could ever compete with it, no matter how engaging" (214). It's not only college students who cycle through their social media applications at a moment of boredom. It's almost everyone who has a smartphone and social media applications. We have spoken to so many mothers who move through this circuit and find themselves immersed in social comparison and doubt because of it. This is just one example where mindfulness can help us recognize our habits and help us to focus on using our personal technological devices as tools when needed. In the place of that circuit, we can cultivate other habits that may make us feel more connected to the present moment.

In Putnam's (2020) "Afterword," he unpacks the concept of alloys, a concept he first introduced to readers in the conclusion of 2000 edition of *Bowling Alone: The Collapse and Revival of American Community*. Putnam explains, an alloy refers "to the crucial fact that most actual networks are neither purely virtual nor purely in-person, but combine both types of networks into novel mixtures with unexpected properties" (2020, 416). He argues for us to move beyond the real versus virtual dichotomy because in social media practice, these two categories exist less frequently in their purest, unadulterated forms (422–23). He continues by explaining that many of the relational networks we form and maintain via social media are not only virtual relationships; they are alloyed relationships. For instance, as Putnam acknowledges, Mark Zuckerberg created Facebook for students to communicate with friends who were part of a campus community. As Putnam states, "your Friends on Facebook were almost certainly also your friends in real life" (422). As we know, the geographic, communal nature of Facebook networks changed when Facebook went global and moved away from the campus-based university setting; however, research conducted about the friend networks people have on Facebook has found that roughly half to two-thirds of people's Facebook friends have some type of in-person ties (Croom, Gross, Rosen, and Rosen 2016, 139). Therefore, we feel it is important to further explore and engage in social media platforms that foster these types of alloyed relationships rather than utilizing or engaging in social media platforms or communication technologies that create and perpetuate pure virtual relationships. One of the authors spoke with young mothers who turned their virtual Facebook group into a group that meets for coffee, with their kids, every month. These mothers said that connection was enhanced in terms of understanding each other's struggles and triumphs in parenting. Context, texture, and nuance were missing from their messages online, and the embodied meeting and seeing of each other helped them all feel less lonely. Finding a time to physically meet was not always easy either, but when they made it a priority, they all reported feeling more supported when they could talk face-to-face.

CONCLUSION

Our research indicates that relying exclusively on social media communities during motherhood intensifies feelings of isolation and loneliness due to lack of social capital and its disembodied nature. Fostering embodied relationships and joining communities that move beyond social media can enrich support and feelings of belonging. We would never discourage a mother from joining a Facebook group, but we are encouraging the recognition of the limitation of social spaces for support and connection. Social comparison for mothers on social media can have deleterious effects. We hope to foreground and highlight an unsettling phenomenon about the relationship between maternal loneliness and frequent social media use, while providing some touchpoints for discussion and change. This chapter contributes to family communication in focusing attention on a previously underrepresented group, recognizing that members of a family are linked in ways that make them interdependent; so, attention to mothers is attention to family as a system. Moving forward, we would like to continue to develop a road map for mindfulness in engagement, with attention to the ways in which online communities can complement our relationships in real life, acknowledging that social spaces, when used with intention and reflection, can be a tool in that communication.

As we put the finishing touches on this chapter, Facebook whistleblower Frances Haugen was getting ready to testify in Congress about Facebook's impact on young users. Pelley (2021) of *60 Minutes* reported that Haugen, who was a product manager at Facebook for two years, released that Facebook covered up the negative impact the platform had on young girls and their body image. Haugen goes on to make the claim that Facebook incentivizes content that is angry, polarizing, and damaging in general. Once again, we see the impact of social media being explored, but mothers are not at the forefront of the conversation. We are collectively recognizing the negative effects of social media on teenagers and starting to think about ways to mitigate that damage. Our hope is to also focus attention on mothers as an underexamined group and to offer a philosophical framework grounded in mindfulness and embodied communication as a response.

NOTE

The authors would like to thank Mattie Updyke for her help cross-referencing this piece.

REFERENCES

Beniamini, Nicole, Melissa DeCesare, Laura Ivey, Melissa Kiesche, Megan Lazovick, and Laura Silvia. 2021. "Moms on Social Media 2019" Edison Research, https://www.edisonresearch.com/moms-on-social-media-2019/#:~:text=Some%20key%20findings%3A,downward%20trend%20among%20U.S.%20moms.

Cacioppo, John T., and Stephanie Cacioppo. 2018. "The Growing Problem of Loneliness." *The Lancet* 391, no. 10119: 426.

Coyne, Sarah A., Brandon T. McDaniel, and Laura A. Stockdale. 2017. "'Do You Dare To Compare?' Associations Between Maternal Social Comparisons on Social Networking Sites and Parenting, Mental Health, and Romantic Relationship Outcomes." *Computers in Human Behavior* 70 (May): 355–400. https://doi.org/10.1016/j.chb.2016.12.081.

Croom, Charles, Bay Gross, Larry D. Rosen, and Brad Rosen. 2016. "What's Her Face(book)? How Many of Their Facebook 'Friends' Can College Students Actually Identify?" *Computers in Human Behavior* 56: 135–141. https://doi.org/10.1016/j.chb.2015.11.015.

Cuddy, Amy. 2015. *Presence: Bringing Your Boldest Self to Your Biggest Challenges.* New York: Little, Brown, and Company.

Dreyfus, Hubert L. 2001. *On the Internet: Thinking in Action.* New York: Routledge.

Eccles, Robert G., and Nitin Nohria. 1992. *Beyond the Hype: Rediscovering the Essence of Management.* Boston: Harvard Business School.

Guy, Batsheva, and Brittany Arthur. 2020. "Academic Motherhood During COVID-19: Navigating Our Dual Roles as Educators and Mothers." *Gender, Work, and Organization* 27, no. 5 (Sept.): 887–899. https://doi.org/10.1111/gwao.12493.

Henderson, Angie, Sandra Harmon, and Harmony Newman. 2016. "The Price Mothers Pay, Even When They Are Not Buying It: Mental Health Consequences of Idealized Motherhood." *Sex Roles* 74: 512–526. http://dx.doi.org/10.1007/s11199-015-0534-5.

Holt-Lunstad, Julianne, Timothy B. Smith, Mark Baker, Tyler Harris, and David Stephenson. 2015. "Loneliness and Social Isolation as Risk Factors for Mortality: A Meta-analytic Review." *Perspectives on Psychological Science* 10, no. 2 (March): 227–237. http://www.jstor.org/stable/44290063.

James, William. 1884. "What Is an Emotion?" (*Mind 9.* Oxford: Oxford University Press) quoted in Amy Cuddy, 2015, *Presence: Bringing Your Boldest Self to Your Biggest Challenges.* New York: Little, Brown, and Company: 175.

Kraut, Robert, Michael Patterson, Vicki Lundmark, Sara Kiesler, Tridas Mukopadhyay, and William Scherlis. 1998. "Internet Paradox: A Social Technology That Reduces Social Involvement and Psychological Well-Being?" *The American Psychologist* 53, no. 9: 1017–1031. https://doi.org/10.1037/0003-066X.53.9.1017.

Lee, Katharine, Konstantina Vasileiou, and Julie Barnett. 2019. "'Lonely Within the Mother': An Exploratory Study of First-time Mothers' Experiences of Loneliness." *Journal of Health Psychology* 24, no. 10: 1334–1344. https://doi.org/10.1177/1359105317723451.

Marso, Andy. 2021. "What Millennials Want Out of Primary Care, and How to Deliver It." *Family Practice Management* 28, no. 3 (May): 29–33. https://www.clinicalkey.com/#!/content/playContent/1-s2.0-S1069564821000204.

Pelley, Scott. 2021. "Whistleblower: Facebook is Misleading the Public on Progress Against Hate Speech, Violence, Misinformation." *60 Minutes*, CBS News, https://www.cbsnews.com/news/facebook-whistleblower-frances-haugen-misinformation-public-60-minutes-2021-10-03/.

Putnam, Robert D. 2000. *Bowling Alone: The Collapse and Revival of American Community.* New York: Simon & Schuster.

———. 2020. *Bowling Alone: Revised and Updated: The Collapse and Revival of American Community*, 2nd edition. New York: Simon & Schuster.

Smith, Dave. 2018. “Shocking Extent of Loneliness Faced by Young Mothers Revealed.” The Co-operative Group, https://www.co-operative.coop/media/news-releases/shocking-extent-of-loneliness-faced-by-young-mothers-revealed.

Tucker, Abigail. 2021. *Mom Genes: Inside the New Science of our Ancient Maternal Instincts.* New York: Gallery Books.

Turkle, Sherry. 2011. *Alone Together: Why We Expect More from Technology and Less from Each Other.* New York: Basic Books.

———. 2015. *Reclaiming Conversation: The Power of Talk in a Digital Age.* New York: Penguin Press.

United States Census Bureau. 2017. “Facts for Features: Mother’s Day: May 14, 2017.” Census Bureau, https://www.census.gov/newsroom/facts-for-features/2017/cb17-ff09-mothers-day.html.

Venker, Suzanne. 2018. “Broken Relationships Are at the Heart of the Suicide Epidemic.” *The Washington Examiner*, https://www.washingtonexaminer.com/opinion/broken-relationships-are-at-the-heart-of-the-suicide-epidemic.

Weis, Robert S. 1985. “Loneliness: What We Know About It and What We Might Do About It.” In *Preventing the Harmful Consequences of Severe and Persistent Loneliness*: Research Planning Workshop, University of California, Los Angeles, Feb. 10–12, 1982, 3–12. Rockville, MD: National Institute of Mental Health.

SECTION III

Transformation

Chapter Nine

"According To Science, This Is Who I Am"

Personal Genome Testing and Adoption Reunions

Melissa Rizzo Weller

Communication in adoptive families is complicated, more so when adult adoptees reunite with their birth families. Although most adoptions today have some element of open communication (Colaner, Halliwell, and Guignon 2014), adoptees from closed adoptions typically have little or no information about their birth families (Miall and March 2005), which may leave adoptees wondering where they came from and who they are. In the United States currently, only 11 states have unrestricted legislation allowing adoptees from closed adoptions to access their original birth certificates (American Adoption Congress 2021), meaning adoptees who want to contact birth family members must find another source of information. The emergence of personal genomic testing (PGT) sites opened a new path for adoptees to connect with their biological families. Genetic databases, such as Ancestry.com and 23andMe, have provided information and hope for millions of adoptees.

This exploration into adoption communication emerges from my reunion with a sibling who was adopted several years before my sisters and me were born. We met my brother when I was almost 40 years old, when he was 43, and have spent the last decade learning how to be a family after growing up in different households. Unquestionably, family communication is complex, and adoptive family communication has additional layers of complexity. In non-adoptive families, siblings have shared experiences and similar relationships with other family members that develop over their early lives.

Conversely, when siblings do not grow up in the same house, there are no (or limited) shared experiences. Thus, the expectation of a typical sibling relationships in flux for siblings in adoptive families. This uncertainty about relationship development and maintenance is likely true across all types of relationships in adoptive families after reunion.

This chapter describes how adoptees reconstruct their personal and family identities after reunion with birth family members through the use of personal genomic testing and the ethical implications for adoptees who utilize personal genomic testing to reunite with birth family members. First, I share the history of closed adoptions in the United States, specifically the Baby Scoop Era—a time of unprecedented adoption. I then provide information about adoptive family communication and reunions, both understudied phenomena in communication studies. Next, we look at identity—both personal and family—and how adoption reunion may impact adult adoptee identities immediately and over time. I also include a discussion of technology in adoption search in reunion, specifically personal genomic testing (PGT). After this review of previous literature, I present the current study by describing participants, a brief methodology, and the results, including excerpts from participants describing their adoption reunion experiences. In the conclusion of this chapter, I provide implications for both family communication and the adoption community. To begin, I discuss the history of closed adoptions in the United States at the start of the twentieth century.

CLOSED ADOPTIONS

At the turn of the twentieth century, shifts in the economy and technological advancements impacted how the United States legally addressed adoption, as well as how adoptive families were perceived in society. In the early 1900s, laws were enacted to seal birth records under the premise of protecting adoptive parents' privacy (Samuels 2013). The first state adoption law passed in 1917 in Minnesota required adoption records to be sealed from public view (Herman 2012). The sealing of records continued in all states from the late 1930s through the 1980s, when all states had legally sealed adoption records (Potter 2013). In the last few decades, laws are changing again to unseal records, giving adoptees access to their original birth certificates (Herman 2012). Currently, only 11 states have laws giving unrestricted access to adult adoptee birth records. The remaining states and District of Columbia have some limitations on access to records (American Adoption Congress 2021).

Adoptees who were born between the end of World War II (late 1940s) and the passing of Roe v. Wade (1972) were part of the Baby Scoop Era (BSE; Wilson-Buterbaugh 2017). In this era, unmarried and/or underaged women and girls had little access to birth control and limited options if they became pregnant. According to Wilson-Buterbaugh (2017), the United States saw up to 4 million babies surrendered for adoption, with 2 million domestic adoptions in the 1960s alone. Unmarried pregnant women were expected to marry quickly or "go away" to have their babies in secret, then surrender their babies for adoption (Fessler 2006). Many women were explicitly told to forget about their baby and move on with their lives, that they could have other children someday (Fessler 2006). Most of the women who surrendered babies during the BSE were white, middle-class women whose families feared the shame and stigma associated with premarital sex and having children out of wedlock (Wilson-Buterbaugh 2017). The United States was not the only country with a surge in adoptions during this time. Other countries, such as Canada (Andrews 2016) and Australia (Fessler 2006), also had soaring adoption statistics during this era.

In this era of adoption, sealed records allowed for adoptive parents to adopt under the expectation that the birth mother would not be able to find their child. Adoptive parents could then raise their children as if they were their own (Wilson-Buterbaugh 2017). Modern adoption was done by matching, where adoptive parents are matched to babies so that "adoption substituted one family for another so carefully, systematically, and completely that natal kinship was rendered invisible and irrelevant" (Herman 2012). Ideally, adoptive parents were matched with a baby, whose ethnicity and other characteristics were close enough to their own, so that the adoption could be invisible. Most adoptions today have some element of open communication (Colaner and Scharp 2016; Hays, Horstman, Colaner, and Nelson 2016), and matching is not as important to adoptive families. The trend toward open adoption, and less secrecy, may contribute to changing laws in many states.

Adoptive Family Communication

Substantial research demonstrating the disparities adoptees face related to medical treatment (May et al. 2016) and mental health (Keyes et al. 2008; 2013) clearly suggests that adoptees' motivations for search and reunion with biological family are literally a matter of life and death. Moreover, adoptees may experience gaps between their personal identity and relational identity layers if they are missing information about their biological families. A phenomenon known as "genetic bewilderment" is often another motivation for adoptees to search for biological family members, which is lack of or uncertain knowledge of their birth parents (Wellisch 1952). Finally, adoptees from closed adoptions seek "genetic mirroring" or seeing physical traits of oneself in others. Adoptees may experience this phenomenon until they have biological children or reunite with birth family members who share physical traits.

Adoptees who experience these identity gaps may feel as if finding birth families will help them "find the missing pieces" of their identity. Modern mediated communication channels allow adult adoptees to search for biological family through Facebook, online search databases, and more recently, personal genomic testing (PGT) sites. According to Baptista et al. (2016), adoptees used PGT due to lack of knowledge related to their family and medical history but hoped to make a connection and reunite with birth family members using their PGT results.

Adoption Reunions

Traditional family reunions provide opportunities for family members to reconnect, relive memories, and celebrate (Coffelt 2018). Rituals are an important part of family reunions, as "knowing your family is knowing yourself" (Sutton 2004, 253). The rituals established in families of origin develop over time and are passed down through generations. However, adoption reunions between adoptees and birth family members are different. Adoption reunions are (usually) first meetings since the adoption among biologically related relatives. Although there is a dearth of recent research regarding reunions between adoptees and birth family members, the following section details some of the early research concerning adoption reunions. Specifically, this research addresses motivations for search and relationship expectations after reunion.

The stigma of adoption may play a crucial role in the decision to search for, and eventually reunite with, birth families (March 1995). Many adoptees struggle with not knowing the circumstances in which they were relinquished. Reuniting with birth mothers can provide a sense of closure and, also, a sense of belonging. The shroud of secrecy that veils most closed adoptions may imply to adoptees that their birth mothers were somehow disgraceful or shameful (Fessler 2006; Wilson-Buterbaugh 2017); reunions can provide adoptees with a more realistic explanation of their birth and adoption situation. Sachdev (1992) posits that secrecy in adoption does not benefit any of the parties involved, which may be partly why more adoptions today have at least some open communication (Hays et al. 2016).

Extant research on adoption reunions focused on relationships between adoptees and adoptive parents. In one study, Campbell, Silverman, and Patti (1991) examined, among other variables, the effect of a reunion on the adoptive parents. While most adoption reunions resulted in little change in adoptee–adoptive parent relationships, those that do might have been the result of uncertainty and insecurity of the adoptive parents themselves. Additionally, Gladstone and Westhues (1998) found that reunions can produce various types of relationships. Their study results showed that satisfaction with contact and emotional closeness influence relationships between adoptees and birth family members.

Other research investigated the biological relationships between adoptees and birth family members. Carsten (2000) examined narratives of kinship in adoption reunions, finding that while reunion can "fill in some of the gaps in a personal biography" (p. 700), the connection between one's past, present, and future is only partial. In another study, Affleck and Steed (2001) found that adoptees and birth families are uncertain about the expectations of an ongoing relationship after reunion. This study showed birth mothers expected to develop a mother-child relationship, while adoptees preferred friendship. This is consistent with Sachdev's (1992) earlier findings, in which he states, "What is clear is that with patience, sensitivity, and understanding, even relationships that do not begin on a positive note have a chance of reviving and blossoming" (p. 66). The discrepancy in expectations can cause a multitude of responses, such as reducing expectations of a relationship or simply withdrawing from contact altogether. Powell and Afifi (2005) assert that adoptees feel uncertainty and ambiguous loss related to their adoption. Reuniting and forming a relationship with birth family members may alleviate or reframe some of that loss. Gaining a "family of heritage" identity may alter or integrate with an adoptee's personal and/or adoptive identity.

From another perspective, Rizzo Weller and Hosek (2020) explored birth mothers' expectations of reunion and found that many birth mothers expected to reunite with their child one they reached adulthood. Privacy rules created at the time of the adoption were often influenced by cultural factors, especially for pregnant women under the age of 18. Birth mothers sometimes felt as if they were giving their child a "better life" if they placed their child for adoption but expected the adoption agency (or other legal entity) to share their contact information with the child once they were adults. Over time, birth mothers in this study acknowledged that the advent of the internet and PGT would render laws blocking access to birth records irrelevant. Adoptees may be more likely to search for birth family members if they believe the contact would be welcomed.

Finally, research explored the roles adoptees expect birth parents to assume after reunion. Passmore and Feeney (2009) explored the difference in the types of relationships that develop between adoptees and birth mothers and fathers after reunion. Relationships after reunion with mothers tend to be more personal, and they are less personal with fathers. The findings showed that adoptees may find resolution of identity issues by gaining information about the adoption from a reunion. Another finding showed that reunions with birth mothers (more than fathers) are more important in gaining a sense of belonging for adoptees. More recently, Scharp and Steuber (2014) examined communication privacy management in reunions between adoptees and birth parents, finding that adoptees expect their birth mothers to be gatekeepers of the information concerning the adoption to maintain a comfortable level of uncertainty. Adoptees may also experience uncertainty regarding the ownership of information about the actual adoption.

The culmination of this research demonstrates multiple motivations and expectations for reunions between adoptees and their birth families. However, we need to further investigate accessibility to adoption records and how the changing state laws and openness in adoption impact communication among members of adoptive families. Adult adoptees who choose to seek out their birth family members sometimes do so in hopes of discovering an identity they have not known yet.

Adoptive Identity

Much of the research exploring adoptive identity emerges from Erikson's (1968) belief that people are born without a sense of identity and develop a 'self' through socialization with others and the world. As we grow, we internalize and reflect upon the stimuli in our ever-changing contexts to make sense of who we are and where we fit into the world. Adoptive identity is more complex because of the inherent uncertainty related to multiple family identities. Colaner, Horstman, and Rittenour (2018) framed adoptive identity through an intergroup lens, social identity theory, to illuminate the complexity of the interconnectedness between personal and family identities.

In this chapter, adoptive identity is examined through the communication theory of identity. According to Hecht (1993), "Identity is inherently a communicative process and must be understood as a transaction in which messages are exchanged" (p. 78). In his foundational piece, Hecht (1993) posited that identities have individual, social, and communal properties and are both enduring and changing. Furthermore, identity has both content and relationship levels of interpretation and prescribe modes of appropriate and effective communication. Colaner, Halliwell, and Guignon (2014) asserted, "CTI has highlighted the complex nature of identity within a variety of contexts, and the theory has potential for informing adoptive identity as embedded in adoptive and birth family relationships" (472). These assumptions are useful to frame identity within adoptive families, as identities during search and reunion may be dynamic and are constructed by the individual adoptee, the adoptive family, and the birth family.

Identity Layers

In addition to the assumptions about CTI, Hecht (1993) describes four frames through which identity can be examined: personal, enactment, relationship, and communal. First, the personal frame is the identity construct "ascribed to the self by others in the social world" (Hecht 1993, 79). Personal identity includes how we define ourselves (Colaner et al. 2014) and the "expectations and motivations" (Hecht 1993, 79) we have about our interactions with others. Adoptees' personal identity may be developed within the adoptive family while growing up and may shift after reunion with birth family members (Powell and Afifi 2005).

The second frame, enactment, asserts that identities are emergent and enacted in social behaviors and symbols (Hecht 1993). This frame demonstrates the "communication of identity" (Colaner et al. 2014, 472) through messages, either as the central focus of the message or simply part of the message (Hecht 1993). For adoptees, enactment may be explicitly stating their status as an adopted person through discourse. Enactment may also occur through more implicit displays, such as taking a family photo with their birth family and posting it to social media. Discourse-dependent family members, specifically in adoptive families, "depend more heavily on discourse processes to establish and maintain their bonds, providing members with a public identity as well as an internal sense of identity" (Galvin and Colaner 2013, 197).

The relationship frame is the third lens, which works in tandem with the enactment frame. According to Hecht (1993), "identity is mutually constructed in social interaction" and "emerges in relationships and becomes a property of the relationship" (79). For adoptees in reunion with their birth families, new roles must be determined, and the nature of the relationship must be ascribed. For example, an adoptee may call their birth mother "Mom" or by her first name, and the introduction may change depending on with whom the adoption is speaking. The relationship is constructed through the agreement of terms of address, which may be different in person than on social media sites. The relationship frame has three levels in which identity emerges. First, "people define themselves in terms of others and shape social behavior to those around them" (Hecht 1993, 80). Adoptees may use "Mom" with their adoptive mother when in her presence, but "adoptive mom" when taking to people outside the family. Second, "people define themselves in terms of their relationships, gaining a sense of self through relationships" (Hecht 1993, 80). Adoptees create an individual identity, similar to children who live with biological parents, and may or may not think of being "adopted" each time family discourse arises. Adoptees who have a loving home growing up may rarely talk about or ask questions about their adoptive status, but they may silently wonder about their birth family. Finally, "relationships, themselves, take on identities and the dyad becomes an entity" (Hecht 1993, 80). The unique communicative behaviors people enact as a couple can be different than the ways they behave alone. We see this identity in social media accounts when partners share an account. Colaner et al. (2014) examined adoptive identity through the relational layer lens, finding "relational layers embedded in both families are present in individual's adoptive identity, contributing particular sources of knowledge, tendencies, and experiences that give weight and context to the personal identity adoptees espouse" (491).

The communal frame is defined as "something held by a group of people which, in turn, bonds the group together" (Hecht 1993, 80). This frame may be the most salient for adoptees in reunion. Adoptees who seek their birth family may be looking to become a member of that family and merge into the family identity. Through the communal frame lens, adoptees may attempt to reconstruct their family identity with members of their birth and/or adoptive family after reunion. According to Hecht (1993), these frames cannot be isolated from each other. As such, all CTI frames can be useful for examining adoptive identity.

TECHNOLOGY IN ADOPTIVE FAMILY COMMUNICATION

For adoptees in closed adoptions, search and reunion is still an important part of identity formation. To aid in their search, many adoptees turn to mediated channels of communication to expedite their search. According to Howard (2012), "The Internet is having a profound, permanent impact on modern adoption" (p. 8). In fact, in a study of 392 adoptees, 88% used the internet to locate adoption information and 76% used the internet to find information regarding adoption laws (Whitesel & Howard, 2013). Additionally, 74% of adoptees in their study used the internet to search for birth family members via various channels, including for-profit and free search sites, search engines, and online public records sites (Whitesel & Howard, 2013).

Today, the internet has provided us with multiple channels for communication, including email, social networking sites, and websites with interactive features. People can form and maintain a wide variety of relationships via mediated channels, including friendships (Sprecher & Hampton, 2017; Yang, Brown & Braun, 2014), romantic relationships (Fox, Warber & Makstaller, 2013; Rochadiat, Tong & Novak, 2017), and relationships with classmates (Swan, 2002) or coworkers (Marshall, Michaels & Mulki, 2007). Adoptees may search for and develop family relationships online, as well. Today, adoptees can search the internet or social networking sites, and send a message to a birth mother (or other family member) within minutes, once they obtain her name from their original birth certificate or other source. Another emerging technology often used in adoption searches is personal genomic testing, otherwise known as genetic or DNA testing.

Personal Genomic Testing

In the previous decade, personal genomic testing (PGT) has emerged as a seemingly simple way for people to find out information about their biological heritage. After purchasing a test through online sites, such as Ancestry.com or 23andMe, consumers submit samples of their DNA and wait for their online results. PGT is used in multiple contexts in health fields, including genetic counseling for gene mutations (McGuire et al. 2009), displaced migrant populations (Lee, Kim & Lee 2016), and suicidality (Petersen et al. 2013).

In the context of adoption, Baptista et al. (2016) found the using PGT by adoptees is a fairly unexplored area of genetic research. However, in their study of 1,607 participants, 80 were adoptees and results indicated approximately half of the adoptees participated in PGT with actionability related to results in mind. Simply put, adoptees used this testing due to lack of knowledge related to their family and medical history. Some participants also commented that PGT would be a potential "long shot to connect with them" (Baptista et al. 2016, 927), referring to birth family members.

In light of this growing consumer practice, some researchers consider PGT unreliable at best, and unethical at worst. For example, Jordens et al. (2009) assert, "PGT provides results that have little or no value as 'health information,' that influence people in unknown ways, with consequences for their health about which we know nothing" (15). In fact, two states (New York and California) investigated "unlicensed practice of medicine" by some companies (McGuire et al. 2009, 3). For adoptees who choose PGT as a method of contact with birth family members, reliable health information may only be part of the attraction. Results from PGT may be the only means for adoptees to know who their biological family members are, and subsequently how to communicate with them.

Ethical Use of Technology

With new technology comes new responsibility for ethical communication. Typically, a person's genetic information is voluntarily added to a PGT database by purchasing a subscription, taking a home collection test, and submitting to the site for analysis and posting to the online database. But what happens when someone has not voluntarily consented to submitting their own DNA? Information accessed via the internet is inherently vulnerable to hackers, data breaches, and other malicious attacks on its security. Although it may be difficult to fathom having your DNA information shared involuntarily online, it is most certainly a possibility. Adult adoptees who know they have a biological sibling may share their connections found via PGT sites in hopes of reunion. This may (in)advertently include information about their birth mother or father, as well as other biological family members. Each person's adoption story is their own; however, because of the vast network of actors in each adoption story, the impact on family privacy, genetic information, and communication can be felt by all the family members involved. In a recent study examining privacy rules, Rizzo Weller and Hosek (2020) found that birth mothers' expectations of privacy changed over time, thus, adult adoptees privacy expectations my change, as well. Sharing PGT results online might seem like a good idea at one point of an adoptee's search journey, but they may change their mind later. With the permanency of information on the internet, such information may near impossible to remove.

Adult adoptees who begin searching for birth family members may struggle with identity and ethical issues related to this unique communicative process. The remainder of this chapter focuses on the experiences of adult adoptees who initiated the search and reunion process utilizing new technology, specifically PGT, to obtain information that could assist them in finding their birth families.

THE CURRENT STUDY

The current study is part of a larger project in which 51 adult adoptees participated in qualitative interviews conducted through in interpretive phenomenological analysis (IPA). According to Smith, Flowers, and Larkin (2009), IPA is "a qualitative research approach committed to the examination of how people make sense of their major life experiences" (p. 1). In line with the IPA process, I asked participates to share their experiences related to reunion with birth family members. Of the total participants in the project, a majority of participants (*n* = 29) engaged in (PGT) with at least one online database. The three sites utilized by participants were Ancestry.com, 23andMe, and Family Tree. A total of 22 participants chose Ancestry.com, one used 23andMe, and one used Family Tree. Additionally, two participants used both Ancestry.com and 23andMe, and three participants used all three PGT sites. The mean age for participants was 49 years old and included 27 female and two male. Additionally, 27 participants identified as white, one as biracial and one as African American. Participants shared their experiences of using PGT to learn about their biological families and in some cases, used their PGT results to contact family members.

In Their Own Words

Exploring family communication in adoptive families from the unique perspective of adult adoptees is crucial for understanding how identities are constructed and reconstructed for adopted people when reuniting with their birth families. Extant literature from the adoptee point of view includes confronting uncertainty (Colaner and Kranstuber 2010), self-esteem and identity (Horstman, Colaner, and Rittenour 2016), identity through names and labels (Docan-Morgan 2017), and meaning of "parent" (Anzur and Myers 2020), all demonstrating the unique positionality of people who had choices made for them at birth yet live with the multiple, shifting identities throughout a lifetime. In this section, I share excerpts from adult adoptees about their experiences using PGT to find birth family members, sometimes as the only way to obtain information they sought.

Building Family Trees

Regardless of the database participants chose, many adoptees understood the implications of submitting their DNA to these sites. Finding a member of their biological family would be life-altering, at minimum, not just for themselves, but also for the family members they find. Marie shared how she prepared herself for a potential match:

> So, I did Ancestry.com, I did DNA, and you know, I knew this was going to leave me, I mean ultimately, I was . . . so, I was looking for my birth parents. But um, and then as I started thinking about it, waiting for the DNA, I was just thinking like, oh, you know, what, you know, preparing myself, I read tons of books and been on all kinds of sites with people and preparing myself for any possible situation, because you never know what's gonna happen. There's many rejections, denials, parents or past some people have families that don't know. So, I really tried to emotionally and mentally preparing myself.

Like Marie, some adoptees submitted their own DNA and found connections to their birth families. These connections were typically distant cousins or aunts and uncles on either the maternal or paternal side. Sometimes, connections to both sides were found. Rarely, adoptees connected directly to a birth parent, which is interesting in itself. Do birth parents of adoption intentionally avoid PGT? Adoptees who located more distant relatives (such as third or fourth cousins) sent messages through the site requesting a phone conversation or more information.

Many recipients of these messages were willing to help create a family tree to trace back to the adoptees' birth parents, when possible. This willingness to help strangers speaks to the unity of the adoption community, as well as the communal aspects of (potential) family support. We often feel empathetic to those in our same situation and are willing to provide informational and emotional support. Additionally, Marie also understood that although she may find a DNA match, she may not experience the reunion she hoped to have.

While many adoptees begin a search to find their birth mother, some DNA searches reveal siblings about whom the adoptees never knew. Lou talks about finding many siblings after using Ancestry.com:

> She had seven children. So, I had siblings and um, about a year ago I sent a letter to the youngest one thinking maybe he'd have the most open mind, you know, have, you know, so I sent it and one I didn't know if I had the right address and two, I didn't know if he got it and just said I'm just going to let this lie and not do anything. Well, I did the DNA tests, ancestry, and I was contacted by a niece and a brother, well they're all actually half brothers and sisters. So, she had the four original before me and then she had me and then she had two more after me. Every single one of her husbands died, passed away. And um, anyways, so now I get the true story from my brother and niece.

Lou's experience with PGT is not uncommon, but she did not anticipate finding any siblings, and she certainly did not expect to find six. Lou's reunion with some of her siblings was quite recent, and she was still piecing together her family's story. She struggled in her search until using Ancestry.com when family members contacted her. Using PGT to build a biological family tree has proven useful for many participants to locate and contact (or be contacted by) birth family members.

Adoptees have (at least) two family trees. The PGT sites create trees for biological families, thus, adoptees may not be able to establish their place in the adoptive family tree, again implying they are not a "real" part of that family. Christine explains her experience trying to establish her place in each tree:

> It's interesting you mentioned the ancestry stuff because both my adoptive family is on it and, and you know, I'm in the tree and so is my biological family and I'm in their tree. Um, and I contacted Ancestry and I said, "Hey, I'm adopted. I'm in two trees and legitimately in two trees. Do you have a way to indicate that?" And you know, they said, "Well we're sorry we can't do it. There's no way to differentiate between biological and adoptive families." And I said, "Well, I really think you should think about that because I'm pretty sure I'm not alone."

Christine's experience demonstrates the pervasiveness of adoptive identity even through technology. The structure of Ancestry.com typically allows for one family tree per user, which makes sense if you are looking for biological relatives. However, adoptees may identify deeply as a member of their adoptive family and want to be part of their family tree, as well.

Integrating Technology

Adoptees without other identifying information may use PGT sites as a starting point in their search. However, once adoptees identify a potential family member, they may use other technologies, such as social media, for initial contact. These technologies can expedite the reunion process once adoptees have identifying information. Mel described using both Ancestry.com and Facebook to find her birth mother and other family members:

> So, I went with Ancestry DNA because of all their TV ads. I thought, well they're going to have a bigger database than and more people are going to see it. I think it's my best bet, and within two weeks of me sending my test, I had the name of my birth mother. I connected with a second cousin. He is the son of my cousin, and what I did is I just wrote a narrative about, took all the redacted information, wrote a narrative. This is what I know about my birth mother, and I put it in a Google Document, and I sent the link to people and said, "If this story sounds familiar to you," you know, gave her approximate age and stuff, "please let me know." And he replied and said, "This sounds like my grandmother's sister." And I said, "Well, your grandmother . . ." On my end, his grandmother was the only one that would have known that I even existed and turned out and she was in, you know, he said, "Well let me talk to my grandmother" and I said, "Can you just give me a maiden name?" Because I knew I could find her if I had a maiden name. And he did. He gave me her full name and so I found her. I found her on Facebook, and I found enough on Facebook to know that it was her. I didn't have to wait very long. The next morning, he sent me her number and said, "She's excited to talk to you, give her call."

Mel continued to say "I'm not much of a phone person, and she's not either, but we still managed to talk for an hour, and it was like we'd known each other all along. It was weird." The combination of old (telephones) and new (Facebook and Ancestry.com) technologies indicate the amount of effort adoptees must undertake to find their family members. New technologies, like PGT and social media, accelerate the reunion process. However, traditional technology, like phones, allow adoptees to make a more personal connection to family members than messaging allows. Hearing a family member's voice for the first time can be an important step for adoptees in discovering their identity in their birth family.

PGT sites have been useful for adoptees in locating and contacting birth family members but was also used by adoptees to find elements of their identity. This technology has also been a way for adoptees to find more information about ethnicity and genetic heritage. Angela shared her experience of having information about her biology that was factual for the first time:

> Well, I think that the biggest thing for me was the very first time we did Ancestry, because I've been told I'm Danish. I'm not Danish. I'm English and 22 percent Irish. You know, Christa [Angela's partner] was like, "You're Irish, you're not Danish." So that was the very first time that like, something was factual. It wasn't just with the first agent or what the agency side because the more you, the more I dive into reunion, like agencies lied all the time. I'm not saying mine did, I'm not saying that what I'm going to find out is different than what I've been told, but I've heard a lot of people were completely fabricated backgrounds and all that stuff. So, this was the first time, once I did the DNA, that was like, okay, according to science, this is who I am. And that, that felt good. I mean, I was very excited to get that and to figure out, okay, where supposedly are my roots, which is interesting because I have a bachelor's degree in British history. There's kind of paralleled that go there. So, then when Yvonne, my birth cousin, and I found each other, I mean to me, it was okay this the first time on earth, I'm 43 years old, I guess I was 42 at that time, this is the first time I know, I know for a fact I am biologically related to someone.

Angela experienced much uncertainty and disappointment in her search. When she discovered her genetic genome, she felt as if she had "facts" about herself for the first time in her life. Angela also understood the adoption process in past (and to some degree, current) decades was not regulated properly and some adoption information was lost or inaccurate, thus, she was wary when she found new information about her own adoption.

The struggles adoptees face when searching for their adoption information is like nothing non-adopted people face. Non-adopted people can learn their ancestry and ethnicity through stories told by their family members. Adoptees who live much of their life without this information, or the ability to verify the accuracy of what they have been told, may be able to reconcile their personal identity once they obtain information from a PGT site. For adoptees, like Angela, this information may be the first piece of their unknown identity. However, not all DNA searches result in finding birth mothers. For some adoptees, only one side of their birth family was matched or had matches who could not provide any information. PGT appears to be a promising avenue for people searching for biological family, yet not every search will be successful.

Discussion

In line with previous research regarding adoption and technology (Whitesel and Howard 2013), participants in this study used technology for information seeking and initiating contact with birth family members through technology, specifically personal genomic testing. Conversely, in the current study PGT was quite successfully in connecting adult adoptees with their birth family members.

Evidence from this study suggests adoptees who take genetic tests and find out their ethnicity experience some identity shift. Using science to confirm or deny ethnicity can affirm one part of adoptees' identity. Although PGT is not completely accurate, some adoptees were comforted by simply knowing their ethnic roots. Additionally, by registering on PGT sites, adoptees left the door open for biological family members to initiate contact. Adoptees who were adopted in closed-record states used PGT as a first step in their search.

Implications for Adoptive Family Communication

Most adoptions now have some form of open communication (Colaner and Scharp 2016), but millions of adoptees from closed adoptions still do not have the information they seek about their biological roots. For adult adoptees, the choice to use PGT as a tool to search for their birth family members is often fraught with uncertainty. The implications of utilizing PGT in search and reunion has several implications for members of an adoptive family, including shifting relational identities. In the broader context of adoptive family communication, PGT has ethical implications related to privacy and transparency.

Broadly, PGT can help adult adoptees initiate and engage in communication with their birth family members. Because of inconsistent and discriminatory legislation related to original birth certificates, many adoptees turn to PGT as the only source of information for finding birth family members. This scientific technology, along with adoption websites and social media, has permanently altered the family communication landscape for people in adoptive families. More specifically, PGT databases provide information to family members seeking information to better understand their own identities. Social media and online databases of adoption records are widely available, often for free or for a small fee. With more channels of access, biologically related people have a greater chance of successfully reuniting. Adoptees with no medical history may opt for PGT as a way to better understand and manage their own health.

Moreover, for many adult adoptees, access to their biological family history is more than just about health. Personal identities are often constructed around the ideals we have related to family. Our identity as a child or a sibling is reflected in the relationships with have with our parents, siblings, and other family members. For adoptees, the existence of another family to which they belong may impact identity construction. Participants in this study often wondered what their lives would be like if they had grown up with their birth families. Most participants were adamant in stating that their interest in discovering their biological roots was not an indication of an unhappy life in their adoptive families. With a few exceptions, adoptees were clear that their relational identities within the adoptive family were separate from the unlived identity in their birth families, an identity they wanted to explore with no implication of dissatisfaction with the adoptive family relationships.

In the current study, participants often struggled with the tension between who they are in their adoptive family and who they would have been or could be in their birth family. Adoptees who want to explore their identity in birth families often turn to PGT as a way to gain information. As participants began their search with this information, some of their adoptive parents were concerned about the experience the adoptee would have upon reunion—fear of being rejected again, but also fear of their "child" being "disloyal" to the family that raised them. Uncertainty for both adoptees and their adoptive parents sometimes strained relationships. Open communication regarding why adoptees wanted to pursue reunion and how meeting their birth families will impact the relationships within the family can help alleviate some of the uncertainty. For non-adopted people, it may be difficult to understand why an adoptee may have an intense desire to meet people who look like them and share other inherited traits. Even when adoptees are happy in their current life, the uncertainty of biological roots often motivates a search. Certainly, not all adopted people are interested in finding their birth families, but those who are often use technology to expediate the process.

Once adoptees connect with their birth family members, their identities often shift again. Some adoptees and family members both find themselves discussing "nature versus nurture" when seeing similar behaviors and habits between them even when not growing up together, such as nonverbal cues like hand gestures, walking style, or nervous tics. On a deeper level, adoptees may feel tensions between the joy of reunion and the sadness of missing out on a lifetime of experiences together, which can be difficult to navigate. Adoptees may struggle to find their place in the family as an in-group, yet an out-group member at the same time. Of course, every family varies in how they develop and maintain relationships, so there is no "right" way to reunite. Adoptees who take the first step in reunion by utilizing PGT have chosen to address their uncertainties and potential identity shifts. Many adoptees know they were adopted for their entire lives, but late-discovery adoptees may be especially vulnerable identity shifts as the sudden knowledge of having entire other family can be understandably overwhelming. Additionally, trans-racial adoptees who reunite with family members who are of their racial or ethnic origin may experience additional cultural shifts as they learn about birth family cultures they may have never been exposed to previously.

Technological advances, such as PGT, in the last three decades have significantly altered the search and reunion process for adoptees. Access to information is timelier and more easily obtained than ever before. For adult adoptees who want information about their adoption but live in states without access to adoption records, PGT may be the tool to help them connect with birth family members who can provide that information.

Implications for Family Communication

While the current study focused on adoption reunions via PGT databases, approximately 26 million people, generally, have used PGT sites, demonstrating the prevalence of interest in biological heritage. Genetic testing is not a new phenomenon, however, access for a substantial part of society is new. In the last decade, awareness of the availability of PGT has grown exponentially, as has the affordability and capabilities of locating ancestors that might not be located otherwise. Another way genetic testing has been used is in prenatal care for the detection of genetic disorders and defects (Kirkscey 2017). Parents may wish to know early in a pregnancy about medical abnormalities, especially if there is a family history of such disorders. Additionally, people with a family history of cancer can now be tested for the genetic mutations of the BRCA to determine their probability of being diagnosed with breast, ovarian, and prostate cancers (Kahán 2020). This technology is here to stay, and accessibility for the public will likely increase, thus we must consider the ethical implications of PGT in family communication.

Beyond health detection uses, PGT can be used by people from families created via medical intervention, such as sperm/egg donation, surrogacy, and IVF. As in adoptive families, some people want to know their biological heritage. As PGT databases grow, ethical implications need greater attention as children from such families grow into adults who often wish to know their biological origins. Moreover, recent news articles report that some people find unexpected information about their family members through DNA testing, such as misattributed parentage (Zhang 2018) and unknown siblings ("Two Siblings Discover Each Other Through DNA Testing—WSJ" n.d.). Family secrets once thought to remain private forever can now be discovered by a simple swab of DNA. Transparency and open communication within families is often successful in family satisfaction (Farr, Grant-Marsney, and Grotevant 2014; Grotevant et al. 2011).

As new technologies for communication emerge, families must consider the advantages and disadvantages of incorporating these channels into their lives. Armed with the knowledge that you cannot 'unsee what you've seen' or 'unknow what you know,' families should be cautious about making private family information public through PGT sites, or otherwise.

REFERENCES

Affleck, M. K., and L. G. Steed. 2001. "Expectations and Experiences of Participants in Ongoing Adoption Reunion Relationships: A Qualitative Study." *American Journal of Orthopsychiatry* 71: 38–48.

American Adoption Congress. 2021. "State Adoption Legislation." American Adoption Congress. January 2021. https://americanadoptioncongress.org/state.php.

Andrews, V. 2016. "Inquiry into Postwar 'Baby Scoop Era' Can Start Healing Process." *Toronto Star* (Canada). http://www.library.ohio.edu/ezpauth/redir/all_weak.php?http%3a%2f%2fsearch.ebscohost.com%2flogin.aspx%3fdirect%3dtrue%26db%3dnfh%26AN%3d6FPTS2016052438198530%26site%3dehost-live%26scope%3dsite.

Anzur, Christine K., and Scott A. Myers. 2020. "'To Meet Her, That Changed Everything': Adult Adoptees' Discursive Construction of the Meaning of 'Parent' Following Birth Parent Contact." *Journal of Family Communication* 20 (1): 1–15.

Baptista, N. M., D. A. Carere, S. A. Broadley, J. S. Roberts, and R. C. Green. 2016. "Adopting Genetics: Motivations and Outcomes of Personal Genomic Testing in Adult Adoptees." *Genetics in Medicine* 18: 924–32. https://doi.org/10.1038/gim.2015.192.

Campbell, L. H., P. R. Silverman, and P. B. Patti. 1991. "Reunions between Adoptees and Birth Parents: The Adoptees' Experience." *Social Work* 36 (4): 329–35.

Carsten, J. 2000. "'Knowing Where You've Come from': Ruptures and Continuities of Time and Kinship in Narratives of Adoption Reunions." *Journal of the Royal Anthropological Institute* 6: 687.

Coffelt, T. A. 2018. "A Paragon of Family Ritual: The Zimmerman Family Reunion." *Communication Studies* 69: 161–79. https://doi.org/10.1080/10510974.2018.1425215.

Colaner, C. W., D. Halliwell, and P. Guignon. 2014. "'What Do You Say to Your Mother When Your Mother's Standing beside You?': Birth and Adoptive Family Contributions to Adoptive Identity via Relational Identity and Relational–Relational Identity Gaps." *Communication Monographs* 81: 469–94.

Colaner, C. W., H. K. Horstman, and C. E. Rittenour. 2018. "Negotiating Adoptive and Birth Shared Family Identity: A Social Identity Complexity Approach." *Western Journal of Communication* 82: 393–415. https://doi.org/10.1080/10570314.2017.1384564.

Colaner, C. W., and H. Kranstuber. 2010. "'Forever Kind of Wondering': Communicatively Managing Uncertainty in Adoptive Families." *Journal of Family Communication* 10: 236–55.

Colaner, C. W., and K. M. Scharp. 2016. "Maintaining Open Adoption Relationships: Practitioner Insights on Adoptive Parents' Regulation of Adoption Kinship Networks." *Communication Studies* 67: 359–78. https://doi.org/10.1080/10510974.2016.1164208.

Docan-Morgan, Sara. 2017. "Korean Adoptees' Discursive Construction of Birth Family and Adoptive Family Identity Through Names and Labels." *Communication Quarterly* 65 (5): 523–48.

Erikson, Erik H. 1968. *Identity, Youth, and Crisis*. New York: W. W. Norton Company.

Farr, R. H., H. A. Grant-Marsney, and H. D. Grotevant. 2014. "Adoptees' Contact with Birth Parents in Emerging Adulthood: The Role of Adoption Communication and Attachment to Adoptive Parents." *Family Process* 53 (December): 656–71. https://doi.org/10.1111/famp.12069.

Fessler, A. 2006. *The Girls Who Went Away*. New York: Penguin Books.

Galvin, K., and C. W. Colaner. 2013. "Created through Law and Language: Communicative Complexities of Adoptive Families." In *Widening the Family Circle*, edited by K. Floyd and M. Morman, 2nd ed., 191–209. Thousand Oaks, CA: Sage Publications, Inc.

Gladstone, James, and Anne Westhues. 1998. "Adoption Reunions: A New Side to Intergenerational Family Relationships." *Family Relations* 47 (2): 177–84.

Grotevant, H. D., M. Rueter, L. Von Korff, and C. Gonzalez. 2011. "Post-Adoption Contact, Adoption Communicative Openness, and Satisfaction with Contact as Predictors of Externalizing Behavior in Adolescence and Emerging Adulthood." *Journal of Child Psychology & Psychiatry* 52: 529–36. https://doi.org/10.1111/j.1469-7610.2010.02330.x.

Hays, A. H., H. K. Horstman, C. W. Colaner, and L. R. Nelson. 2016. "'She Chose Us to Be Your Parents': Exploring the Content and Process of Adoption Entrance Narratives Told in Families Formed through Open Adoption." *Journal of Social & Personal Relationships* 33: 917–37. https://doi.org/10.1177/0265407515611494.

Hecht, M. L. 1993. "2002—A Research Odyssey: Toward the Development of a Communication Theory of Identity." *Communication Monographs* 60: 76.

Herman, E. 2012. "Adoption History in Brief." The Adoption History Project. 2012. http://pages.uoregon.edu/adoption/topics/adoptionhistbrief.htm.

Horstman, H. K., C. W. Colaner, and C. E. Rittenour. 2016. "Contributing Factors of Adult Adoptees' Identity Work and Self-Esteem: Family Communication Patterns and Adoption-Specific Communication." *Journal of Family Communication* 16: 263–76. https://doi.org/10.1080/15267431.2016.1181069.

Howard, J. 2012. "Untangling the Web: The Internet's Transformative Impact on Adoption." Evan B. Donaldson Adoption Institute.

Jordens, C. F. C., I. H. Kerridge, and G. N. Samuel. 2009. "Direct-to-consumer Personal Genome Testing: The Problem is Not Ignorance--It Is Market Failure." *The American Journal of Bioethics: AJOB* 9 (6–7): 13–15. https://doi.org/10.1080/15265160902874411.

Kahán, Zsuzsanna. 2020. "[Medical Treatment Options in BRCA-Associated Cancers]." *Magyar Onkologia* 64 (1): 13–24.

Keyes, M. A., S. M. Malone, A. Sharma, W. G. Iacono, and M. McGue. 2013. "Risk of Suicide Attempt in Adopted and Nonadopted Offspring." *Pediatrics* 132: 639–46. https://doi.org/10.1542/peds.2012-3251.

Keyes, M. A., A. Sharma, I. J. Elkins, W. G. Iacono, and M. McGue. 2008. "The Mental Health of U.S. Adolescents Adopted in Infancy." *Archives of Pediatrics & Adolescent Medicine* 162: 419–25. https://doi.org/10.1001/archpedi.162.5.419.

Kirkscey, Russell. 2017. "Patient Decision Aids for Prenatal Genetic Testing: Probability, Embodiment, and Problematic Integration." *Health Communication* 32 (5): 568–77. https://doi.org/10.1080/10410236.2016.1140500.

Lee, Richard M., Oh Myo Kim, and Heewon Lee. 2016. "Unpacking Reasons for Genetic Testing of Adoptees." *American Journal of Bioethics: AJOB* 16 (12): 39–40. https://doi.org/10.1080/15265161.2016.1239793.

March, K. 1995. "Perception of Adoption as Social Stigma: Motivation for Search and Reunion." *Journal of Marriage & Family* 57: 653–60. https://doi.org/10.2307/353920.

May, T., K. A. Strong, K. L. Zusevics, J. Jeruzal, M. H. Farrell, Alison LaPean Kirschner, Arthur R. Derse, James P. Evans, and Harold D. Grotevant. 2016. "Does Lack of 'Genetic-Relative Family Health History' Represent a Potentially Avoidable Health Disparity for Adoptees?" *American Journal of Bioethics* 16: 33–38. https://doi.org/10.1080/15265161.2016.1240255.

McGuire A. L., C. M. Diaz, T. Wang, and S. G. Hilsenbeck. 2009. "Social Networkers' Attitudes toward Direct-to-Consumer Personal Genome Testing." *American Journal of Bioethics* 9 (6/7): 3–10. https://doi.org/10.1080/15265160902928209.

Miall, C. E., and K. March. 2005. "Community Attitudes toward Birth Fathers' Motives for Adoption Placement and Single Parenting." *Family Relations* 54 (October): 535–46. https://doi.org/10.1111/j.1741-3729.2005.00341.x.

Passmore, Nola L., and Judith A. Feeney. 2009. "Reunions of Adoptees Who Have Met Both Birth Parents: Post-Reunion Relationships and Factors That Facilitate and Hinder the Reunion Process." *Adoption Quarterly* 12 (2): 100–119. https://doi.org/10.1080/10926750902978865.

Petersen, Liselotte, Thorkild I. A. Sørensen, Per Kragh Andersen, Preben Bo Mortensen, and Keith Hawton. 2013. "Genetic and Familial Environmental Effects on Suicide—An Adoption Study of Siblings." *PLoS ONE* 8 (10): 1–1. https://doi.org/10.1371/journal.pone.0077973.

Potter, J. E. 2013. "Adopting Commodities: A Burkean Cluster Analysis of Adoption Rhetoric." *Adoption Quarterly* 16: 108–27. https://doi.org/10.1080/10926755.2013.787573.

Powell, K. A., and T. D. Afifi. 2005. "Uncertainty Management and Adoptees' Ambiguous Loss of Their Birth Parents." *Journal of Social & Personal Relationships* 22: 129–51.

Sachdev, Paul. 1992. "Adoption Reunion and After: A Study of the Search Process and Experience of Adoptees." *Child Welfare* 71 (1): 53–68.

Samuels, E. J. 2013. "Surrender and Subordination: Birth Mothers and Adoption Law Reform." *Michigan Journal of Gender & Law* 20: 33–81.

Scharp, K. M., and K. R. Steuber. 2014. "Perceived Information Ownership and Control: Negotiating Communication Preferences in Potential Adoption Reunions: Privacy Management." *Personal Relationships* 21: 515–29. https://doi.org/10.1111/pere.12046.

Smith, J. A., P. Flowers, and M. Larkin. 2009. *Interpretive Phenomenological Analysis*. Thousand Oaks, CA: Sage.

Sutton, C. R. 2004. "Celebrating Ourselves: The Family Reunion Rituals of African-Caribbean Transnational Families." *Global Networks* 4: 243–57. https://doi.org/10.1111/j.1471-0374.2004.00091.x.

"Two Siblings Discover Each Other Through DNA Testing—WSJ." n.d. Accessed October 7, 2021. *Wall Street Journal.* https://www.wsj.com/articles/two-siblings-discover-each-other-through-dna-testing-11576764007.

Weller, Melissa Rizzo, and Angela M. Hosek. 2020. "Birth Mothers' Experiences of Privacy Turbulence in Relation to Closed Adoption Information." *Journal of Family Communication* 20 (3): 250–64. https://doi.org/10.1080/15267431.2020.1761807.

Wellisch, E. 1952. "Children without Genealogy: A Problem of Adoption." *Mental Health* 12: 41–42.

Whitesel, A., and J. A. Howard. 2013. "Untangling the Web II: A Research-Based Roadmap for Reform." Evan B. Donaldson Adoption Institute. https://www.adoptioninstitute.org/wp-content/uploads/2013/12/2013_12_UntanglingtheWeb2.pdf.

Wilson-Buterbaugh, K. 2017. *The Baby Scoop Era: Unwed Mothers, Infant Adoption, Forced Surrender*. Karen Wilson-Buterbaugh.

Zhang, Sarah. 2018. "When a DNA Test Shatters Your Identity." *The Atlantic*. July 17, 2018. https://www.theatlantic.com/science/archive/2018/07/dna-test-misattributed-paternity/562928/.

Chapter Ten

Family Communication Disrupted by Incarceration and the Role of Technology

An Overview

Tiffany Petricini

In 2013, *Sesame Street* debuted a character, Alex, whose father was in prison. This would be event that might normally go unnoticed by anyone other than the viewers, however major US media outlets picked up on the story and sensationalized it. Alex appeared only in that single episode in 2013. Later, he was incorporated in a short video produced by *Sesame Street* as part of an outreach project, but his character was not incorporated regularly. Unfortunately, this was one of the few instances in which children of incarcerated parents and their stories were represented in the media in any significant form. While media representations of these children are rare, the phenomenon of children being affected by this issue is relatively common. Research from 2009 noted that one in 12 children will go through the trauma of parental incarceration in their lifetime (Wildeman, 2009). Wildeman, Haskins, and Poehlmann-Tynan (2018) noted that research about the effects of parental incarceration has been picked up in the field of psychology, family science, criminology, and sociology. The trio argued that while research is picking up steam in many other fields, there are two areas "in which research has moved at a glacial pace" (2018, p. 5). These are interdisciplinary studies and intervention research. Communication studies is another field in which research is lacking, and within the media ecology realm, it is completely absent. Communication studies are well-suited to the task of filling in the current gaps, however, as our field is by nature interdisciplinary and our theories aim to be applied.

Operating from the family communication approach by Sussman, Stenmetz, and Petersons (2013), there is no research that this author could find that examines the nature of family communication in a prison setting. Traditional communication theories applied to groups and dyads have yet to be examined in this marginalized population. The disruption of incarceration can cause immense strain on families, but it also offers the possibility for reflection and change for intervention that many families desperately need. Communication studies should be invested in researching this phenomenon in more depth.

This chapter will attempt to help begin the conversation related to the above gaps in the family communication literature by giving a brief overview of the research related to families with incarcerated members and attempting to situate the role of communication studies as it applies to this phenomenon and its related complexities. It will also examine the role of technology in families that fall within the scope of incarceration. There is a pressing need for this research. Haskins and Turney (2018) wrote that sociologists often study three effects: "trauma, stigma, and/or strain" (p. 13). Nguyen (2011) defined trauma "a fissure in experience which introduces the subject (and vicariously the observer-society) to something unknowable, intolerable, and incomprehensible" (p. 28). The trauma that is associated with parental incarceration goes beyond disruption of the family system and has broader societal implications.

Hagan and Dinovitzer (1999) focus on the trauma associated specifically with the removal of fathers. Trauma can result in cognitive and developmental delays and hindrances to children's psychological and social development (Haskins and Turney, 2018). Wakefield and Apel (2018) have argued that the effects of the incarceration process on the children of incarcerated parents is often overlooked, and Hagan and Dinovitzer claimed that this "may be the least understood and most consequential implication of the high reliance on incarceration in America" (1999, p. 22). While there is plenty of focus on prison reform and rehabilitation studies in the academic literature, especially in the field of criminal justice and law, the resources to assist children are lacking and require more attention. Therefore, understanding the complexities of family communication is one path to illuminating the overlooked and understudied phenomenon of incarceration's effect on families' communication. This chapter will begin by discussing family communication and briefly overviewing the vast field of literature related to family relationships and incarceration. It will then explore barriers to family communication when one or more members of the unit is incarcerated and finish with a discussion of the role of technology in family of this specialized subset.

FAMILY COMMUNICATION, TECHNOLOGY, AND INCARCERATION: A BRIEF OVERVIEW

Communication serves as more than mere information exchange in family units. Families serve as the primary location for human support and nurturance (Koerner and Fitzpatrick 2002), and they act as the primary agent of socialization. Family communication serves as the center from which expectations about the world, and self, emanate. Societal transformations over the last 100 years have been astronomical, as have been the correlative technological shifts that followed and preceded these transformations. Family communication scholars recognize that these cultural transformations have had an effect on family systems (Fitzpatrick and Vangelisti, 1995). Due to these shifting boundaries, some researchers have advocated for scholars to transition their conceptual framework of family from a scientific definition to a transactional one (Noller and Fitzpatrick, 1993). From this perspective, family could be defined as "a group of intimates who generate a sense of home and group identity and who experience a shared history and shared future" (Koerner and Fitzpatrick, 2002, p. 71). Because of this, this chapter operates from an approach in which family is defined as above, and any family unit in which at least one member is incarcerated in the central focus and in particular, the development on children within the family is of particular interest to this author.

There are two considerations that are important, said Fitzpatrick and Ritche (1993), when exploring family communication—intersubjectivity and interactivity. The pair defines intersubjectivity as "the sharing of cognitions among participants in a communicative event" and interactivity as "the degree to which symbol creation and interpretation are linked" (p. 73). Explorations of intersubjectivity must approach the cognitive while those grounded in interactivity explore the "behavioral element that accounts for how family members create, shape and maintain the social unit through their interactions" (p. 73). Studies grounded in these approaches are lacking in communication studies about families affected by incarceration.

Children learn to understand and make sense of their world from both the direct relational experiences and grounded in what they see and observe in their social world, for example via stories in their media. Communication is foregrounded in these sense-making processes (Fiske and Taylor, 1991; Koerner and Fitzpatrick, 2002). The specific communicative patterns of families impact children's development significantly, for example the encouragement of equal participation within family conversations and conformity orientation (McLeod and Chaffee, 1972; Fitzpatrick and Ritchie, 1994; Ritchie and Fitzpatrick, 1990). A family's orientations to conversation and conformity have been found to impact conflict management abilities within the individual family members (Koerner and Fitzpatrick, 1997a). In addition, long-lasting impacts on resilience and future family and romantic relationships have been noted (Fitzpatrick and Koerner, 1996; Koerner and Fitzpatrick, 1997b). How children learn control and restraint also have been correlated with family communication patterns (Fitzpatrick, Marshall, Leutwiler, and Krcmer, 1996).

Threads in the media ecology and computer-mediated communication tradition often pit online and offline communication against each other, yet the reality of our everyday communication is less polarized. Most of our relationships, including our family affairs, are hybridized. Technology has transformed several arenas of human experience, and in this chapter the intention is to identify and examine the ways in which technology is woven into the communication patterns in family systems in which one or more members of the family unit is incarcerated grounded in the existing literature.

Both scholars and institutions have been slowly recognizing the shifting role that media and technology play in family life. Connell, Lauricella, and Wartella point out that between 1995 and 2013, the American Academy of Pediatrics completely shifted their stance on technology use in families from screen-time limits to co-use (2015). In fact, in 2016 they began encouraging video chat for all children. Technology use is now a regular part of all family communicative patterns. Rudi, Walkner and Dworkin reported that the most frequent form of communication between adolescents and parents, even when technology was available, was still talking in person. Roughly 95% of 15-year old adolescents could access the internet in 2017 (Gottschalk, 2019).

The literature, generally, has focused on the negative outcomes related to technology and Gottshalk has noted that it has been "unbalanced with potential positive outcomes" (p. 22). How children and adolescents use technology is under-discussed and often misconceptualized. A statement by the American Academy of Pediatrics in 2016 noted that TV use had decreased overall in the last decade when observing children of school age. The passive model of technology use that plagued many lamenting years of scholarship has become irrelevant, as children and adolescents now engage in the participatory media of web 2.0. Technology has been shown to help with relationships in several unique and novel ways. Liu, Inkpen, and Pratt, 2015, for example, have shown that technology has been used to reduce feelings of loneliness and alienation in children who have chronic illnesses. Technology, like video-chatting, has also been shown to help children with autism (Goldsmith and LeBlanc, 2004).

Lanigan (2009) has proposed that there are four general categories when understanding the ways in which technology has impacted family life. They are "technology characteristics, individual traits, family factors, and extrafamilial influences" (p. 589). Some of the ways in which technology have affected human life, Lanigan (2009) explains, have led us to an "unprecedented level of contact" (p. 589) in which communication is near instantaneous and low cost, and they also all for communication "instantly in contexts where a conversation is not possible" (p. 589). One article's authors deemed cell phones "umbilical cords" (Palen, Salzman, and Youngs, 2001). Lanigan does not, though, that technology has also introduced new problems into the family system. Some problems with technology within families include boundary maintenance, time, and family function distortion.

Incarceration is, put simply, the state of being imprisoned. This chapter specifically examines the nature of incarceration within family settings, meaning that at least one family member is in a jail or prison. Because research is lacking in the field of communication studies, much of the research is this arena is in criminal justice and law studies. Studies done on communication patterns within families in which at least one parent is incarcerated have argued that strong communicative support can lead to "positive offender change" and also that the risks that the children face in these families are decreased (Swanson, Lee, Sansone and Tatum, 2013, p. 454; Adalist-Estrin, 1996; Hairston, 1988). Studies on communication within family systems has often examined gender-role specific relationships, like mother-child (Swanson, Lee, Sansone and Tatum, 2013; Owen, 1998; Pollock-Byrne, 1990; Sandifer, 2008; Surratt, 2003; Hoffmann, Byrd, and Kightlinger, 2010; Mignon and Randsford, 2012) however, there are several studies that examine the communication between incarcerated fathers and children (Hairston, 1998; Lanier, 1993; Maldonado, 2006). Multiple studies have shown that familial support leads to better outcomes when the incarcerated family members are released from prison (Kubrin and Stewart, 2006; La Vigne, Naser, Brooks, and Castro, 2005; Nevin and Stewart, 2005; Petersilia, 2003).

Of particular interest to technology and communication scholars should be outcomes for children. The nature of children's relationship to media and the implications of technology use on the developing child and human flourishing is contested, yet what is not challenged is the importance of the parent-child relationship. One set of researchers have even gone so far to argue that the parent-child relationship is the most important relationship that is disrupted when a family member is incarcerated (De Claire and Dixon, 2017, p. 186). The disruption of this relationship and the communication that guides it can have negative impacts on a family's future.

Research has suggested that the children most likely to have an incarcerated parent are between the ages of five and fourteen years old (Glaze and Maruschak, 2008; Murphey and Cooper, 2015; Travis, McBride, and Solomon, 2005). A 2016 statement on media use by the American Academy of Pediatrics drew from research by Common Sense Media and noted that children over eight years old spend an average of two hours a day watching television shows, most likely through streaming services on their smartphones. Rarely will these children encounter the narratives and representations of children of incarcerated parents in their daily viewing. Orgad (2012) showed that images, narratives, and all forms of representation affect the way that we come to understand ourselves and others. Orgad wrote that "they nourish a wide and deep understanding and feeling that guide and frame people's actions and practices" (p. 4) and the communicative pathways for families that experience incarceration are informed by these understandings and feelings that are often misguided.

Children with incarcerated parents face several significant challenges. Not only are they traumatized in the events leading up to their parent's incarceration, but they are retraumatized by lack of policy to protect their well-being and by the social stigma that they encounter. Rudd, Neuendorf, Atkin, Romano, Gross, and Ray (2019) consider children of incarcerated parents to be a "marginalized special population" (p. 243), but caution is necessary here because this does not mean that the problem itself is minor or affects few. A Pew Report in 2010 found that children of incarcerated parents have less earning potential over their lifetime in general, which of course affects the larger community as a whole. Also, a second study showed that children who have classmates with incarcerated parents also experience negative effects (Turney and Goodsell, 2018).

No matter what the size of the population affected, the effects can be severe. Nesmith and Ruhland (2008) call for more academic consideration of this population in order to understand the negative effects on children as well as provide pathways for caregivers, communities, and social services to better help them. The known impacts on the life of a child who undergoes having an incarcerated parent are already vast. Nesmith and Ruhland explained that the child-parent bond is harmed, which can lead to "traumatic stress and inadequate quality of care" (p. 1120). This trauma, the pair noted, can lead to "fear, anxiety, sadness and grief," which can in turn lead to "reactive behaviors such as physical and verbal aggression and withdrawal" (p. 1120), and it is no surprise considering that the children have no means of being proactive and are generally powerless over their situation.

BARRIERS TO FAMILY COMMUNICATION IN PRISON SETTINGS

Despite numerous studies showing that positive communication can lead to better outcomes for families, there are still a plethora of challenges and barriers that diminish if not completely prevent free-flowing communication among family members when one member is incarcerated. In 2004, a study done by a group of researchers of 12,633 prisoners showed that over half had children under the age of 18 that they had not seen since the date of their incarceration (Hairston, Rollin, and Jo, 2004). Every day missed is another day missed to helping the child achieve a milestone and build a healthier parent-child relationship. Nesmith and Ruhland (2008) argued that "The developmental changes that occur over that additional five years of childhood can be monumental, further exacerbating the difficulties separated parents have in staying connected to their children" (p. 1120). Maintaining frequent healthy communication is imperative.

There are several reasons that children are unable to visit with their parents. Horgan and Poehlmann-Tynan (2020) highlighted several of the ways that children of incarcerated parents maintained contact prior to the COVID-19 pandemic, including: in-person visits, letters, phone calls, and email. There are several problems with the above media, however. The duo explained that phone calls, for example, are difficult for young children for cognitive and emotional reasons. Likewise, letter writing and email are impossible for children who lack literacy. In-person visits are the optimal way in which children can interact with their parents, however there are multiple drawbacks. In some instances, the inmates are allowed no contact with their visitors, and it is even possible that they must interact through a glass. The process of setting up visits often takes a considerable amount of time and is not available until the parent is in a more permanent setting. In addition, it is difficult for children to find the means to visit, based on previous statistics about distance from prisons.

Thombre, Montague, Maher, and Zohra noted that the separation and consequent disruption of the child's life due to multiple stages of the incarceration process, including leaving and returning, can lead to significant confusion and emotional damage "if not handled properly" (2009, p. 68). They continued "Many of these children face dramatic imbalance as a result of lack of parent communication and usually have no one else to whom they can turn" (p. 69). Lack of parental communication is associated with a slew of negative consequences, both short-term and very long-lasting (Thombre et al., 2009). Thombre et al. (2009) explained that one of the most important benefits to parental communication is to ensure that children do not fall victim to the prison system themselves, and the best way to combat this is through incarcerated parents educating their children about their situations.

Hairston (2007) explained that some of the reasons that many children do not get to see their parents are: "prison rules and restrictions," distance, "increased family tensions, and the effects of stigma" (p. 6). There are gender and ethnic differences, specifically that mothers often communicate more with children as do African Americans. Hairston (2007) found that the most common mode of contact was mail, followed by phone calls and finally in-person. They noted, however, that only about one quarter of incarcerated parents saw their children in person. One of the most major problems with phone calls, of course, as Hairston (2007) notes, is the cost of a collect call. Hairston (2007) noted some the early adoption of virtual visits, but at the time of writing, they noted little research dedicated to policies, technology, and the effects on families.

Hairston, Rollin, and Jo (2004) found that the odds of children who lived within 50 miles of their parents visiting them in prison were still roughly half, and the likelihood of children who lived farther away became less as distance increased. Horgan and Poehlmann-Tynan (2020) provided a good literature review about the benefits of visitation on the children, and they also provide a good representation of the negatives associated with visitation. For example, they wrote, "Harsh treatment by correctional staff, lack of privacy, long waits, and security procedures can also contribute to low-quality visits" and to add to this, it can stress the children, also (p. 402). In a series of interviews with incarcerated fathers, Pierce (2013) identified three themes associated with barriers: the phone call expense, poor visitation conditions, and distance from family.

Citing McClure and Barr (2017), Horgan and Poehlmann-Tynan (2020) explained that video chat is near optimal for it is "suited to the diverse communication competencies of children across developmental levels" (p. 402). They added that screen time is not equal, with some elements of screen time benefiting children. The duo noted that "The World Health Organization (2019) has identified lack of access to the internet and digital technology as an area of concern regarding equity in human development that needs addressing across the globe, especially in low resource areas" (p. 403). It should not replace in-person visits, but given the issues associated with in-person visits, it can prove to be more beneficial in many circumstances.

Davies, Brazzell, La Vigne, and Shollenberger showed that in addition to systemic barriers, families can face barriers in communicating when technological issues get in the way. For example, if limiting a child's access to technology is used as a punishment, the barrier is significant. As Reed and Reed (1997) pointed out, children who have incarcerated parents rarely if ever have any control at all about contact with their parent and "have no voice because they are invisible to larger society" (p. 152). The assigned caregivers to the children also play a significant role in facilitating contact (Tasca, 2016). In another series of interviews of families with incarcerated members, research suggested that in-person visits are extremely difficult and can decline due to increased financial burdens and decreased emotional capacity to handle the stress of visits.

Continuing contact between family members leads to more successful outcomes, such as decreased recidivism rates (Reed and Reed, 1997). Not only does it improve the life of the child, but Christian (2009) suggested that strengthening "family connections can yield positive societal benefits in the form of reduced recidivism, less intergenerational criminal justice system involvement, and promotion of healthy child development" (p. 1). Multiple studies have shown this to be true, that the emotional, cognitive, and physical development of children with incarcerated parents can be affected positively by continuing contact with incarcerated parents (Edin, Nelson, and Paranal, 2004; Klein, Bartholomew, and Hibbert, 2002; La Vigne, Nasar, Brooks, and Castro, 2005; Sack and Seidler, 1978, Stanton, 1980).

Tewksbury and DeMichele (2005) have noted that institutional policies have changed since 1971. Their research suggests that barriers to physical visitation had been reduced yet telephone policies were relaxed. Pierce (2015) pointed out that often, barriers are more than just arbitrary, and multiple goods must be navigated by administrators, such as protecting the inmates, staff, and families from harm. Some scholars have pointed out the complicated issue of visitation. In one titled, "Should Children Visit Their Parents in Prison," Sack and Seidler argued that visitations themselves can be traumatic, and children's well-being may not be prioritized.

New media technology can help reduce the exposure to the various facets of in-person visits that might cause undue stress to children. It can also help overcome developmental barriers associated with older media used to facilitate contact between parents and children. Ballagas, Kaye, Ames, Go and Raffle have noted that children under five have a difficult time with phone conversations (2009). In 2017, authors De Claire and Dixon noted that one of the benefits of letter-writing was to minimize the stress parents faced when children came to visit them. Video chat also benefits younger children due to its ability to hold children's attention longer than phone calls and engage in more play. It also allows for a more natural group communication orientation than phone calls.

Technology does not just assist facilitating visits, but can also provide benefits in other ways. Access to information generally can be "life-sustaining," one prison librarian explained (Austin, 2020). There are many advantages to guiding technology use within prisons. Austin notes that many families and friends read books together and share information about books. Rudd et al. (2019) explored conflict styles and highlighted that communication during prison time can be a valuable tool to develop skills with positive outcomes and eliminate problematic communicative parenting methods, like authoritative parenting methods. By attempting to reduce barriers at the institutional level that prevent families from communicating, social support and familial bonds can be enriched and fostered leading to better outcomes for all of the family members involved (Carlson and Cervera, 1991; Lanier, 1993; Tewksbury and DeMichele, 2005).

IMPLICATIONS

While there is no substitute for families being together, in person, as we see above, there are multiple reasons why technologically mediated communication could be a good alternative or even better than face-to-face visits for children, especially, when adults are incarcerated. This is one area in which family communication scholars can invest significantly more time and resources to study. Technology can offer viable solutions to some of the barriers of communication that these families face. Study after study has shown that maintaining bonds with family is correlated with positive outcomes like decreased recidivism (De Claire and Dixon, 2017; Hale, 1988; La Vigne, Nasser, Brooks and Castro, 2005; Hairston, 1988; May, Sharma, and Stewart, 2008; Niven and Stewart, 2005). Larger societal implications related to studying this phenomenon with an eye on communication studies include reduced recidivism, less stigma, and new directions in communication research generally.

In a thorough review of family interventions, the researchers concluded that very little scholarship had been dedicated over the last 50 years to family services and communication practices in prisons. The researchers do note that this could be due to many significant challenges, including: "limited engagement with families, high participant drop-out rates, prisoner concerns about confidentiality and practical barriers, such as lack of therapeutic room space or geographical distance that families travelled to visit the prison" (Rudi et al., 2017, p. 27). Previous barriers that might have seemed problematic potentially became moot after the recent modifications due to the COVID-19 pandemic.

There is no doubt that COVID-19 impacted family communication across the globe. In a special issue of the *Journal of Family Communication*, the editors listed some of the ways in which family life and communication were challenged and altered, including parents working from home, child care, routine readjustment, development stressors, etc. It also had impacts on families already affected by incarceration. One of the first modifications to protect prisoners and staff during the COVID-19 pandemic was to immediately suspend outside visits (Heard, 2020). Lawyers, religious personnel, and other important visitors beyond the scope of family were also prevented from visits at this time. One of the most significant challenges during the time of COVID-19 was the shutdown of visitation for families. Communication policies were greatly affected, including the offering of free phone and video calls (Dallaire, Shlafer, Goshin, Hollihan, Poehlmann-Tynan, Eddy, and Adalist-Estrin, 2021). Penn State researchers found that there are numerous benefits to video communication between incarcerated parents and children. Beyond the obvious of eliminating the barriers of distance, it also provides a more realistic representation visually of the parents (Stickel, Prins, and Kaiper-Marquez, 2021). There are drawbacks, however. Citing a 2017 and 2015 study, the trio note that technology issues like internet outages can cause problems and video visits tend to be shorter (Cramer, Goff, Peterson, and Sandstrom, 2017; Poehlmann-Tynan, Runion, Burnson, Maleck, Weymouth, Pettit, and Huser, 2015). This is another avenue that family communication scholars should pursue.

In an investigation of well-being and technology, a pediatric nursing scholar wrote:

> Technology became essential during the Covid-19 pandemic. During a time of isolation and social distancing, the world relied on technology to learn, live, and stay connected. Technology is best used to leverage and maintain social, physical, emotional, intellectual, and spiritual well-being for children, in an environment where children are co-engaged with an adult. (p. 89)

Deeper explorations and conversation about the well-being of children of incarcerated parents is necessary, particularly with a lens on the experience of the children. Their voices are almost completely absent in all of the literature.

Skora Horgan and Poehlmann-Tynan have pointed out that although in-person visits are the most meaningful and rich, with COVID-19 the reliance on video chat grew. The pair explained the restrictions associated with "traditional media" that children face, related to physical and cognitive development (2020). Of course, the issue can become exploitative when facilities refuse to do in-person visits anymore because of the cost-saving elements of video chat. For-profit prison agencies are notorious for the exploitation, and video chat can also be unattainable for many families with exorbitant costs (Skora Horgan and Poehlmann-Tynan, 2020). This is one final area that communication and technology ethicists might dive into in more depth.

There are likely infinite more possibilities for study from a family communication approach that have been forgotten in this section. The aim of this chapter was to survey the current literature frame a communication framework related to families affected by incarceration and technology. There are numerous directions that might be taken by communication scholars who have an interest in this field. One area that deserves more attention is whether or not all families, regardless of offender sentence, benefit from more communication. The implications from the field of family communication theory in general need to be explored in more detail in our field.

The literature across disciplines associated with the effects of incarceration on families is vast, and the modest attempt above to overview it has likely left many excellent studies and works out that deserve mention and exploration. After giving an overview, the chapter attempted to examine current and past barriers to communication for affected families. Finally, the hope was to offer some important insights into the role of technology within family units generally and this specialized subset. While currently there is a gap in research in this area, hopefully this chapter and book will inspire more thorough research into this important disruption to family life and the various ways technology might serve as bridge and continuator.

REFERENCES

Adalist-Estrin, A. (1996). Incarcerated fathers. *Family & Corrections Network Report*, *8*(1), 8–10.

Addams, J., Hairston, C. F., Rollin, J., and Jo, H. (2004). Family Connections During Imprisonment and Prisoners' Community Reentry.

American Academy of Pediatrics. (1999). Media education. Pediatrics, 104, 341–343.

———. (2013). Policy statement on children, adolescents, and the media. Pediatrics, 132, 957–961. 10.1542/peds.2013–2656.

———. (2016). Media and young minds. *Pediatrics*, 138(5), e20162591

Austin, J. (2020). Information access within carceral institutions. *Feminist Media Studies*, *20*(8), 1293–1297.

Ballagas, R., Kaye, J. J., Ames, M., Go, J., and Raffle, H. (2009, June). Family communication: phone conversations with children. In *Proceedings of the 8th international Conference on Interaction Design and Children* (pp. 321–324).

Carlson, B. E., and Cervera, N. J. (1991). Incarceration, coping, and support. *Social Work*, *36*(4), 279–285.

Christian, S. M. (2009, March). Children of incarcerated parents. Washington, DC: National Conference of State Legislatures.

Connell, S. L., Lauricella, A. R., and Wartella, E. (2015). Parental co-use of media technology with their young children in the USA. *Journal of Children and Media*, *9*(1), 5–21.

Cramer, Lindsey, Margaret Goff, Bryce Peterson, and Heather Sandstrom. 2017. *Parent-child Visiting Practices in Prisons and Jails*. Washington, DC: Urban Institute.

Dallaire, D. H., Shlafer, R. J., Goshin, L. S., Hollihan, A., Poehlmann-Tynan, J., Eddy, J. M., and Adalist-Estrin, A. (2021). COVID-19 and prison policies related to communication with family members. *Psychology, Public Policy, and Law*.

Davies, E., Brazzell, D., Nancy, G. La Vigne, and Shollenberger, T. (2008). *Understanding the Needs and Experiences of Children of Incarcerated Parents: Views From Mentors." Urban Institute Research Report. Washington, DC: Urban Institute.*

De Claire, K., and Dixon, L. (2017). The effects of prison visits from family members on prisoners' well-being, prison rule breaking, and recidivism: A review of research since 1991. *Trauma, Violence, & Abuse*, *18*(2), 185–199.

Edin, K., Nelson, T. J., Paranal, R., Patillo, M., Weiman, D., and Western, B. (2004). *Imprisoning America: The social effects of mass incarceration.* New York: Russell Sage Foundation.

Fiske, S. T., and Taylor, S. E. (1991). *Social cognition* (2nd ed.). New York: McGraw-Hill.

Fitzpatrick, M. A., and Koerner, A. F. (1996, July). Family communication schemata and social functions of communication. Paper presented at the International Research Colloquium on Communication Research, Moscow, Russia.

Fitzpatrick, M. A., and Ritchie, L. D. (1993). Communication theory and the family. In P. Boss, W. Doherty, R. LaRossa, W. Schumm, and S. Steinmetz (Eds.), *Sourcebook of Family Theories and Methods: A Contextual Approach* (pp. 565–585). New York: Plenum.

———. (1994). Communication schemata within the family: Multiple perspectives on family interaction. *Human Communication Research, 20*, 275–301.

Fitzpatrick, M. A., and Vangelisti, A. L. (1995). *Explaining family interactions*. Sage.

Fitzpatrick, M. A., Marshall, L. J., Leutwiler, T. J., and Krcmar, M. (1996). The effect of family communication environments on children's social behavior during middle childhood. *Communication Research, 23*, 379–406

Genty, P. M. (2012). Moving beyond generalizations and stereotypes to develop individualized approaches for working with families affected by parental incarceration. *Family Court Review*, *50*(1), 36–47.

Glaze, L. E., and Maruschak, L. (2008). Parents in prison and their minor children (Report No. NCJ22984). Washington, DC: Bureau of Justice Statistics. Retrieved from http://bjs.ojp.usdoj.gov/content/pub/pdf/pptmc.pdf.

Goldschmidt, K. (2020). The COVID-19 pandemic: Technology use to support the wellbeing of children. *Journal of Pediatric Nursing*, *53*, 88.

Goldsmith, T. R., and LeBlanc, L. A. (2004). Use of technology in interventions for children with autism. *Journal of Early and Intensive Behavior Intervention*, *1*(2), 166.

Gottschalk, F. (2019). Impacts of technology use on children: Exploring literature on the brain, cognition and well-being.

Hagan, J., and Dinovitzer, R. (1999). Collateral consequences of imprisonment for children, communities, and prisoners. In M. Tonry and J. Petersilia (Eds.), *Prisons* (pp. 121–162). University of Chicago Press.

Hairston, C. F. (1998). The forgotten parent: Understanding the forces that influence incarcerated fathers' relationships with their children. *Child Welfare*, *77*(5), 617.

———. (2007). Focus on children with incarcerated parents: An overview of the research literature. https://repositories.lib.utexas.edu/bitstream/handle/2152/15158/AECasey_Children_IncParents.pdf?sequence=2

Hairston, C. F., Rollin, J., and Jo, H. (2004). Family connections during imprisonment and prisoners' community reentry.

Hale, D. C. (1988). The impact of mother's incarceration on the family system: Research and recommendations. In F. E. Hagan and M. B. Sussman (Eds.), *Deviance and the family* (pp. 143–154). New York: Haworth.

Haskins, A. R., and Turnkey, K. (2018) The Demographic landscape and sociological perspectives on parental incarceration and childhood inequality. In C. Wildeman, A.R. Haskins, and J. Poehlmann-Tynan (Eds.). *When parents are incarcerated: Interdisciplinary research and interventions to support children* (pp. 9–28), American Psychological Association.

Heard, C. (2020). Commentary: assessing the global impact of the COVID-19 pandemic on prison populations. *Victims & Offenders*, *15*(7–8), 848–861.

Hoffmann, H. C., Byrd, A. L., and Kightlinger, A. M. (2010). Prison programs and services for incarcerated parents and their underage children: Results from a national survey of correctional facilities. *Prison Journal*, *90*(4), 397–416.

Klein, S. R., Bartholomew, G. S., and Hibbert, J. (2002). Inmate family functioning. *International Journal of Offender Therapy and Comparative Criminology*, *46*(1), 95–111.

Koerner, A. F., and Fitzpatrick, M. A. (1997a). Family type and conflict: The impact of conversation orientation and conformity orientation on conflict in the family. *Communication Studies, 48*, 59–78.

———. (1997b, May). You never leave your family in a fight: The impact of families of origins on conflict-behavior in romantic relationships. Paper presented at the annual conference of the International Communication Association, Montreal, Canada.

———. (2002). Toward a theory of family communication. *Communication theory*, *12*(1), 70–91.

Kubrin, C. E., and Stewart, E. A. (2006). Predicting who reoffends: The neglected role of neighborhood context in recidivism studies. *Criminology*, *44*(1), 165–197.

La Vigne, N. G., Naser, R. L., Brooks, L. E., and Castro, J. L. (2005). Examining the effect of incarceration and in-prison family contact on prisoners' family relationships. *Journal of Contemporary Criminal Justice*, *21*(4), 314–335.

Lanier, C. S. (1993). Affective states of fathers in prison. *Justice Quarterly*, *10*(1), 49–66.

Lanigan, J. D. (2009). A sociotechnological model for family research and intervention: How information and communication technologies affect family life. *Marriage & Family Review*, *45*(6–8), 587–609.

Liu, L. S., Inkpen, K. M., and Pratt, W. (2015, February). "I'm Not Like My Friends": Understanding How Children with a Chronic Illness Use Technology to Maintain Normalcy. In *Proceedings of the 18th ACM Conference on Computer Supported Cooperative Work & Social Computing* (pp. 1527–1539).

Maldonado, S. (2006). Recidivism and paternal engagement. *Family Law Quarterly*, *40*(2), 191–211.

May, C., Sharma, N., and Stewart, D. (2008). Factors linked to reoffending: A one year follow-up of prisoners who took part in Resettlement Surveys 2001, 2003 and 2004. Research Summary5. London, England: Ministry of Justice

McClure, E., and Barr, R. (2017). Building family relationships from a distance: Supporting connections with babies and toddlers using video and video chat. In *Media exposure during infancy and early childhood* (pp. 227–248). Cham, Switzerland: Springer.

McLeod, J. M., and Chaffee, S. H. (1972). The construction of social reality. In J. Tedeschi (Ed.), *The social influence process* (pp. 50–59). Chicago: Aldine–Atherton.

Mignon, S. I., and Ransford, P. (2012). Mothers in prison: Maintaining connections with children. *Social Work in Public Health, 27*(1–2), 69–88.

Murphey, D., and Cooper, P. M. (2015). Parents behind bars: What happens to their children?

Nesmith, A., and Ruhland, E. (2008). Children of incarcerated parents: Challenges and resiliency, in their own words. *Children and Youth Services Review, 30*(10), 1119–1130.

Nevin, S., and Stewart, D. (2005). Resettlement outcomes on release from prison in 2003. London, England: Home Office.

Nguyen, L. (2011). The ethics of trauma: Re-traumatization in society's approach to the traumatized subject. *International journal of group psychotherapy, 61*(1), 26–47.

Niven, S., and Stewart, D. (2005). Resettlement outcomes on release from prison in 2003. Research findings 248. Home Office. Research summary. London, England: Ministry of Justice.

Noller, P., and Fitzpatrick, M. A. (1993). *Communication in family relationships.* Hoboken, NJ: Prentice-Hall.

Orgad, S. (2014). *Media representation and the global imagination.* Hoboken, NJ: John Wiley & Sons.

Owen, B. (1998). In the mix: Struggle and survival in a women's prison. Albany, NY: SUNY Press.

Palen, L., Salzman, M., and Youngs, E. (2001). Discovery and integration of mobile communication in everyday life. *Personal and Ubiquitous Computing*, 5, 109–122.

Petersilia, J. (2003). *When prisoners come home: Parole and prisoner reentry.* New York: Oxford University Press.

Pierce, M. B. (2015). Male inmate perceptions of the visitation experience: Suggestions on how prisons can promote inmate–family relationships. *Prison Journal, 95*(3), 370–396.

Poehlmann, J. (2005). Incarcerated mothers' contact with children, perceived family relationships, and depressive symptoms. *Journal of the Division of Family Psychology of the American Psychological Association* (Division 43), 19, 350–357. doi:10.1037/0893–3200.19.3.35

Poehlmann-Tynan, J., Runion, H., Burnson, C., Maleck, S., Weymouth, L., Pettit, K., and Huser, M. 2015. Young Children's Behavioral and Emotional Reactions to Plexiglas and Video Visits with Jailed Parents. In *Children's Contact with Incarcerated Parents*, edited by J. Poehlman-Tynan, 39–58. Cham, Switzerland: Springer.

Pollock-Byrne, J. M. (1990). *Women, prison & crime*. Pacific Grove, CA: Brooks/Cole Publishing Company.

Reed, D. F., and Reed, E. L. (1997). Children of incarcerated parents. *Social Justice*, *24*(3 (69), 152–169.

Ritchie, L. D., and Fitzpatrick, M. A. (1990). Family communication patterns: Measuring interpersonal perceptions of interpersonal relationships. *Communication Research,* 17(4), 523–544.

Roberts, Anna, Juliana Onwumere, Andrew Forrester, Vyv Huddy, Majella Byrne, Catherine Campbell, Manuela Jarrett, Patricia Phillip, and Lucia Valmaggia. "Family intervention in a prison environment: A systematic literature review." *Criminal Behaviour and Mental Health* 27, no. 4 (2017): 326–340.

Rudd, J. E., Neuendorf, K. A., Atkin, D. J., Romano, A., Gross, C., and Ray, G. (2019). The incarcerated parent: Examining mother-child conflict at the margins through a bio-ecological lens. *Journal of Family Communication*, 19(3), 243–260.

Rudi, J. H., Walkner, A., and Dworkin, J. (2015). Adolescent–parent communication in a digital world: Differences by family communication patterns. *Youth & Society*, *47*(6), 811–828.

Sack, W. H., and Seidler, J. (1978). Should children visit their parents in prison? *Law and Human Behavior*, *2*(3), 261–266.

Sandifer, J. L. (2008). Evaluating the efficacy of a parenting program for incarcerated mothers. *Prison Journal*, *88*(3), 423–445.

Skora Horgan, E., and Poehlmann-Tynan, J. (2020). In-home video chat for young children and their incarcerated parents. *Journal of Children and Media*, *14*(3), 400–406.

Stanton, A. M. (1980). *When mothers go to jail*. Lanham, MD: Lexington Books.

Stickel, T., Prins, E., and Kaiper-Marquez, A. (2021). 'The video is an upgrade from them all': how incarcerated fathers view the affordances of video in a family literacy programme. *Learning, Media and Technology*, *46*(2), 174–189.

Surratt, H. L. (2003). Parenting attitudes of drug-involved women inmates. *Prison Journal*, *83*(2), 206–220.

Sussman, M. B., Steinmetz, S. K., and Peterson, G. W. (Eds.). (2013). *Handbook of Marriage and the Family*. Springer Science & Business Media.

Swanson, C., Lee, C. B., Sansone, F. A., and Tatum, K. M. (2013). Incarcerated fathers and their children: Perceptions of barriers to their relationships. *Prison Journal*, *93*(4), 453–474.

Tasca, M. (2016). The gatekeepers of contact: Child–caregiver dyads and parental prison visitation. *Criminal Justice and Behavior*, *43*(6), 739–758.

Tewksbury, R., and DeMichele, M. (2005). Going to prison: A prison visitation program. *Prison Journal*, *85*(3), 292–310.

The Pew Charitable Trusts, 2010. Collateral Costs: Incarceration's Effect on Economic Mobility. Washington, DC: The Pew Charitable Trusts.

Thombre, A., Montague, D. R., Maher, J., and Zohra, I. T. (2009). If I could only say it myself: How to communicate with children of incarcerated parents. *Journal of Correctional Education*, 66-90.

Travis, J., McBride, E. C., and Solomon, A. L. (2005). *Families left behind: The hidden cost of incarceration and reentry*. Washington, DC: Urban Institute.

Turney, K., and Goodsell, R. (2018). Parental incarceration and children's wellbeing. *The Future of Children, 28*(1), 147–164.

Wakefield, S., and Apel, R. J. (2018) Criminological perspectives on parental incarceration. In C. Wildeman, A. R. Haskins, and J. Poehlmann-Tynan (Eds.). *When parents are incarcerated: Interdisciplinary research and interventions to support children* (pp. 29–52), American Psychological Association.

Wildeman, C. (2009). Parental imprisonment, the prison boom, and the concentration of childhood disadvantage. *Demography, 46*, 265–280. 280. http://dx.doi.org/10.1353/dem.0.0052

Wildeman, C., Haskins, A. R., and Poehlmann-Tynan, J. (2018) Introduction: Invigorating research and practice on children of incarcerated parents. In C. Wildeman, A. R. Haskins, and J. Poehlmann-Tynan (Eds.). *When parents are incarcerated: Interdisciplinary research and interventions to support children* (pp. 3–8), American Psychological Association.

World Health Organization. (2019). *Stronger collaboration, better health: Global action plan for healthy lives and well-being for all*. Geneva, Switzerland: World Health Organization.

Yousman, B. (2013). Challenging the media-incarceration complex through media education.

Zurcher, J. D., Webb, S. M., and Robinson, T. (2018). The portrayal of families across generations in Disney animated films. *Social Sciences*, 7(3), 47.

Chapter Eleven

Strengthening Families through Web-Based Interventions

Developing and Assessing Feasibility of the "Parenting Now!: Talking About Alcohol" Program

Michelle Miller-Day, Anne E. Ray, Michael L. Hecht, and Rob Turrisi

INTRODUCTION

Underage drinking is a significant public health concern in the United States (Centers for Disease Control and Prevention, 2020) and has only worsened during the COVID-19 pandemic (Dumas et al., 2020). This chapter discusses the process of developing and testing the feasibility of a web-based intervention to reduce alcohol use and related harm among adolescents aged 14 to 18 by enhancing parents' knowledge surrounding the topic of teen alcohol and alcohol use and enhancing parental communication skills. The web-based intervention program titled "Parenting Now!: Talking About Alcohol" builds on an existing parent-based intervention developed by Dr. Rob Turrisi (Turrisi et al., 2001) with demonstrated effectiveness in three separate NIH-funded random control trials (Turrisi et al., 2001, 2009, 2013;Varvil-Weld et al., 2014). The intervention initially targeted only college-bound youth, was limited in terms of accessibility/ flexibility, offering hard-copy and PDF formatted documents to parents, and limited in terms of design, and not interactive. By developing a web-based version of this intervention and harnessing e-learning technology, the program (a) more effectively targets parents of all high school youth, regardless of post-graduation plans, (b) harnesses technology for broader reach and more dynamic presentation using a powerful pedagogical model of interactive media effects (Sundar, 2007) and (c) provides opportunities for tailoring the intervention based on parent-child communication style (Miller-Day, 2008; Miller-Day & Kam, 2010).

The chapter first provides some background on teen alcohol use and family communication as a tool for teen substance use prevention. The focus of the rest of the chapter will highlight and discuss the original parent-based intervention developed by Turrisi et al. (2001), the processes involved in adapting the original print-based intervention for digital implementation, the usability of the intervention, challenges faced, and finally discuss how harnessing technology for parenting interventions can broaden their reach and impact.

FAMILY COMMUNICATION AS A TOOL FOR YOUTH ALCOHOL USE PREVENTION

Youth Alcohol (Mis)Use

Underage drinking continues to be a significant public health concern in the United States with excessive drinking responsible for more than 3,500 deaths and 210,000 years of potential life lost among people under the age 21 each year (Alcohol-Related Disease Impact Application, 2020). Moreover, underage drinking cost the United States $24 billion in 2010 (Sacks et al., 2015) with approximately 119,000 emergency rooms visits by persons aged 12 to 21 for injuries and other conditions linked to alcohol in 2013 (Naeger, 2017). Results from national epidemiologic studies suggest that alcohol use escalates in later adolescence (ages 17–20) (Substance Abuse and Mental Health Services Administration [SAMHSA], 2014) and, in the United States, alcohol is the most commonly used substance among young people (Center for Behavioral Health Statistics and Quality, 2020). Data from several national surveys document the illicit use of alcohol among young people (Johnston et al., 2020). A SAMHSA report (2014) revealed that there is a substantial increase in alcohol use midway through adolescence: with rates of past 30-day use, one or more binge episodes, and heavy use (5+ binge episodes) reported as 22.7%, 13.1%, and 2.7% among 16- to 17-year-olds and these rates jump to 43.8%, 29.1%, and 8.5%, respectively for 18- to 20-year-olds. Among the indicators of riskiest use, binge use more than doubles and heavy drinking more than triples in this age-group (SAMHSA, 2014). This is concerning as alcohol use, particularly risky use, has myriad consequences for adolescents, the people around them, and society as a whole. Individual-level consequences are physical, emotional, and social in nature including death from injuries, engagement in risky sexual behavior, increased risk of sexual and physical assault, academic failure, and changes in brain functioning, which may last into young adulthood (Esser et al., 2019; Miller et al., 2007; U.S. Department of Health and Human Services, 2016). On a societal level, costs of underage drinking are estimated at $24.3 billion (Sacks et al., 2015).

Given these costs and consequences of alcohol use discussed in this section, it is important to understand that underage drinking is preventable. Prevention is understood as any activity designed to avoid substance abuse and reduce its health and social consequences. Primary prevention strategies are implemented prior to the onset of substance use with the intention of preventing or reducing the risk. Since the average age of actual onset of experimentation and alcohol use tends to begin during adolescence, prevention efforts often target youth in late childhood or early adolescence (Hopfer, Davis, Kam, Shin, Elek, & Hecht, 2010).

Family Communication as a Tool for Prevention

Research has shown that parents have a potentially powerful role to play in reducing the scope of the problems associated with youth alcohol use (Choi et al., 2017; Pettigrew et al., 2017; Turrisi et al., 2000b; Wood et al., 2004, 2010). Research has consistently linked family-based factors with the initiation and escalation of substance use. For example, a number of studies have found that effective parental monitoring of adolescent activities can reduce risk for substance use (Branstetter et al., Koning et al., 2020; Van Ryzin et al., 2012) and research supports a link between parent-adolescent relationship quality and adolescent substance use (Hummel et al., 2013). It is effective parent-youth communication, however, that shows some of the most promise for effectively preventing alcohol misuse among youth (Kam et al., 2015a; Kam et al., 2015b; Kam & Middleton, 2013; Miller-Day & Dodd, 2004; Miller-Day & Kam, 2010; Reimuller et al., 2011; Zaharakis et al., 2015).

Within the field of family communication, an early generation of substance-use related research focused on addiction and the role of interpersonal communication in reinforcing substance use dependence (Le Poire, 1992, 1995; Thomas & Seibold, 1996). The next generation of substance-use related family communication research was firmly fixed in examining parent-youth communication about substances and substance use (Kam & Miller-Day, 2017). At the turn of the century, greater attention was paid to the central role of communication within the family and substance use outcomes. Miller-Day (2002, 2005a, 2005b, 2007, 2008) conducted research on how parents talk with youth about substances and substance use and the effectiveness of those conversations. This "drug talk" research was then further developed by Miller-Day and colleagues, qualitatively exploring the contexts of drug talks (Miller-Day & Dodd, 2004), adolescents' interpretation of their parent's anti-drug messages within the context of past and current parental use (Ebersole et al., 2014) and the development of an instrument to measure targeted parent-child communication about alcohol (Miller-Day & Kam, 2010). Identifying the construct labeled as "targeted parent–child communication about substances" refers to one-time and ongoing, direct and indirect conversations specifically against substance use. Such conversations may include warning offspring about the negative consequences to substance use, discussing others who were in trouble because of using substances, providing suggestions for avoiding substance-use offers, or clearly stating disapproval of substance use. Given the anti-substance-use messages that characterize targeted parent–youth communication, youth who discuss substances and substance use with parents are more likely to develop anti-substance-use perceptions, and in turn, less likely to use substances. The development of the Miller-Day and Kam (2010) instrument to assess parent-youth conversations about alcohol was notable because it opened the door to a new line of research empirically assessing targeted parent-youth communication about a number of illicit substances.

This led to a third generation of substance use related family communication research conducted by Kam and Cleveland (2011) examining parent-adolescent communication about substances as a protective factor against adolescent substance use (Kam & Cleveland, 2011; Kam et al., 2015a; Lee & Kam, 2015; Miller-Day & Kam, 2010), but also examined ethnic similarities and differences between non-Latin Whites and Latinx in their parent-youth communication about substances (Kam & Cleveland, 2011; Kam & Middleton, 2013; Kam et al., 2014a; Kam et al., 2014b; Kam & Yang, 2014). This line of research contributed a great deal to understanding parent-youth communication about substance use, revealing that anti-substance-use parent-youth communication has the potential to protect against the negative effects of certain cultural stressors that Latinx early adolescents face. Ebersole et al.'s (2014) investigation revealed how parents' mixed messages about substance use impedes the effectiveness of anti-substance use messages and how contradictory messages from parents may attenuate the protective nature of targeted parent–child communication.

More recently, there was a special issue of the *Journal of Family Communication* (Kam & Miller-Day, 2017) dedicated to research on substance use prevention, intervention, and coping from a family communication perspective. This special issue extends previous research in the field of family communication by identifying different subgroups of substance-specific prevention communication (SSPC) occurring between parents and their adolescent offspring (Choi et al., 2017) and examining these subgroups over time based on family communication environments and adolescent substance use. This study revealed that SSPC differs according to one's family communication environment. Based on family subgroups, four profiles emerged: *Active-Open* (i.e., high SSPC, high expressiveness, high structural traditionalism, relatively high avoidance), *Passive-Open* (i.e., low SSPC, high expressiveness, medium-to-relatively-high structural traditionalism, medium-to-relatively-low avoidance), *Active-Silent* (i.e., high SSPC, low expressiveness, medium-to-relatively-high structural traditionalism, relatively high avoidance), and *Passive-Silent* (i.e., low SSPC, low expressiveness, low structural traditionalism, low avoidance). After tracking adolescents' changes in alcohol and tobacco use over a two-year period, they found that the Passive-Silent profile engaged in significantly greater alcohol and tobacco use than the other profiles. By contrast, Active-Open adolescents exhibited the lowest rates of alcohol and cigarette use over the two-year period, thereby leading Choi and colleagues to conclude that substance-use prevention programs might encourage high SSPC, high expressiveness, and low traditionalism and low levels of topic avoidance in families.

Similar to Choi and colleagues, other research emphasizes the importance of considering substance specific parent-child prevention communication in predicting early adolescents' lifetime alcohol use. In Pettigrew et al.'s (2017) study of nearly 500 Nicaraguan early adolescents, they report that an expressive family environment was associated with SSPC and significantly lower levels of reported adolescent alcohol use. What was particularly fascinating about Pettigrew et al.'s findings is that family expressiveness was not significantly directly related to lifetime alcohol use; instead, it was only significantly indirectly related to lifetime alcohol use *through SSPC*. Moreover, in another study by Pettigrew and colleagues (2018), they found that parents who directly address the topic of alcohol use with their adolescent in an open and responsive manner were most effective in delaying onset of use and decreasing amount of use among adolescents and they encouraged scholars and practitioners to find ways to encourage parent's direct communication about substances with their adolescents, especially in families where the family communication environment may not be palatable open and expressive discourse surrounding such a topic. Consistent with past research by Miller-Day and Kam (2010), SSPC has been shown to play a unique and powerful role in adolescent alcohol use prevention.

In almost all of the family communication reviewed in this section there were calls from scholars for family-based prevention interventions to assist parents in communicating with their adolescents about alcohol and other substance use. These calls encouraged the development of prevention interventions to teach parents how to promote active, open communication about substances with their teens. These calls have been heeded by few. One notable exception is the development of the *A Parent Handbook for Talking with College Students about Alcohol* by Dr. Turrisi and colleagues (2001).

ORIGINAL EVIDENCE-BASED INTERVENTION

A Parent Handbook for Talking with College Students about Alcohol, developed by Dr. Turrisi and colleagues (Turrisi et al., 2001), is the prototype we used for the development of the current digital intervention. The *Parent Handbook* is a brief guide for parents derived from his research on both college student decision-making about alcohol use and parent-child communication (Turrisi, 1999; Turrisi et al., 2000ab; Turrisi & Jaccard, 1992). The *Parent Handbook* spans several conceptual domains. The first domain introduces the problem of underage drinking and related harm to help motivate parents to talk with their teen. The next domain focuses on relationship building and specific strategies that parents can use to improve communication channels with their teen. The final domain is an in-depth discussion of the risks of underage drinking alcohol-related consequences (whom is most at risk, decision making, peer influences, positive and negative reasons why some teens drink, alternatives to drinking, driving under the influence, and riding with an impaired driver). Ultimately, the *Parent Handbook* provides parents with: 1) skills to improve parenting, reducing barriers to communication; 2) skills to guide teens on choosing friends, peer pressure, and decision making; and 3) information for specific topics to discuss about drinking, DUI, and riding with drinking drivers.

The *Parent Handbook* is the only evidence-based, "brief" parent intervention that has undergone the rigor of multiple, well-controlled clinical trials (Turrisi et al., 2001, 2009, 2010, 2013), with several independent replications (Doumas et al., 2013; Ichiyama et al., 2009; Testa et al., 2010). As a result, the recent Surgeon General's Report on Alcohol, Drugs, and Health highlights the *Parent Handbook* as one of two prevention approaches that met rigorous criteria to be considered "efficacious" for preventing college student drinking and consequences (U.S. Department of Health and Human Services, 2016). In addition, the National Institute on Alcohol Abuse and Alcoholism's College AIM Matrix has stated that the handbook is an "effective" intervention to produce changes in attitudes or behaviors related to alcohol use rather than the environments in which alcohol use occurs.

The data show that the *Parent Handbook* not only prevents nondrinking teens' onset of use when they come to college campuses, but it also reduces the drinking of those students who come to college with established high-risk drinking habits (Turrisi et al., 2013; Turrisi & Ray, 2010). However, the current format is limited in several ways. It reaches only college students. Prevention research is clear that there also is a need to address prevention earlier in adolescence than college and among the larger population consisting of all high-school students (i.e., those who are headed for employment or the military) (Harford et al., 2002; Turissi et al., 2009). This is particularly important given that 33.8% of graduating high school students do not enroll in college immediately following graduation (National Center for Education Statistics, 2016). Moreover, the current format is limited in terms of efficiency and engagement in that has only been available in hard copy and pdf formats and does not fully utilize technology, therefore limiting its usability in a digital age where people are used to accessing content on the go and at convenient intervals through their devices. One of the most exciting developments in terms of the delivery of prevention interventions is the use of technology as a platform for delivery (Kiluk et al., 2019), yet few interventions maximize use of technology to deliver prevention interventions. Hence, funds were secured from the National Institute on Alcohol Abuse and Alcoholism to adapt the analog intervention for digital delivery.

PARENTING NOW!: TALKING ABOUT ALCOHOL

REAL Prevention, LLC adapted the *Parent Handbook* to digital format and branded it *Parenting Now!: Talking about Alcohol*. Currently, *Parenting Now!: Talking about Alcohol* (referred to as PN henceforth) is the only digitized, "brief" parent intervention developed from an evidence-based program. While other interventions such as the Strengthening Families intervention (Kumpfer, 1998) use DVD or CD-ROM formats, none fully capitalizes on digital media.

In its initial phase of development, PN is an educational web-based training that aims to equip parents with the necessary tools and skills to effectively communicate with their teens about alcohol use (Figure 1). The design of the program is comprised of two modules. The goal of the first module is to introduce the importance of parental communication in adolescents' alcohol use choices and to determine the user parenting communication style. The goal of module 2 is to guide the user through talking with their teens about alcohol depending on their parenting communication style.

Module 1: Parents Make a Difference

The first activity in this module is titled "Fact or Myth?" In this activity a variety of illustrated characters produce thought bubble content expressing

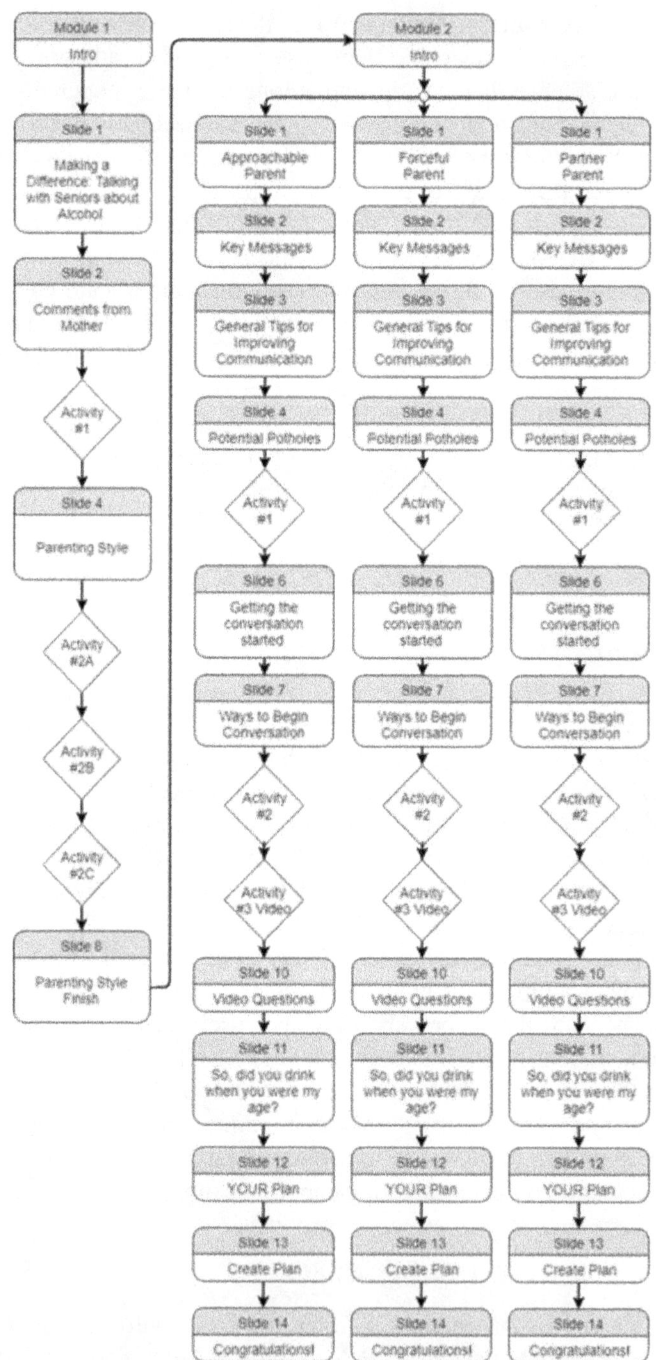

Figure 11.1 Initial Program Design Flow

certain common myths. The user clicks on each character to reveal the fact. For example:

Mother: "My daughter is not interested in drinking." (Click to reveal: Over 90% of students try alcohol outside the home before graduating from high school.)

Father: "My son has learned about the negative effects of alcohol in school." (Click to reveal: Although many students do learn about alcohol in their classes on health, research shows that many important issues do not get covered.)

Mother: "My son will not listen to me." (Click to reveal: National surveys reveal that parents are the number one source that students turn to for important information [even if they can't admit that publicly!])

Mother: "I have taught my daughter our family values such as honesty and responsibility. I assume she knows how to drink responsibly." (Click to reveal: This is a risky assumption. Teens' brains are not fully developed and don't make the same connections that are obvious to adults. The development of the decision-making part of the brain is not fully accomplished until around the age of 25.)

Father: "I don't think it's a big deal if he drinks a controlled amount of alcohol at certain events, as long as I am around to supervise." (Click to reveal: Studies consistently show that when parents permit their student to drink—even when supervised—they tend to more often and heavier once they are outside the home.)

The second activity in the first module is the "Parenting Communication Style Quiz." Building off the profiles identified in the Choi et al. (2017) study of parent-teen substance-specific prevention communication (SSPC), the parenting communication style quiz includes items from both SSPC and family communication environment measures. SSPC was measured using seven items adapted from Miller-Day and Kam's (2010) Targeted Parent-Child Communication about Substances scale. Items ask how frequently they engaged in various conversational strategies such as lecturing, warning of dangers, commenting on media portrayals of drinking and smoking, indirectly hinting, and soliciting youths' opinions about alcohol or tobacco use (1 = never, 2 = occasionally, 3 = quite often, 4 = all the time). Family communication environment was measured using Fitzpatrick and Ritchie's (1994) Family Communication Environment Inventory (FCEI). This included thirteen Likert-type items measuring participants' perceptions of family communication schemata within three dimensions: expressiveness [Partner parent] (four items: e.g., "My child can tell me almost anything"), structural traditionalism (four items: e.g., "I often hear myself say things like "My ideas are right and you should not question them."), and avoidance (six items: e.g., "In my family it is better to avoid conflicts than engage in them"). Responses to these items are on 5-point scales ranging from 1 (strongly disagree) to 5 (strongly agree). The internal reliability of these subscales were acceptable: expressiveness (.82), structural traditionalism (.84), and conflict avoidance (.84). The four original styles identified in Choi et al. (2017) were *Active-Open* (i.e., high SSPC, high expressiveness, high structural traditionalism, relatively high avoidance), *Passive-Open* (i.e., low SSPC, high expressiveness, medium-to-relatively-high structural traditionalism, medium-to-relatively-low avoidance), *Active-Silent* (i.e., high SSPC, low expressiveness, medium-to-relatively-high structural traditionalism, relatively high avoidance), and *Passive-Silent* (i.e., low SSPC, low expressiveness, low structural traditionalism, low avoidance). However, based on advice from our advisory group and a review of the scholarly literature, we assessed that passive-silent parents would be unlikely to seek out an intervention such as PN and so we did not provide a specific module for that style.

Module 2: Talking about Alcohol: It's up to You to Start the Dialogue

After identifying the parenting communication style of the parent user (Active-Open, Passive-Open, and Active-Silent), the content of module 2 was tailored to match the preferences of the user's particular style. Module 2 consists of content focusing on goals for talking with your teen about alcohol, general tips for improving your communication with your teen and potential potholes when communicating with your teen. This module includes five activities. Activity 1 is the "Knowledge Challenge." Activity 2 focuses on "Ways to Begin the Conversation." Activity 3 is titled "Keep the Conversation Going." Activity 4 includes a "Video Conversation and Knowledge Check" which provides a video model of an actual parent-teen conversation about alcohol along with a review of prior content. Finally, activity 5 involves the user developing "My Communication Plan." Once users have completed both learning modules, they have access to the entire menu and can revisit any content they wish.

Currently, there are no known equivalent programs that aim to increase effective communication between parents and their teens about alcohol use via parent-adolescent communication style tailoring. This training is the first of its kind and has potential to help increase effective communication between parents and their teens about safe alcohol use and reduce problematic drinking behaviors among teens. PN has learning modules, interactive activities, and voiceover narration detailing instructions for participants.

In terms of instructional design, PN adheres to a VODEPS approach that our team created during previous technology developments—(V) visually engage the learner, (O) provide an overview of the level content, (D) define terms and learning objectives, (E) demonstrate and provide examples, (P) practice skills, and (S) summarize the level (Miller-Day, 2017). PN is a mobile web application. The digital format enables parents to access the information from their computers or tablets, making the content easily accessible and readily available.

PROCESS OF DEVELOPING A DIGITAL INTERVENTION

Adapting Existing Content

Translating Turrisi and colleague's and Miller-Day and colleague's basic research and adapting the prototype *Parent Handbook* (2001) into the *Parenting Now!: Talking about Alcohol* parent intervention was a process involving many players. Miller-Day (in press) points out that conducting translational research is a collaborative process. She states:

> At its core, "translation means relating an insight from basic scientific investigation to something that is useful for promoting the well-being of one or more humans" (Evans, 2012, p. 23). The 'something useful' might be an innovation such as a program (e.g., intervention, training, campaign), practice (e.g., guideline recommendations, message design strategies, skill, procedure, service), product (e.g., toolkits, mobile app, or other technology), or policy (Miller-Day, in press, p. 10–11) . . . and it includes collaboration and developing partnerships to develop those innovations and carefully test them. (Miller-Day, in press, p. 31)

For our PN digital intervention, the content of the curriculum was adapted from basic research and Turrisi et al.'s handbook (2001) in collaboration with many. Our collaboration included parents across the United States who participating in formative and evaluation research, program development and evaluation by the authors, and design and technology development by the creative team at Klein Buendel, Inc. This process was aided by an expert panel consisting of Dr. Jerod Stapleton (web-based health interventions), Dr. Caitlin Abar (parent-teen communication and adolescent alcohol prevention), and Mr. Andrew Wiss (mobile technology).

Our process of adapting existing information for the content of the digital program included two stages of additional research. First, we surveyed parents of teens to capture current data on strategies parents were using to address alcohol use with their teens, identify prototypical narratives to include in the digital learning modules, and gauge parents' interest in the intervention. Next, all surveyed parents were asked to participate in a follow-up paid interview study. For those who consented, project team members contacted them to schedule a follow up focus group interview.

Survey

A total of 278 parents of 16- to 20-year-old teens were recruited through (1) a Facebook announcement, (2) the D.A.R.E. America national program, (3) a Qualtrics survey panel, (4) military organizations, and (4) Universities completed the survey (75% female, 25% male) with the following ethnic breakdown: 76% White, 17% Black or African-American, 5% Hispanic or Latino, 1% Asian, and 1% Other. The age distribution of their children was: 16 (24%), 17 (29%), 18 (28%), 19 (24%), and 20 (17%). Our sample reported that 72% of their high school aged children planned to attend college following graduation (72%). This is similar to national data based on Bureau of Labor statistics (i.e., 67% actually attending).

The parenting communication style was determined by a combination of measures including the SSPC and FCEI subscales. An Active-Open style consisted of high SSPC, high expressiveness, high structural traditionalism, relatively high avoidance, a Passive-Open style consisted of low SSPC, high expressiveness, medium-to-relatively-high structural traditionalism, medium-to-relatively-low avoidance, and the Active-Silent style consisted of high SSPC, low expressiveness, medium-to-relatively-high structural traditionalism, relatively high avoidance).

Eighty-one percent reported an Active-Open style with their teen (e.g., communication about alcohol, open exchange of ideas, joint problem solving); 8% reported a Passive-Open style (e.g., indirect or low levels of communication about alcohol, strict rules; punishment should rules be broken); and 7% reported an Active-Silent style (e.g., communication about alcohol, high avoidance of conflict). Reflecting the basic research, there were distinctions across parent-teen communication styles, with (a) parents of all communication styles gathering and sharing alcohol information from the web or television with their teen; (b) parents with an Active-Open style discussing the effects of alcohol on decision-making, addiction, sexual risk, social pressure and drinking, the effect of alcohol on the body, refusal strategies, keeping your drink "safe," alternative activities to drinking, and having a safety plan; parents with a Passive-Open style discussing moderation of use, telling the teen to pace him or herself if drinking alcohol, and telling them to eat food when drinking alcohol; (c) parents with an Passive-Open and Active-Silent styles offered tangible rewards for non-use; and (d) parents with an Active-Silent style reported communication about alcohol with their teens, but that communication was infrequent and brief.

After being shown a visual mock-up of the planned modules and content topics based on the *Parent Handbook*, parents reported on their interest in the program. Overall, parents were very interested in the overall PN program, with an overall mean rating of 3.47 (SD = .65) on a 4-point scale (high scores are positive) and ratings on scales measuring the core modules were all above 4.29 (1–5 scale, with 5 as positive).

Focus Group Interviews

Our team wanted to allow participants to expand on their survey responses and collectively share their ideas and experiences, therefore we scheduled online focus group interviews to follow-up on survey responses. If a parent could not meet in a focus group session, they were interviewed individually. Of the 278 parents surveyed, 32 (28 female, 4 male) parents participated in follow-up interviews. Eight different parent focus groups included a total of 19 participants with the remaining 13 parent participants interviewed individually. The parents participating in the interviews represented a variety of parent-teen communication styles with 75% (n = 24) identified as having an Active-Open style, 22% (n = 7) having a Passive-Open style, and 3% (n = 1) having an Active-Silent style.

Focus group sessions were homogeneous, including parents who identified similar communication styles and included individuals across the United States, therefore focus group interviews were conducted using video conferencing software (Zoom) so that all participants, facilitator, and notetakers could see one another, interact, and share their screens as needed. Each Zoom meeting was video-and audio-recorded. Participants were sent reminders and instructions for the technology one week ahead, along with text/phone/ or email reminders 24–48 hours before their scheduled interview. Interviews ranged from 55 minutes to 70 minutes in length.

In the focus group discussions, we specifically sought to explore in more depth how parents using different communication styles approached conversations about alcohol with their teens. One of the key pieces of information that guided our module development was parents' suggestion to rename the parent-teen communication styles to facilitate user understanding. Based on specific suggestions from participants, we re-labeled the parent-teen communication styles in the following way. Those parents identified as having an Active-Open style were now referred to as "Partner Parents," those with a Passive-Open style were now referred to as "Forceful Parents," and those with an Active-Silent style were now referred to as "Avoidant Parents." Within each of these styles we were able to collect the accounts from parents about their unique strategies for addressing alcohol use with their teens.

Topics that emerged in these conversations included the effects of alcohol on decision-making, addiction, and sexual risk; social pressure and drinking; the body; refusal strategies; keeping your drink safe; alternative activities; having a safety plan; discussing family history; hosting parties; legal issues; other drugs including nicotine and marijuana; and friends' problems. Moreover, approximately 34% (n = 11) of the parents in the interview portion of our research reported that the "alcohol talks" in their households were linked in some way to a parent or other family member who had a problem with alcohol addiction. Key narratives emerged from the parents participating in the focus group interviews including "My teen will not be like me," "Cautionary tales will convince them," "Just give them a sip and they won't be curious," "Give them the tools they need to make the best decisions," and "Tone [of the conversation] is everything." The information gained in this formative research was then used to inform specific examples, practice scenarios, and mock situations in module 2 of the digital intervention.

Personalization of Content

The formative research results and the content of the *Parent Handbook* (Turrisi et al., 2001) informed the development of three versions of module 2. After completing module 1 activities, including the parenting communication style assessment, the programming identified the user as a partner parent, forceful parent, or avoidant parent. Partner parent style is characterized by communication that is open, bidirectional, and expressive, has shared decision-making, and provides explanations. Forceful parent style is characterized by communication that emphasizes parental authority, tends to be unidirectional from parent to child, and is focused on gaining compliance. Avoidant parent style is characterized by communication that is avoidant of sensitive topics and conflict, with a belief that parents do not influence adolescent choices.

None of these parenting communication styles was discussed in the intervention as qualitatively better or worse than the others, but within module 2 all topics were addressed with a slightly different approach. For example, in activity 2, "Ways to begin the conversation [about alcohol]" users were provided with a sampling of key messages to convey that matched their parenting communication style. For example, Partner Parents were offered messages that emerged in our formative research such as "I am interested in your life," "I care about you and want to understand you," and "I want to help you." Whereas avoidant parents were offered message possibilities such as "I want you to live your own life, but I plan to remain interested in you as you live that life," "I care about you and even if we don't always talk openly, I want to understand you," and "I respect your privacy and desire to be independent." Additionally, in activity 4 there were video models provided of parent-teen conversations, with three separate videos depicting parental approaches from each parenting communication style.

Optional Content

"Optional content" was also developed for the intervention. The purpose of optional content was to provide specific interest material to parents. These include topics such as "other drugs including nicotine and marijuana," "Facts you don't know," "Binge drinking 101," "Recognizing if your child has a problem," "Hosting underage parties," "Legal issues related to underage drinking," and "Alternatives to drinking." We also developed a partner website to provide consistently updated information pertaining to this optional content.

Expert Panel Feedback

Once the prototypes for PN and the accompanying website were developed, three members of our expert panel were invited to provide feedback to guide any revisions before commencing on the final development of the program and usability study. The expert panelists were asked to provide feedback on the intervention modules and the website regarding logos, content, design, organization, usability, the use of animated explainer videos, and any additional feedback that would assist us in revising the program. Based on this feedback we made some changes such as font sizes, visual effects adjustments, adding information about the developers for credibility, adding audio instructions, providing users with information letting them know that the following material in module 2 "was tailored to help parents who communicate like you," with most changes focused on minimizing too much text on any one page and eliminating confusing information from the website.

FEASIBILITY OF THE INTERVENTION

To determine the feasibility of implementing the PN program to parents of teens, an independent evaluator conducted ten in-depth interviews (IDI) with a convenience sample of participants recruited from a list provided by two universities and the evaluators own social network. The interviews were all conducted on the Zoom meeting platform. Participants were sent an invitation email with instructions about the study, how to complete informed consent online, and details on how to join the meeting. Interviews were scheduled over email.

At the beginning of each Zoom IDI session, Dr. Evans confirmed that the participant had completed informed consent (all 10 had done so in advance) and provided a brief introduction to the Parenting Now! program and the feasibility study. Then Dr. Evans and the participant went through the two modules of PN content and completed all screens and activities. After each of the two modules, Dr. Evans paused and asked a series of open-ended questions. Participants then received a brief technology usability questionnaire with close-ended questions (Brooke, 1996). Nine out of the ten completed the questionnaire.

The findings from this usability data supported the feasibility of the PN program. The feedback from the ten in-depth interviews some concerns about content, but most concerns focusing on graphics and navigability. The quantitative data from those who participated in the usability study was positive,

Table 11.1. Descriptive Statistics: Usability of Parenting Now!: Talking about Alcohol

	N	*Min.*	*Max.*	*Mean*	*SD*
I think that I would like to use this program.	9	3	5	4.78	.67
I found the program unnecessarily complex.	9	4	5	4.67	.50
I thought the program was easy to use.*	9	5	5	5	.0
I think that I would need the support of a technical person to be able to use this program.*	9	5	5	5	.0
I found the various functions in this program were well integrated.	9	4	5	4.78	.44
I thought there was too much inconsistency in this program.	9	4	5	4.89	.33
I would imagine that most people would learn to use this program very quickly.	9	4	5	4.78	.44
I found the program very cumbersome to use.	9	5	5	5	.0
I felt very confident using the program.*	9	3	5	4.56	.88
I needed to learn a lot of things before I could get going with this program.	9	4	5	4.67	.50

Notes: Reverse coded: 2,4,6,8,10; Likert 1–5 scale

* Perfect Score

supporting the feasibility of this technology. The statistics below provide support for the usability of this program.

CHALLENGES AND CHANGES

Despite the process of closely adapting the material in the *Parent Handbook* (Turrisi et al., 2001) for source material, adding tailoring for parenting communication style, and receiving positive interest and feedback from users on the content, design, and usability of the program, we are currently concerned with the complexity of the program. We originally sought to develop a *brief* intervention, and while no one activity takes longer than eight minutes, we believe all the content and activities across both modules may still be too long and complex. So, we are currently in the second phase of development which includes creating a mobile app of the program specifically for very brief informational sessions and this will include only four sections: What should I know about alcohol use and teens? How can I improve my communication? How do I start the conversation? What should I say when talking about alcohol? The focused content in the app will hit on some of the core pieces of information from the more complex program. A mobile web app functions similar to a native app on a smartphone or tablet computer. However, a mobile web app runs through the phone's/computer's web browser controlled by an external web server rather than running on the local device. There are several advantages to this approach:

1. Mobile web apps can be mobile device responsive to ensure cross-platform compatibility
2. User experience is like a native mobile app, but content can be updated much more quickly than native apps that need to download/install a revised version
3. Mobile web apps avoid the need to program for multiple operating systems (e.g., iOS or Android for smartphones/tablet computers), speeding development, and
4. Use of mobile web app facilitates evaluation because it can be better tracked from the web servers than from a native app.

Additionally, we have begun to question the value-added for the cost of creating tailored modules for different parenting communication styles. The cost of developing one module versus three separate modules makes the simpler intervention more cost effective. It is unclear, however, if the tailored program would be more effective in promoting a sense of efficacy in parents in planning and carrying out their conversations about alcohol. Research would still be needed to determine if tailoring compared to no-tailoring have differential effects on a host of variables such as parental efficacy, satisfying conversations, and impacts of the conversations on teen alcohol use. Additional funding will be needed to address these issues.

IMPLICATIONS, DISCUSSION, AND FUTURE DIRECTIONS

Harnessing technology for parenting interventions can broaden their impact and reach. Shifting from the original information-based, print *Parent Handbook* to an interactive, skill-building intervention via the e-learning format enhances learning opportunities. With the paper-based format, parents were asked to read a handbook and then communicate with their teens about alcohol, with no skill building activities or ways to offer tailored feedback to reinforce positive communication skills. Thus, as we turn toward technology use, we shift from simply telling parents what works best to giving them actual opportunities to apply what they've learned and practice their own skills. The shift to digital technologies allows us to move from a passive, didactic, information-based approach (e.g., parents read content) to an interactive, skill-building approach where parents not only read content, but participate in activities to apply knowledge, practice skills, and receive tailored feedback and additional coaching in topic areas of their choosing. The technology allows us to utilize a more sophisticated pedagogical model to enhance engagement and skill development while individualizing the experience. That is, program interactivity enhances the overall communication of the message through increased user engagement, which leads to better message processing and impacts on cognition, attitude, and behavior (Sundar, 2007). Additionally, the distribution of materials and keeping content updated is much simpler and cost effective with digital technologies. Traditional print versions of parent information limits pedagogy to didactic delivery and restricts dissemination because they are cumbersome and costly. With digital technology a user can click on an app or link and be taken directly into the program without having to store files on their own device. This can ensure rapid dissemination to a much larger market than currently occurs with most contemporary parent interventions.

Finally, we believe that the time has come to harness digital technologies in the field of family communication to provide more detailed analytics about *how* parents and families are using our interventions. Analytics such as total time spent accessing the digital program, time spent on each module and activities within modules, and number of activities and modules completed can easily be obtained with digital technologies. This is the kind of detail we need to understand dosage and actual exposure to our programs and if deviations from receiving the full program impact expected outcomes. Most importantly, however, we believe that all parents and families deserve accessible resources that can be custom tailored, enable them to engage fully and interact with information, practice skills, and be exposed to prosocial models of behavior. Through digital technologies, quality family communication information can reach the most inaccessible corners of the world through digital technology. This is the promise and future of interventions seeking to improve family communication across the globe.

REFERENCES

Alcohol-Related Disease Impact Application (2020). Centers for Disease Control and Prevention website. https://nccd.cdc.gov/DPH_ARDI/default/default.aspx.

Branstetter, S. A., Furman, W., & Cottrell, L. (2009). The influence of representations of attachment, maternal–adolescent relationship quality, and maternal monitoring on adolescent substance use: a 2-Year Longitudinal Examination. *Child Development*, *80*(5), 1448–1462.

Brooke, J. (1996). SUS: A Quick and Dirty Usability Scale. In: P. W. Jordan, B. Thomas, B. A. Weerdmeester & I. L. McClelland (Eds.), *Usability Evaluation in Industry*. London: Taylor & Francis. (Also see http://www.cee.hw.ac.uk/~ph/sus.html.)

Centers for Disease Control and Prevention (2020). Underage drinking. https://www.cdc.gov/alcohol/fact-sheets/underage-drinking.htm.

Choi, H. J., Miller-Day, M., Shin, Y., Hecht, M. L., Pettigrew, J., Krieger, J. L., . . . & Graham, J. W. (2017). Parent prevention communication profiles and adolescent substance use: a latent profile analysis and growth curve model. *Journal of Family Communication*, *17*(1), 15–32.

Doumas, D. M., Turrisi, R., Ray, A. E., Esp, S. M., & Curtis-Schaeffer, A. K. (2013). A randomized trial evaluating a parent based intervention to reduce college drinking. *Journal of Substance Abuse Treatment*, *45*(1), 31–37. doi:10.1016/j.jsat.2012.12.008.

Dumas, T. M., Ellis, W., & Litt, D. M. (2020). What does adolescent substance use look like during the COVID-19 pandemic? Examining changes in frequency, social contexts, and pandemic-related predictors. *Journal of Adolescent Health*, 67(3), 354–361.

Ebersole, D. S., Miller-Day, M., & Raup-Krieger, J. (2014). Do actions speak louder than words? Adolescent interpretations of parental substance use. *Journal of Family Communication, 14,* 328–351. doi: 10.1080/15267431.2014.945699.

Esser, M. B., Guy, G. P., Zhang, K., Brewer, R.D. (2019). Binge drinking and prescription opioid misuse in the U.S., 2012–2014. *American Journal of Preventive Medicine, 57*, 197–208.

Fitzpatrick, M. A., & Ritchie, L. D. (1994). Communication schemata within the family: Multiple perspectives on family interaction. *Human Communication Research, 20*(3), 275–301.

Harford, T. C., Wechsler, H., & Muthén, B. O. (2002). The impact of current residence and high school drinking on alcohol problems among college students. *Journal of Studies on Alcohol, 63*(3), 271–279.

Hopfer, S., Shin, Y., Davis, D., Elek, E., Kam, J. A., & Hecht, M. L. (2010). A review of elementary school-based substance use prevention programs: Identifying program attributes. *Journal of Drug Education, 40*(1), 11–36.

Hummel, A., Shelton, K. H., Heron, J., Moore, L., & van den Bree, M. B. (2013). A systematic review of the relationships between family functioning, pubertal timing and adolescent substance use. *Addiction, 108*(3), 487–496.

Ichiyama, M. A., Fairlie, A. M., Wood, M. D., Turrisi, R., Francis, D. P., Ray, A. E., & Stanger, L. A. (2009). A randomized trial of a parent-based intervention on drinking behavior among incoming college freshman. *Journal of Studies on Alcohol and Drugs, Supp 16*, 67–76. doi:10.15288/jsads.2009.s16.67.

Johnston, L. D., Miech, R. A., O'Malley, P. M., Bachman, J. G., Schulenberg, J. E., & Patrick, M. E. (2020). Monitoring the Future National Survey results on drug use 1975–2019: Overview, key findings on adolescent drug use. Ann Arbor: Institute for Social Research, University of Michigan.

Kam, J. A., Basinger, E. D., & Abendschein, B. (2015a). Do adolescent perceptions of their parents drinking alcohol undermine or enhance what parents say about alcohol? The interaction between verbal and nonverbal messages about alcohol use. *Communication Research.* Published online first on January 6, 2015. doi:10.1177/0093650214565922.

Kam, J. A., Castro, F. G., & Wang, N. (2015b). Parent-child communication's attenuating effects on Mexican-heritage early-stage adolescents' depressive symptoms and substance use. *Human Communication Research, 41,* 204–225. doi: 10.1111/hcre.12043.

Kam, J. A., & Cleveland, M. J. (2011). Perceived discrimination as a risk factor for Latina/o youth's substance use: Do parent-and peer-based communication and relationship resources act as protective factors? *Health Communication, 26,* 111–124. doi: 10.1080/10410236.2010.539180.

Kam, J. A., & Middleton, A. V. (2013). The associations between parents' references to their own past substance use and youth's substance-use beliefs and behaviors: A comparison of Latino and European American youth. *Human Communication Research, 39,* 208–229. doi:10.1111/hcre.12001.

Kam. J. A., & Miller-Day, M. (Eds) (2017). A family communication perspective on substance use prevention, intervention, and coping [Special Issue]. *Journal of Family Communication, 17* (1), 1–88.

Kam, J. A., Potocki, B., & Hecht, M. L. (2014a). Encouraging Mexican-heritage youth to intervene when friends drink: The role of targeted parent-child communication against alcohol. *Communication Research, 14,* 544–664. doi: 10.1177/0093650212446621.

Kam, J. A., Wang, N., & Harvey, J. (2014b). Latino and European American early adolescents' exposure to music with substance-use references: Examining parent-child communication as a moderator. *Journal of Adolescence, 37,* 185–196. doi: 10.1016/j.adolescence.2013.12.001.

Kam, J. A., & Yang, S. (2014). Explicating how parent-child communication increases Latino and European American early adolescents' intentions to intervene in a friend's substance use. *Prevention Science, 15,* 536–546. doi:10.1007/s11121-013-0404-8.

Kiluk, B. D., Ray, L. A., Walthers, J., Bernstein, M., Tonigan, J. S., & Magill, M. (2019). Technology-delivered cognitive-behavioral interventions for alcohol use: A meta-analysis. *Alcoholism: Clinical and Experimental Research, 43*(11), 2285–2295.

Koning, I., de Looze, M., & Harakeh, Z. (2020). Parental alcohol-specific rules effectively reduce adolescents' tobacco and cannabis use: A longitudinal study. *Drug and Alcohol Dependence, 216*, 108–226.

Kumpfer, K. L. (1998). Selective prevention interventions: the strengthening families program. *Drug Abuse Prevention through Family Interventions*, *177*, 160–207.

Le Poire, B. A. (1992). Does the codependent encourage substance dependent behavior: Paradoxical injunctions in the codependent relationship. *International Journal of the Addictions, 27,* 1465–1474. doi: 10.3109/10826089209047363.

Le Poire, B. A. (1995). Inconsistent nurturing as control theory: Implications for communication-based treatment research and treatment programs. *Journal of Applied Communication Research, 22,* 60–74. doi: 10.1080/00909889509365414.

Miller, J.W., Naimi, T. S., Brewer, R. D., Jones, S. E. (2007) Binge drinking and associated health risk behaviors among high school students. *Pediatrics, 119*, 76–85.

Miller-Day, M. (2002). Parent-adolescent communication about alcohol, tobacco, and other drug use. *Journal of Adolescent Research, 17*, 604–616. doi:10.1177/074355802237466.

———. (2005a). U.S. parent-offspring discourse about alcohol and other drugs. *Language and Communication Journal, 10*, 10–18.

———. (2005b). Effective parent-child communication: A preventive measure. *Counselor,* 6(1), 70–71.

———. (2007). Talking with your kids about alcohol and other drugs: Are parents the anti-drug? In L. B. Arnold. (Ed.), *Family communication: Theory and research* (pp. 335–343). Boston, MA: Allyn & Bacon.

———. (2008). Talking to youth about drugs: What do late adolescents say about parental strategies? *Family Relations, 52,* 1–12. doi:10.1111/j.1741-3729.2007.00478.x.

Miller-Day, M. (2017). *Feasibility study of D.A.R.E. Mobile elementary prevention program.* Report presented to the Scientific and Executive D.A.R.E. Boards.

Miller-Day, M. (in press). *Translational research: Moving from discovery to practice*. Cognella.

Miller-Day, M., & Dodd, A. (2004). Toward a descriptive model of parent-offspring communication about alcohol and other drugs. *Journal of Social and Personal Relationships, 21,* 73–95. doi: 10.1177/0265407504039846.

Miller-Day, M., & Kam, J. A. (2010). More than just openness: Developing and validating a measure of targeted parent-child communication about alcohol. *Health Communication, 25,* 293–302. doi:10.1080/10410231003698952.

Naeger, S. (2017). Emergency department visits involving underage alcohol use: 2010 to 2013. Substance Abuse and Mental Health Services Administration, Rockville, MD.

National Center for Education Statistics (2016). *Fast facts: Back to school statistics.* Retrieved from http://nces.ed.gov/fastfacts/display.asp?id=372.

Pettigrew, J., Miller-Day, M., Shin, Y., Krieger, J. L., Hecht, M. L., & Graham, J. W. (2018). Parental messages about substance use in early adolescence: Extending a model of drug-talk styles. *Health Communication, 33*(3), 349–358.

Pettigrew, J., Shin, Y., Stein, J. B., & Van Raalte, L. J. (2017). Family communication and adolescent alcohol use in Nicaragua, Central America: A test of primary socialization theory. *Journal of Family Communication, 17*(1), 33–48.

Reimuller, A., Hussong, A., & Ennett, S. T. (2011). The influence of alcohol-specific communication on adolescent alcohol use and alcohol-related consequences. *Prevention Science, 12,* 389–400. doi: 10.1007/s11121-011-0227–4.

Sacks, J. J., Gonzales, K. R., Bouchery, E. E., Tomedi, L. E., & Brewer, R. D. (2015). 2010 national and state costs of excessive alcohol consumption. *American Journal of Preventive Medicine*, *49*(5), e73-e79.

Substance Abuse and Mental Health Services Administration (2014). *Results from the 2013 National Survey on Drug Use and Health: Summary of national findings* (HHS Publication No. SMA 14–4863, NSDUH Series H-48). Retrieved from http://www.samhsa.gov/data/sites/default/files/NSDUHresultsPDFWHTML2013/Web/NSDUHresults2013.pdf.

Sundar, S. S. (2007). Social psychology of interactivity in human-website interaction. *The Oxford Handbook of Internet Psychology*, 89–104.

Testa, M., Hoffman, J. H., Livingston, J. A., & Turrisi, R. (2010). Preventing college women's sexual victimization through parent based intervention: A randomized controlled trial. *Prevention Science, 11*(3), 308–318. doi:10.1007/s11121-010-0168–3.

Thomas, R. W., & Seibold, D. R. (1996). Communicating with alcoholics: A strategic influence approach to personal intervention. In E. B. Ray (Ed.), *Communication and disenfranchisement: Social health issues and implications* (p. 405–432). Mahwah, NJ: Routledge.

Turrisi, R. (1999). Cognitive and attitudinal factors in the analysis of alternatives to binge drinking. *Journal of Applied Social Psychology, 29*(7), 1512–1535. doi:10.1111/j.1559-1816.1999.tb00150.x.

Turrisi, R., Abar, C., Mallett, K. A., & Jaccard, J. (2010). An examination of the mediational effects of cognitive and attitudinal factors of a parent intervention to reduce college drinking. *Journal of Applied Social Psychology*, *40*(10), 2500–2526. doi:10.1111/j.1559-1816.2010.00668.x.

Turrisi, R., & Jaccard, J. (1992). Cognitive and attitudinal factors in the analysis of alternatives to drunk driving. *Journal of Studies on Alcohol*, *53*(5), 405–414. doi:10.15288/jsa.1992.53.405.

Turrisi, R., Jaccard, J., Taki, R., Dunnam, H. & Grimes, J. (2001). Examination of the short-term efficacy of a parent intervention to reduce college student drinking tendencies. *Psychology of Addictive Behaviors*, 15, 366–372. doi:10.1037/0893-164X.15.4.366.

Turrisi, R., Larimer, M. E., Mallett, K. A., Kilmer, J. R., Ray, A. E., Mastroleo, N. R., . . . & Montoya, H. (2009). A randomized clinical trial evaluating a combined alcohol intervention for high-risk college students. *Journal of Studies on Alcohol and Drugs*, *70*(4), 555. doi:10.15288/jsad.2009.70.555.

Turrisi, R., Mallett, K. A., Cleveland, M. J., Varvil-Weld, L., Abar, C., Scaglione, N., & Hultgren, B. (2013). Evaluation of timing and dosage of a parent-based intervention to minimize college students' alcohol consumption. *Journal of Studies on Alcohol and Drugs*, *74*(1), 30. doi:10.15288/jsad.2013.74.30.

Turrisi, R., Padilla, K. K., & Wiersma, K. A. (2000a). College student drinking: an examination of theoretical models of drinking tendencies in freshmen and upperclassmen. *Journal of Studies on Alcohol*, *61*(4), 598–602. doi:10.15288/jsa.2000.61.598.

Turrisi, R., & Ray, A. E. (2010). Sustained parenting and college drinking in first-year students. *Developmental Psychobiology*, *52*(3), 286–294. doi:10.1002/dev.20434.

Turrisi, R., Wiersma, K. A., & Hughes, K. K. (2000b). Binge-drinking-related consequences in college students: Role of drinking beliefs and mother–teen communications. *Psychology of Addictive Behaviors*, *14*(4), 342. doi:10.1037/0893-164X.14.4.342.

U.S. Department of Health and Human Services (HHS), Office of the Surgeon General (2016). *Facing addiction in America: The Surgeon General's report on alcohol, drugs, and health*. Washington, DC: HHS.

Van Ryzin, M. J., Fosco, G. M., & Dishion, T. J. (2012). Family and peer predictors of substance use from early adolescence to early adulthood: An 11-year prospective analysis. *Addictive Behaviors*, *37*, 1314–1324. doi: 10.1016/j.addbeh.2012.06.020.

Varvil-Weld, L., Scaglione, N., Cleveland, M. J., Mallett, K. A., Turrisi, R., & Abar, C. C. (2014). Optimizing timing and dosage: Does parent type moderate the effects of variations of a parent-based intervention to reduce college student drinking? *Prevention Science*, *15*(1), 94–102. PMCID: PMC3688671. doi:10.1007/s11121-012-0356-4.

Wood, M. D., Mitchell, R. E., Read, J. P., & Brand, N. H. (2004). Do parents still matter? Parent and peer influences on alcohol involvement among recent high school graduates. *Psychology of Addictive Behaviors, 18*(1), 19–30. doi:10.1037/0893-164X.18.1.19.

Wood, M. D., Fairlie, A. M., Fernandez, A. C., Borsari, B., Capone, C., Laforge, R., & Carmona-Barros, R. (2010). Brief motivational and parent interventions for college students: a randomized factorial study. *Journal of Consulting and Clinical Psychology*, *78*(3), 349–361. doi:10.1037/a0019166.

Zaharakis, N. M., Taylor, K. A., & Kliewer, W. (2015). What do urban Black mothers tell their adolescents about alcohol and other drugs? *Journal of Research on Adolescence, 25,* 75–80. doi: 10.1111/jora.12094.

Chapter Twelve

Embracing the Transition to Social Media in Parent–Teen Communication

Melissa Rizzo Weller, Angela M. Hosek, and Jessica Cherry

The continuous evolution of social networking sites (SNS) has provided families with new channels to communicate information and build relationships. Families who integrate SNS into family life increase the potential channels and content for family communication (Kanter, Afifi, and Robbins 2012). Current researchers have demonstrated that low levels of parent–teen communication result in behavioral issues and delinquency (Stouthamer-Loeber et al. 2002), depressive symptomatology (Yu et al. 2006), and substance use (Kelly, Comello, and Hunn 2002). As a result, parents may be seeking new ways to increase levels of communication with their teens. Conversely, positive communication between parents and teens results in more family cohesion, adaptability, and satisfaction (Barnes and Olson 1985). Moreover, Racz, Johnson, Bradshaw, and Cheng (2017) found that positive parent–teen communication improved "youth behavioral and socio-emotional functioning" (199). These positive outcomes for frequent communication are encouraging for families to maintain positive relationships and overall family satisfaction. We argue that parents who embrace the social media their teens are using as a way to initiate conversations and maintain relationships may be able to improve communication in the family.

The current generation of adolescents are largely parented by the generation who lived as teenagers without social media but have raised their children within the current media landscape including internet, email, and social media as forms of communication. Recent scholarship has shown that 71%

of teens are active on more than one social media site and 90% of teens (with a cell/smartphone) use text messaging apps (Lenhart 2015), clearly demonstrating the pervasiveness of new technology into family communication. Moreover, approximately 84% of adults ages 18–29 who use social media, which is similar to the 81% of adults ages 30–49 who use social media, and greater than adults ages 50–64 (73%) and adults 65 and older (45%) who use social media (Auxier and Anderson 2021). When considering the frequency of social media use by both adults and teens, it is imperative we understand how families can use social media and other mediated channels to improve communication among family members.

In this chapter we continue exploring family communication between parents and teens through mediated channels. More specifically, we want to understand how teens use social media as a tool for sharing information and ideas with their parents. As the authors of this chapter, we have particular interest to understand the ways in which social media can be used to engage family communication between children and parents, in particular, surrounding difficult conversations. Although each with unique perspectives, we are collectively women who have either had, will have, or hope to have teenage children.

Melissa has four children, aged 24, 19, 16, and 15. As a parent belonging to the first generation who is raising children with social media, Melissa has embraced new ways of communicating with her children via social network sites and text messaging. She is especially interested in how adolescents might use content from apps, such as TikTok, to initiate and engage in difficult conversations.

Angela has four children ranging in age from 11 to one year old. Angela is interested in how to build useful, accessible, appropriate, and open channels of communication with her children using social media to supplement and support face-to-face conversations she and her partner have with their children about topics such as racism, gender identity, politics, finances, sex, and sexuality.

Jessica hopes to have children in the future. As a prospective parent, Jessica is interested in understanding how social media can help facilitate conversations with her future children. She is especially fascinated in the development and advancement of social media and how these emerging platforms, such as TikTok, may impact engaging and open communication between parents and their children.

CHAPTER ROAD MAP

With the continual evolution of mediated communication, social media, and digital communication, it is important to understand how communication in family contexts, specifically between parents/caregivers and their children has evolved, as well. In this chapter, we will explore how parents communicate with their teens through mediated communication channels. First, we present extant literature on family communication and social media. Then, we share some of the most popular social media applications used by both teens and parents. Next, we examine how parent and teen communication can be viewed and explored through five theoretical lenses: family communication patterns, communication privacy management, media richness theory, social presence theory, and social influence theory. To conclude the chapter, we provide practical implications for family communication in social media contexts and future directions for scholarship on family communication in mediated spaces.

Family Communication and Social Media

The family has long been heralded as one of the most influential relationships in the lives of children (Braithwaite et al. 2010). As a primary socializing force, families provide scripts that guide the development of their children's worldviews, values, and beliefs (Hosek 2015). Family relationships develop differently than other interpersonal relationships due to the physical closeness of family members within the home. Often, family members have more frequent communication over longer periods of time beginning from birth, in traditional family households.

In recent decades, children often have closer relationships with their parents who are heavily involved in their lives than in previous generations (Howe and Strauss 2007). To maintain these relationships, many families use both online and face-to-face forms of communication (Caughlin and Sharabi 2013). In these highly enmeshed relationships, it makes sense that families may use social media as a point of connection. Child and Westermann (2013) contend that social media is rife with opportunities for family interaction. Although children may feel vulnerable about engaging with parents on sites like Facebook (Child and Petronio 2011), the medium offers families an easy way to stay in touch (Child and Westermann 2013). Adolescence and the transition to adulthood relationships with family members continue; yet are often different in form than when the child was younger (Madsen and Collins 2018). Mediated technologies play a vital role in connecting parents and children (Vitak 2014). For example, researchers have shown that children are more likely to engage in video chats than phone calls with their parents, because the video feature keeps them more engaged (Ames et al. 2010). Teens may not be as eager to communicate via video chat with their parents to preserve their privacy or prefer to keep the conversation short.

Often, young adults struggle to express themselves authentically and to present their true selves (Dou, Pan, and Jiang 2020). As teens work to find their identities, the affordances of social media, such as asynchronicity, may allow for more uninhibited communication between teens and parents. Asynchronicity is the lack of real-time interaction online (Suler 2004). This allows both the message sender and receiver to process the message and form an appropriate response. Even if these responses are sent quickly, the sender is afforded time to craft a message that forms the impression they choose. O'Sullivan (2000) asserts, "Interaction initiators who perceive that an episode is potentially threatening or supportive of their own or their partner's self-presentation are expected to strive to maximize rewards and minimize costs" (411). Thus, teens who want to initiate conversation related to sensitive subjects may prefer mediated channels to reduce uncertainty while avoiding some of the awkward nonverbal cues present in face-to-face communication. The communicative processes used to maintain relationships include both strategic and routine efforts which are either explicitly or implicitly enacted (Billedo, Kerkhof, and Finkenauer 2015). We see this in family communication when members use mediated channels for everyday tasks, such as requesting items from the grocery store, and strategic messaging, such as asking for a later curfew through a text to avoid confrontation.

Research conducted to examine how families utilize technology to communicate include a substantial amount focused on negative outcomes of social media use in families. Parents' technology rules and adolescents' responses to these rules often create tensions within the family. For example, Blackwell et al. (2016) found tensions between parents and adolescents related to technology use include obscurity of personal device use, attention expectations and management, adolescence and work, and family time. While these tensions have always been present, they have been reinterpreted in relation to the new technology, including cell phones and social networking sites.

Another study focused on teens and parents' privacy perspectives for new technology (Cranor et al. 2014). Findings showed that teens and parents all believed that teens should have some semblance of privacy related to their devices and online presence. However, the gap between knowledge of the technology, inaccurate parental expectations for communication, and generational differences regarding appropriate use of technology contributed to disagreement between teens and parents on technology usage. Similarly, Blackwell et al. noted that mutual trust and parental acceptance were predictors for reduced secrecy and more frequent disclosures, establishing that teens' privacy can be maintained with effective communication between parents and teens.

Much of the research exploring family communication in mediated contexts focuses on either private, text-only messages or public messaging on social media sites. In this chapter, we are interested in the ways teens can share public content from social media sites in private messages with their parents as a way to open lines of communication about difficult topics. This type of communication may strengthen the bond between teen and parent, as well as provide a channel for teens to initiate conversations that may be uncomfortable. Moreover, teens may share public content posted to their friends' social media profiles with their parents as a way to connect over common or risky behaviors among peer groups. In the following section, we describe some of the most popular social media apps and usage among teens that might facilitate these conversations.

Popular Social Media Applications

The most popular social media applications differ among age-groups, not surprisingly. According to Auxier and Anderson (2021), 72% of adults aged 18–29 report using social media and 81% of adults aged 30–49 use social media. The most popular apps for adults aged 18–28 are Instagram (71%), Facebook (70%), Snapchat (65%), and TikTok (48%), while adults aged 30–49 use Facebook (70%), Instagram (48%), Snapchat (~22%), and TikTok (~22%). In a study by Anderson and Jiang (2018), the most popular online platforms reported for teens aged 13–17 are Instagram (72%), Snapchat (69%), and Facebook (51%).

TikTok. Launched in China in 2016, TikTok is a video-sharing app where users create content sound tracked to popular music and largely focuses on dancing, lip-syncing, and other physical activities (Iqbal 2020; Jenson 2020). With well over 800 million users globally, the app has become one of the most used apps in the last few years (Iqbal 2020). The affordances of TikTok allow users opportunities to preserve and share content across SNS, including private messages (e.g., iMessage). Additionally, users often incorporate social messages intended to inform audiences about current events (e.g., voting) and social issues (e.g., sex, climate change), as well as the "silly normativity" of dancing and comedy (Kennedy 2020).

Instagram. The online photo-sharing app Instagram was introduced in 2010 by Kevin Systrom and Mike Krieger as a visual storytelling app to "empower the community on Instagram to connect with their interests and passions" ("About Us," n.d.). Instagram grew to a billion-dollar business in less than two years, when it was purchased by Facebook and shifted to a publicly traded company. The app garnered over 25,000 users on the first day and had over 100,000 downloads at the end of their first week (Blystone 2020).

Snapchat. According to their website, Snapchat is a "camera company" built upon the belief that "reinventing the camera represents our greatest opportunity to improve the way people live and communicate" ("Snap Inc." 2021). Launched in 2011, Snapchat is a messaging app noted for its feature that disappears snaps after the receiver views the message (Krogager and Degn 2020). Snapchat has a private friends list and a multitude of "filters" that allow senders to edit pictures before sending.

Facebook. Launched in 2004, Mark Zuckerberg's Facebook was initially intended to be a social networking site for students at Harvard University (Hall 2021). The site soared to popularity and in 2012, Facebook went public. Today, Facebook has over 3 billion users who post stories, pictures, and connect with friends and family on their Wall ("Company Info" 2021).

Each social networking site has unique features and allow users to curate a personal profile and select with whom users connect. Regardless of the SNS, children and parents can utilize content to initiate conversations and strengthen relationships. We now turn to communication theories as a way to better understand parent–teen communication in mediated spaces.

FAMILY COMMUNICATION THEORIES

These popular social media apps are rich with sharable content related to a vast range of topics, including family matters. In the next section of this chapter, we explore theoretical approaches to exploring parent–teen communication through social media. We include two interpersonal communication theories: family communication patterns and communication privacy management, and two mediated communication theories: social presence theory and media richness theory. We discuss how sharing content can be a catalyst for parent-adolescent conversations that may not have occurred otherwise through these lenses. To begin we apply Family Communication Patterns and Communication Privacy Management to parent and teen communication.

Family Communication Patterns

Family Communication Patterns Theory (FCPT) is parsimonious and can be applied to a variety of different family communication contexts (Koerner, Schrodt, and Fitzpatrick 2018). The simplicity of this theory and its ability be applied to various contexts makes it very useful for the study of parents and young adults use of social media. In fact, the original theory was created to understand media's impact on families (McLeod and Chaffee 1972; 1973).

Therefore, this theory offers a useful lens to study families and technology due to its simplicity and constant evolving applicability. Family communication literature is rich with a variety of contexts where FCP has been applied, subsequently, it is essential to explore how FCPT applies to family communication through social media and technology.

Family communication patterns theory is an overarching theory of parent-child family communication that functions to create a shared construction of reality (Koerner, Schrodt, and Fitzpatrick 2018). The theory was originally developed by McLeod and Chaffee (1972; 1973) and was created to understand how media messages impact families. Fitzpatrick and Ritchie later altered McLeod and Chaffee's model to become a more general family communication theory, since the creation of shared reality is not solely based on how family process the media they consume. Fitzpatrick and Ritchie argued that FCPs are essential to how families understand relationships, behaviors, and interpret theirs and other family members interactions (Koerner and Fitzpatrick 2002). Sensemaking is still key to the theory, with the reconceptualization and introduction of the new terms created the Family Communication Patterns Theory (FCPT; Ritchie and Fitzpatrick 1990). Conformity and conversation orientation were identified after Fitzpatrick and Richie reconceptualized McLeod and Chaffee's model. Conformity orientation is defined by the extent to which families encourage alignment with similar beliefs, attitudes, and values (Koerner and Fitzpatrick 2002). Conversation orientation is defined by the extent to which families encourage and accept discussion about a variety of different topics (Koerner and Fitzpatrick 2002). It is important to note that these orientations are not divorced from one another but interact with each other to create different type of families.

There are four different types of families formed though conversation and conformity orientation, consensual, pluralistic, protective, and laissez-faire (Koerner and Fitzpatrick 1997). Consensual families are high in conversation and conformity orientation, resulting in families that value open communication as well as conformity to families' beliefs and values (Koerner and Fitzpatrick 1997). Pluralistic families are high in conversation and low in conformity orientation, resulting in families that value open communication about various topics and engage in conflict more freely (Koerner and Fitzpatrick 1997). Protective families have high conformity and low conversation orientation, resulting in lack of open communication and emphasis on parental authority (Koerner and Fitzpatrick 1997). Finally, laissez-faire families have low conversation and conformity orientation. Parents lack engagement in decision making or discussions while children lack emotional connections with their families and avoid conflict (Koerner and Fitzpatrick 1997).

While FCPT has been applied to various aspects of family communication, including family privacy invasions (Kennedy-Lightsey and Frisby 2016; Ledbetter 2019), financial support and credit card behaviors (Thorson and Kranstuber Horstman 2014), and family identification and FCPT (Phillips et al. 2018) there is still much to explore when applying FCP to the use of technology, such as social media and family communication.

Family Communication Patterns and Technology

There have been many advances in technology since the original framing of FCP. As such, with the growth of new technology and social media, it is important to understand how all these platforms impact family communication and interaction. With the introduction of new apps, such as TikTok, the usage of these apps has shifted. In the year 2020, TikTok was the second most installed non-gaming app, followed by Facebook, WhatsApp, and Instagram (Chan 2020). With how much social media changes and evolves over the years, it is important to understand the impact, if any, social media has on families and their communication patterns, making FCPT a fitting theory to explore these connections.

Scholars argue that we need to understand how information and communication technologies impact family communication and found that when using information and communication technologies in conjunction with face-to-face communication can help improve happiness in families (Wang et al. 2015) Participating in media together relates to co-orientation and greater connectivity, since the objective for using the media is the same (Padilla-Walker, Coyne, and Fraser 2012). However, family connection through social media sites may be seen negatively if parents' communication is seen as intrusive. Parent–child communication via social media is more complex than other mediums (Padilla-Walker et al. 2012), especially since different social media sites have different usage rules. Due to the complexity of social media usage between parents and children, and the increased connectivity that can result from using media, FCPT is useful to explore how parent–child communication and the relationship is impacted by joint use of various social media sites.

The type of media used, when parents choose to engage in media, and how parents feel about media in general can have an impact on interactions. Perception of social media and how parents feel about the use of social media can influence how the family functions (Procentese, Gatti, and Di Napoli 2019). If parents have positive associations with social media and interacting with their family, it can help create improved family functioning and open communication within the family (Procentese et al. 2019). Families are incorporating media and shared viewing into family traditions and using it to talk about serious issues and broach serious, difficult-to-discuss topics

(Coyne et al. 2014). However, many adolescents do not report that their parents discuss difficult topics, which could mean parents just think they are engaging with their children or that children are not picking up on when parents are trying to engage in serious discussions (Coyne et al. 2014). How does sharing social media content through private messaging alter or enhance these perceptions? Hence, when investigating the use of technology within families, we must consider the type of social media being used, joint use of media within families, and parent and child perceptions of social media use and the messages sent.

Current research has started to explore FCPT and how conversation and conformity orientations apply to online communication with parents and young adults. According to Koerner and Fitzpatrick (2002) parents' communication competence may have an impact on how open communication is valued (conformity vs conversation orientations) within family. The type of family communication patterns may affect how parents and children use technology (Rudi, Walkner, and Dworkin 2015). According to Wang, Roaché, and Pusateri (2019), family rules and norms learned in face-to-face communication can be easily applied to young adults' online communication. However, the communication patterns experienced within families can have an influence on the attitudes of online communication in children (Ledbetter 2010). Online behaviors used to maintain young adult friendships are linked to conversation and conformity orientation (Ledbetter 2009). Individuals tend to be more comfortable disclosing online depending on the conformity and conversation-orientation within their family (Ledbetter 2010). Belonging to a pluralistic family (Koerner and Fitzpatrick 1997), might result in less disclosure online because these families already have open conversations within the family (Ledbetter 2010). Since communicating online allows for more control, conformity orientation would not make online communication more difficult (Ledbetter 2009). Overall, this research highlights how family communication patterns relate to motivations and outcomes of using social media to connect with young adult children. Therefore, future research on FCP and technology should continue to explore additional areas, including how communication that occurs via social media is influenced by FCP, how FCP influences engagement in different types of social media (Instagram vs. TikTok), and how FCP and social media use relates to relational satisfaction.

Clearly, FCP is useful for examining how parents and teens communicate, generally, but also through mediated channels. We turn now to communication privacy management as another theory to guide our analysis of parent and teen communication.

Communication Privacy Management

Disclosure is an important factor in family relationships, especially as children age. Disclosure can promote or inhibit bonds between family (Solomon and Roloff 2018). Communication privacy management theory (CPM) offers a thorough approach to understanding boundary management surrounding the disclosures of private information that may occur in families (CPM; Petronio 2002; 2013). In all, CPM outlines the ways in which people develop privacy ownership and control over their information and how they experience privacy turbulence surrounding violations of those expectations.

In general, people believe they can control who has access to their private information. In this way, owners attempt to control their private information by creating privacy rules (based on gender, culture, motivations, contextual needs, and cost-benefit ratio calculations). These criteria can be divided into core criteria and catalyst criteria. Core criteria are the "stable gauges" that reflect the consistency in the way people reveal and conceal their information (Petronio 2013). However, privacy turbulence occurs when boundaries are not adequately managed in ways that clarify what is public and what is private information (Petronio 2013).

Although, sharing social media content among parents and teens is not directly managing private information, it nonetheless invokes disclosures of feelings, topics, and emotions that are personal in nature that one family member desires to discuss with another. As such, using CPM to examine parent-child communication through social media can offer opportunities to determine what catalyst criteria parents and teens use in the decision-making process to reveal or conceal certain content. For example, calling back to our earlier discussion, do certain FCP result in different types of rules surrounding the types of content children will share with their parents? How do teens manage disclosure around certain topics when sharing social media content that might evoke other conversations about the child's or parents own behaviors? For example, potentially risky behaviors such as drinking, sex, or drugs, or politically charged topics (e.g., racism, vaccinations, sexism) that children want to bring up to have a conversation with family members who have different opinions. Finally, CPM can be used to explore how people manage privacy boundaries surrounding information that is shared by others. For example, a teen sharing a TikTok video that a neighborhood friend made about their house party while the parents were out of town. In this example, how do parents navigate the co-ownership of information with their children that involve other close contacts? These questions broaden the scope of CPM theory and offer new directions for research surrounding revealing and concealing in families.

Now, we turn to theories developed explicitly for mediated communication channels. The following section examines parent–teen communication through media richness theory, social presence theory, and social influence theory.

COMPUTER-MEDIATED COMMUNICATION THEORIES

Computer-mediated communication (CMC) is an expanding area of communication research as new media are consistently emerging. As such, communication in families has also expanded into digital, social, and interactive media. The affordances of CMC have great appeal for convenience and mobility of remaining in contact with family. These affordances are inherent in mediated communication, but the advantages and disadvantages of each are dependent on context. Along with asynchronicity, social media and private messaging have affordances that make communicating through these channels appealing for teens. Mobility, or the convenience of having access to mediated communication wherever they are, means more frequent communication, which can be beneficial in emergency or important situations. Another affordance we posit as vital for positive parent–teen communication is the concept of filtered-out cues. According to Ramirez and Zhang (2007):

> Any reduction in the number of nonverbal and contextual cues available to communicators inherently hinders their ability to form social connections. Reductions in visual, aural, and contextual cues are predicted to produce less awareness of one's partner and colder, less personalized communication, both of which are detrimental to relationship formation. (290)

However, we argue that for teens trying to communicate with parents through mediated channels, having fewer nonverbal cues may be beneficial. The degree to which affordances, such as cues filtered out, is dependent on the situation and the communication partners. The affordances of social media allow family communication to develop differently. The use of TikTok, Snapchat, and Instagram allow family members to share pictures, articles, and memes through private and public messaging (i.e., posting on their Instagram or Facebook feed), which can enhance text-only communication. The following section applies media communication theories to parent and teen communication. We begin with media richness theory.

Media Richness Theory

Media richness theory posits that the richer the media used for communication, the more effective the communication (Daft and Lengel 1986; Daft and Wiginton 1979). Originally developed to focus on organizational communication, media richness theory has four subdimensions: (1) the number of cue systems; (2) the immediacy of feedback; (3) the potential for natural language; and (4) message personalization (Walther 2011). Moreover, message complexity and ambiguity should determine media richness appropriateness. As mediated communication traveled from the office to the home, media richness theory became a useful tool for exploring interpersonal and mediated communication (Dennis and Kinney 1998).

However, defining "richness" may not be as objective as the original theory postulates. Fulk, Schmitz, and Ryu (1995) argue that "richness is not just inherent in the medium, but that it is partly socially constructed" (281). Effective communication channels may be varied across families and contexts in that there likely is not one best way to communicate. In fact, Cramer and Mabry (2015) assert that when sending complex, ambiguous messages, families choose channels that meet multiple subdimensions. For most relational partners today, multiple channels of communication are used as maintenance tools. Thus, richness, as conceptualized previously, may not be the strongest determinant of communication channel selection. For teens who want to initiate conversation with a parent about sensitive material, such as drinking or depression, a less-rich media may be more beneficial. Teens may feel like they can be open and honest when they do not have to look their parent in the eye. Social media platforms like TikTok, curate content about an endless number of topics that teens could share as conversation starters with their parents. For example, during the summer of 2020 when George Floyd was murdered, Melissa's daughter shared a TikTok with her through a text message about the video circulating online. They texted about the current racial climate in the United States and eventually, her daughter came out of her room to have a face-to-face conversation in more detail. This conversation would likely not have occurred without TikTok and may not have continued if the initial interaction made her daughter feel uncomfortable in her inquiry. The immediate response capability of messaging allows parents to respond to teens' messages in an appropriate manner for the urgency of the initial message.

Media richness theory has questionable support from empirical data yet continues to be a popular way to explore mediated communication. As such, we present a second theory of CMC to gain another perspective on parent–teen communication: social presence theory.

Social Presence Theory

Media richness theory asserts more effective communication comes from richer channels, such as face-to-face communication. In the same vein, Walther (2011) states, "The fewer the number of cue systems a system supported, the less warmth and involvement users experienced with one another" (445). However, this may not always be true for parent–teen dynamics. We argue that less rich channels, such as direct messages and texts, might result in communication about sensitive topics that teens are hesitant to bring up to their parents. Through the lens of social presence theory, we explore how parents and teens can have a sense of closeness through mediated channels.

Social presence theory explains how family members can be physically separated yet still feel "together" in some sense (Short, Williams, and Christie 1976). Parents and teens can use mediated channels to communicate when physically separated. Teens may text or message parents for a ride home, to ask permission to do something with friends, or in an emergency situation. Mediated communication is a logical means for efficient and often immediate communication. But how do parents and teens use mediated channels when they are physically close, such as in the same house or in the same building? What reasons would families use technology to communicate when they are in close quarters?

People who meet for the first time online may develop an idealized version of their communication partner. According to Walther (2011), "CMC may facilitate impressions and relationships online that exceed the desirability and intimacy that occur in parallel off-line interactions" (460). Walther's hyperpersonal model helps us explain how online relationships may develop more quickly and more intensely than in-person relationships (2011). In communication among family members who reside in the same household, the hyperpersonal model may not apply as Walther's intended conceptualization. The model may develop, however, in such a way that teens see their parent through an idealized lens when communicating through text because of the missing nonverbal cues. Teens cannot see facial expressions or hear verbal exasperation when discussing intense messages with their parent through CMC, which may allow them to feel closer to their parents. Parents can use the asynchronous advantage to pause and reflect on a response message that will encourage their children to continue the conversation via text, which may not be possible when communicating face-to-face. The disinhibition effect posits that people behave differently online and in mediated spaces than they do in person (Suler 2004). This concept may explain why children communicate differently with their parents through text. The lack of nonverbal cues could be a catalyst for teens to initiate serious discussions with parents when they are uncertain about a reaction.

Social Influence Theory

Media richness theory and social presence theory focus on the degree of media richness as a determinant of how effective or useful messages are. According to Walther (2011), "In a world where we know our communication partners by photo if not by face, plain-text CMC with no additional multimedia is, in some corners, being retro-conceptualized as never having been quite good enough, especially in comparison with the more presence-bearing media that seem (for now) to be here to stay" (446). Yet, in families where relationships are established, plain-text CMC may be useful, if not preferred, in some scenarios. To address this concept, we posit social influence theory may be the ideal lens through which to understand parent and teen communication in mediated channels.

According to Walther (2011), "social influence theory predicts that one's strong ties have more influence on one's perception of CMC richness than do one's weak ties" (456). Parents and teens have established relationships before turning to mediated channels to communicate. Thus, the richness of the media is often irrelevant for relationship development. However, relationship maintenance may be enhanced through mediated communication for parents and teens, as we know interpersonal relationships today are most often maintained through both mediated and face-to-face channels (Caughlin and Sharabi 2013). Affordances such as mobility and cues-filtered-out may actually be beneficial in relational maintenance strategies. First, the mobility of CMC today allows parents and teens to connect regardless of their physical location. If a teen is arguing with a friend or fails a test at school, parents are only a text message away. Moreover, parents can text message teens who camp out in their bedrooms when they want them to emerge and interact with the family. Second, cues-filtered-out may be important for teens who want to talk to parents about sensitive subjects but are not certain how to begin.

Parents who establish open lines of communication with their teens may be successful for topics that feel comfortable and safe for teens. By using mediated channels, teens may feel like they can approach sensitive subjects such as sex or drug use without the nonverbal cues that may be intimidating or judgmental. Additionally, teens may want to talk about pressing social issues but are not confident they have the vocabulary or understanding to have a discussion. Teens may share memes, TikTok videos, or Instagram photos to initiate a conversation about their content without needing the perceived closeness through richer media. In fact, teens may redefine what we think of rich media as the evolution of mediated communication continues. The following section includes how we see the future of mediated communication research, as it relates to families and communication through social media.

FUTURE DIRECTIONS

Exploring family communication and technology in the context of parents and teens and social media is rife for research exploration. In this section we share several areas for future researchers to consider in this area. First, future researchers should explore parents' use of social media as a form of interacting with their children. Given the plethora of social media platforms being used by young adults, it is important to discover how parents might use these platforms to engage with their children. Parents may engage in social media in order to connect with their children (Padilla-Walker, Coyne, and Fraser 2012), but it is important to better understand why parents may choose to use different social media platforms and how this engagement might impact the family relationship. Future researchers might explore how this engagement can by be used for relational maintenance and how it might impact relational satisfaction. Additionally, researchers can explore parental motivation to engage in communication, or not, with their children via social media. In doing so, this might illuminate reasons why parents resist or approach this form of communication with their teens and give rise to ways to mitigate or reinforce their concerns from an empirical standpoint.

Additionally, researchers can also explore the young adult perspective on sharing content from social media with their parents. While parents might think they are engaging with their children via social media, young adults do not seem to agree (Coyne et al. 2014). Families are starting to use media as a reward and include it in family traditions (Coyne et al 2014), but it is also important to understand how young adults perceive this incorporation, how it applies to direct messaging via social media, and how it might impact the family relationship. Identifying young adults' perceptions of the messages their parents share with them on social media, researchers can gain greater insight into how parents might be able to better communicate with their children using mediated content about difficult topics. This research can also highlight some of the positives of using social media, which is a switch from the usual negative tone surrounding the use of media (Barnes and Olson 1985; Racz et al. 2017).

Exploring the issues that arise from posts that originate outside of the family offers new insight into privacy and social networking communication. For example, how, if at all, do young adults share information that originates from their friends social media feeds with their parents and what motivations and implications arise from sharing others content. How, if at all, does sharing about their friendship networks impact the family dynamic? How does sharing social media stories and posts with parents impact the friend dynamic between young adults? These questions enhance the boundaries of privacy management and co-ownership of information into new areas. Relatedly, future researchers can address the parental role of reluctant confidant that results when children share social media posts of other young adults to which they are relationally linked. In some cases, parents might find posts dangerous or inappropriate. If a parent knows these children or their parents, how do parents manage ownership of that knowledge, especially if the parents of the children in the post are friends? How, if at all, does gaining knowledge from social media blur privacy lines between parents, children, and friend networks? These ideas point to important privacy considerations that arise as parents and children share social media content with each other.

Implications for Parent–Teen Communication

In this chapter, we have identified five theories through which research can and should continue exploring communication between parents and teens in mediated contexts. Social and other interactive media are constantly evolving, as does communication in families, particularly teens and parents. In this section, we present implications for using mediated channels to share information and maintain relationships within the family.

To begin, much of the early research on social media and teens focused on the negative impacts. For example, research on social media applications demonstrates negative outcomes for behaviors such as virtual lying (Dumas et al. 2020), depression (Lin et al. 2016), and difficulty with emotion regulation and perceived stress (Rasmussen et al. 2020). As new media evolves and more research is conducted, we are seeing more positive influences in communication. Many parent or community groups on Facebook regularly share the evils of social media. For parents of younger children, it may be wise to limit access and monitor accounts whenever possible. Unrestricted access can introduce younger children to explicit and dangerous content. However, some younger media users will have secret accounts, such as Finstas, which are "fake Instagram accounts" typically with a fake name and limited audience (Duffy and Chan 2019) where users post content they are not comfortable sharing with the larger audience on their main accounts. Some teens allow their parents to follow their main accounts to comply with family rules but create Finstas to maintain privacy boundaries from their parents. According to Duffy and Chan (2019), "young people are socialized to anticipate digital surveillance from various social institutions" (132), including from their family. Thus, parents cannot rely on communicating with their teens through social media for relationship maintenance. True relationship work may develop through private modes, such as direct messaging or texts. For example, Snapchat is touted as a dangerous social media app because of the affordance of disappearing messages (Krogager and Degn 2020). However, the filter feature may be enticing for parents and teens to share silly pictures as a way of keeping in touch when they are not physically in the same space.

Parents of teens with access to a mobile device will likely find it challenging to keep their teen off social media. The pervasiveness of social media apps has soared over the last decade. In fact, 95% of teens now report they have a smartphone or access to one and 45% of teens say they are online on a near-constant basis (Anderson and Jiang 2018). With 70% of adults of all ages using at least one app daily, we clearly need to continue studying how parents and teens can maintain positive relationships through mediated channels. As such, how can parents embrace these new media as a way to maintain relationships with their teens, if they desire to do so? Sign on! Parents who familiarize themselves with social media and can incorporate content into private messages with their children may strengthen the relationships. In general, many contemporary interpersonal relationships are maintained using both face-to-face and mediated channels (Caughlin and Sharabi 2013). The transition between channels is called modality switching or, "the progressive change in the primary forms of communication" (Sprecher and Hampton 2017, 4). This switching of channels or mediums may counter the hyperpersonal model, as people develop relationships and discover the (potentially) multiple selves of those with whom they are communicating. According to Aloia and Warren (2019), "online relational maintenance behaviors are direct forces shaping the quality of parent–child relationships regardless of standard for face-to-face communication" (53). This means that parents should continue using mediated channels to communicate with their teens to reinforce quality interactions.

Yet, "sign on" with caution. Recently, researchers have found that parents who venture into social media may overstep their children's privacy boundaries. Parents may post pictures or other information about their children to demonstrate pride or adoration. Of course, too much "sharenting" is also a problem, excessive posting of pictures and status updates of children via social media channels. According to Siibak and Traks (2019), too much sharing by parents online can cause distress in parent-child relationships as children experience a loss of privacy. Children may feel "embarrassed, annoyed, and frustrated when parents share their private experiences" (117). Thus, parents should consider communicating with their child about a comfortable level of disclosure online to maintain healthy relationships regarding the use of social media. While it may be beneficial for teens to share content with their parents to improve relational satisfaction, parents who share personal content about their child publicly on social media may be violating their privacy boundaries. Parents should post with caution as the permanency of the internet may be a point of contention in their relationships with their children.

CONCLUSION

Mediated communication continues to evolve, as do the relationships between parents and teens who utilize the channels. Relational satisfaction, strong bonds, and open communication can result from an understanding of how mediated channels can facilitate—and prohibit—growth in communication. Moreover, understanding that all mediated communication channels are not equal will benefit parents as they try to navigate the teenage years. Parents who are willing to participate in sharing social media content as a catalyst for engaging communication may fare better than those who do not embrace emerging mediated tools.

REFERENCES

"About Us." n.d. Instagram. instagram.com/about/us.

Aloia, Lindsey Susan, and Ron Warren. 2019. "Quality Parent–Child Relationships: The Role of Parenting Style and Online Relational Maintenance Behaviors." *Communication Reports* 32 (2): 43–56. https://doi.org/10.1080/08934215.2019.1582682.

Ames, M. G., J. Go, J. J. Kaye, and M. Spasojevic. 2010. "Making Love in the Network Closet: The Benefits and Work of Family Videochat." In, 145–54. ACM Press. https://doi.org/10.1145/1718918.1718946.

Anderson, M., and J. Jiang. 2018. "Teens, Social Media & Technology 2018." *Pew Research Center: Internet, Science & Tech* (blog). May 31, 2018. https://www.pewresearch.org/internet/2018/05/31/teens-social-media-technology-2018/.

Auxier, Brooke, and M. Anderson. 2021. "Social Media Use in 2021." *Pew Research Center: Internet, Science & Tech* (blog). April 7, 2021. https://www.pewresearch.org/internet/2021/04/07/social-media-use-in-2021/.

Barnes, Howard L., and David H. Olson. 1985. "Parent—Adolescent Communication and the Circumplex Model." *Child Development* 56 (2): 438. https://doi.org/10.2307/1129732.

Billedo, C. J., P. Kerkhof, and C. Finkenauer. 2015. "The Use of Social Networking Sites for Relationship Maintenance in Long-Distance and Geographically Close Romantic Relationships." *Cyberpsychology, Behavior, and Social Networking* 18: 152–57. https://doi.org/10.1089/cyber.2014.0469.

Blackwell, Lindsay, Emma Gardiner, and Sarita Schoenebeck. 2016. "Managing Expectations: Technology Tensions among Parents and Teens." In *Proceedings of the 19th ACM Conference on Computer-Supported Cooperative Work & Social Computing*, 1390–1401. CSCW '16. New York: Association for Computing Machinery. https://doi.org/10.1145/2818048.2819928.

Blystone, D. 2020. "The Story of Instagram: The Rise of the #1 Photo-Sharing Application." Investopedia. 2020. www.investopedia.com/articles/investing/102615/story-instagram-rise-1-photo0sharing-app.asp.

Braithwaite, D. O., B. W. Bach, L. A. Baxter, R. DiVerniero, J. Hammonds, A. M. Hosek, and B. Wolf. 2010. "Constructing Family: A Typology of Voluntary Kin." *Journal of Social and Personal Relationships* 27: 388–407.

Caughlin, J. P., and L. L. Sharabi. 2013. "A Communicative Interdependence Perspective of Close Relationships: The Connections between Mediated and Unmediated Interactions Matter: Interdependence of Communicative Modes." *Journal of Communication*, n/a-n/a. https://doi.org/10.1111/jcom.12046.

Chan, Julia. 2020. "Top Apps Worldwide for April 2020 by Downloads." Sensor Tower Blog. 2020. https://sensortower.com/blog/top-apps-worldwide-april-2020-by-downloads.

Child, J. T., and S. Petronio. 2011. "Unpacking the Paradoxes of Privacy in CMC Relationships: The Challenges of Blogging and Relational Communication on the Internet." In *Computer Mediated Communication in Personal Relationships*, edited by K. B. Wright and L. M. Webb, 21–40. Peter Lang.

Child, J. T., and D. A. Westermann. 2013. "Let's Be Facebook Friends: Exploring Parental Facebook Friend Requests from a Communication Privacy Management (CPM) Perspective." *Journal of Family Communication* 13: 46–59. https://doi.org/10.1080/15267431.2012.742089.

"Company Info." 2021. Facebook. 2021. https://about.facebook.com/company-info/.

Coyne, S. M., L. M. Padilla-Walker, A. M. Fraser, K. Fellows, and R. D. Day. 2014. "'Media Time = Family Time': Positive Media Use in Families with Adolescents." *Adolescent Research* 29: 663–88. https://doi.org/10.1177/0743558414538316.

Cramer, E. M., and E. A. Mabry. 2015. "Exploring the Interaction of Media Richness and Family Characteristics in Computer-Mediated Communication." In *Family Communication in the Age of Digital and Social Media*, edited by C. J. Bruess, 99–116. Peter Lang Publishing, Inc.

Cranor, L. F., A. L. Durity, A. Marsh, and B. Ur. 2014. "Parents' and Teens' Perspectives on Privacy in a Technology-Filled World." Presented at the Symposium on Usable Privacy and Security (SOUPS).

Daft, Richard L., and Robert H. Lengel. 1986. "Organizational Information Requirements, Media Richness and Structural Design." *Management Science* 32 (5): 554–71.

Daft, Richard L., and John C. Wiginton. 1979. "Language and Organization." *Academy of Management Review* 4 (2): 179–91. https://doi.org/10.5465/AMR.1979.4289017.

Dennis, Alan R., and Susan T. Kinney. 1998. "Testing Media Richness Theory in the New Media: The Effects of Cues, Feedback, and Task Equivocality." *Information Systems Research* 9 (3): 256–74. https://doi.org/10.1287/isre.9.3.256.

Dou, Y., Y. Pan, and S. Jiang. 2020. "Talk to Me, Don't Text Me: Face to Face Communication Generates Greater Closeness than Texting among Generation Z in China." *PsyArXiv*. https://doi.org/10.31234/osf.io/7angu.

Duffy, Brooke Erin, and Ngai Keung Chan. 2019. "'You Never Really Know Who's Looking': Imagined Surveillance across Social Media Platforms." *New Media & Society* 21 (1): 119–38. https://doi.org/10.1177/1461444818791318.

Dumas, Tara M., Matthew A. Maxwell-Smith, Paul F. Tremblay, Dana M. Litt, and Wendy Ellis. 2020. "Gaining Likes, but at What Cost? Longitudinal Relations between Young Adults' Deceptive like-Seeking on Instagram, Peer Belonging and Self-Esteem." *Computers in Human Behavior* 112 (November): 106467. https://doi.org/10.1016/j.chb.2020.106467.

Fulk, Janet, Joseph Schmitz, and Daehee Ryu. 1995. "Cognitive Elements in the Social Construction of Communication Technology." *Management Communication Quarterly* 8 (3): 259–88. https://doi.org/10.1177/0893318995008003001.

Hall, M. 2021. "Facebook." Britannica. 2021. https://www.britannica.com/topic/Facebook.

Hosek, A. M. 2015. "Education and Family Communication." In *The Sage Handbook of Family Communication*, edited by L. Turner and R. West, 2nd ed., 293–305. Sage Publications.

Howe, N., and W. Strauss. 2007. *Millennials Go to College*. LifeCourse Associates.

Iqbal, M. 2020. "TikTok Revenue and Usage Statistics (2021)." Business of Apps. 2020. https://www.businessofapps.com/data/tik-tok-statistics/.

Jenson, K. 2020. "What Makes These Librarians TikTok?" *School Library Journal* 66: 32–34.

Kanter, Maggie, Tamara Afifi, and Stephanie Robbins. 2012. "The Impact of Parents 'Friending' Their Young Adult Child on Facebook on Perceptions of Parental Privacy Invasions and Parent-Child Relationship Quality." *Journal of Communication* 62: 900–917. https://doi.org/10.1111/j.1460-2466.2012.01669.x.

Kelly, K. J., M. L. G. Comello, and L. C. P. Hunn. 2002. "Parent-Child Communication, Perceived Sanctions against Drug Use, and Youth Drug Involvement." *Adolescence* 37 (148): 775–87.

Kennedy, Melanie. 2020. "'If the Rise of the TikTok Dance and e-Girl Aesthetic Has Taught Us Anything, It's That Teenage Girls Rule the Internet Right Now': TikTok Celebrity, Girls and the Coronavirus Crisis." *European Journal of Cultural Studies* 23 (6): 1069–76. https://doi.org/10.1177/1367549420945341.

Kennedy-Lightsey, Carrie D., and Brandi N. Frisby. 2016. "Parental Privacy Invasion, Family Communication Patterns, and Perceived Ownership of Private Information." *Communication Reports* 29 (2): 75–86.

Koerner, A. F., P. Schrodt, and M. A. Fitzpatrick. 2018. "Family Communication Patterns Theory: A Grand Theory of Family Communication." In *Engaging Theories in Family Communication: Multiple Perspectives*, edited by D. O. Braithwaite, E. A. Suter, and K. Floyd, 2nd ed., 142–53. Routledge.

Koerner, Ascan F., and Mary Anne Fitzpatrick. 1997. "Family Type and Conflict: The Impact of Conversation Orientation and Conformity Orientation on Conflict in the Family." *Communication Studies* 48 (1): 59–75. https://doi.org/10.1080/10510979709368491.

———. 2002. "Toward a Theory of Family Communication." *Communication Theory* 12: 70.

Krogager, Stinne Gunder Strøm, and Hans-Peter Degn. 2020. "Snapchat: A Space for Intimate and Boundary-Pushing Transactions." *Interactions: Studies in Communication & Culture* 11 (3): 377–92. https://doi.org/10.1386/iscc_00031_1.

Ledbetter, Andrew M. 2009. "Family Communication Patterns and Relational Maintenance Behavior: Direct and Mediated Associations with Friendship Closeness." *Human Communication Research* 35 (1): 130–47. https://doi.org/10.1111/j.1468-2958.2008.01341.x.

Ledbetter, Andrew M. 2019. "Parent-Child Privacy Boundary Conflict Patterns During the First Year of College: Mediating Family Communication Patterns, Predicting Psychosocial Distress." *Human Communication Research* 45 (3): 255–85. https://doi.org/10.1093/hcr/hqy018.

Ledbetter, Andrew M. 2010. "Family Communication Patterns and Communication Competence as Predictors of Online Communication Attitude: Evaluating a Dual Pathway Model." *Journal of Family Communication* 10 (2): 99–115. https://doi.org/10.1080/15267431003595462.

Lenhart, A. 2015. "Teens, Social Media & Technology Overview 2015." *Pew Research Center: Internet, Science & Tech* (blog). 2015. https://www.pewresearch.org/internet/2015/04/09/teens-social-media-technology-2015/.

Lin, L. Y., J. E. Sidani, A. Shensa, A. Radovic, E. Miller, Jason B. Colditz, Beth L. Hoffman, Leila M. Giles, and Brian A. Primack. 2016. "Association Between Social Media Use and Depression Among U.S. Young Adults." *Depression & Anxiety (1091–4269)* 33 (4): 323–31. https://doi.org/10.1002/da.22466.

Madsen, S. D., and W. A. Collins. 2018. "Personal Relationships in Adolescence and Early Adulthood." In *The Cambridge Handbook of Personal Relationships*, edited by A. L. Vangelisti and D. Perlman, 135–47. Cambridge University Press.

McLeod, J. M., and S. H. Chaffee. 1972. "The Social Construction of Reality." In *The Social Influence Process*, edited by J. Tedeschi, 50–59. Aldine-Atherton.

———. 1973. "Interpersonal Approaches to Communication Research." *American Behavioral Scientist* 16: 469–99.

O'Sullivan, P. B. 2000. "What You Don't Know Won't Hurt Me: Impression Management Functions of Communication Channels in Relationships." *Human Communication Research* 26: 403–31.

Padilla-Walker, Laura M., Sarah M. Coyne, and Ashley M. Fraser. 2012. "Getting a High-Speed Family Connection: Associations Between Family Media Use and Family Connection." *Family Relations* 61 (3): 426–40. https://doi.org/10.1111/j.1741-3729.2012.00710.x.

Petronio, S. 2002. *Boundaries of Privacy: Dialectics of Disclosure*. Albany, NY: State University of New York Press.

Petronio, Sandra. 2013. "Brief Status Report on Communication Privacy Management Theory." *Journal of Family Communication* 13 (1): 6–14. https://doi.org/10.1080/15267431.2013.743426.

Phillips, Kaitlin E., Andrew M. Ledbetter, Jordan Soliz, and Gretchen Bergquist. 2018. "Investigating the Interplay Between Identity Gaps and Communication Patterns in Predicting Relational Intentions in Families in the United States." *Journal of Communication* 68 (3): 590–611. https://doi.org/10.1093/joc/jqy016.

Procentese, Fortuna, Flora Gatti, and Immacolata Di Napoli. 2019. "Families and Social Media Use: The Role of Parents' Perceptions about Social Media Impact on Family Systems in the Relationship between Family Collective Efficacy and Open

Communication." *International Journal of Environmental Research & Public Health* 16 (24): 5006. https://doi.org/10.3390/ijerph16245006.

Racz, Sarah Jensen, Sarah Lindstrom Johnson, Catherine P. Bradshaw, and Tina L. Cheng. 2017. "Parenting in the Digital Age: Urban Black Youth's Perceptions about Technology-Based Communication with Parents." *Journal of Family Studies* 23 (2): 198–214. https://doi.org/10.1080/13229400.2015.1108858.

Ramirez Jr, Artemio, and Shuangyue Zhang. 2007. "When Online Meets Offline: The Effect of Modality Switching on Relational Communication." *Communication Monographs* 74 (3): 287–310. https://doi.org/10.1080/03637750701543493.

Rasmussen, Eric E., Narissra Punyanunt-Carter, Jenna R. LaFreniere, Mary S. Norman, and Thomas G. Kimball. 2020. "The Serially Mediated Relationship between Emerging Adults' Social Media Use and Mental Well-Being." *Computers in Human Behavior* 102 (January): 206–13. https://doi.org/10.1016/j.chb.2019.08.019.

Ritchie, L. D., and M. A. Fitzpatrick. 1990. "Family Communication Patterns: Measuring Intrapersonal Perceptions of Interpersonal Relationships." *Communication Research* 17 (4): 523–44. https://doi.org/10.1177/009365090017004007.

Rudi, Jessie H., Amy Walkner, and Jodi Dworkin. 2015. "Adolescent–Parent Communication in a Digital World: Differences by Family Communication Patterns." *Youth & Society* 47 (6): 811–28. https://doi.org/10.1177/0044118X14560334.

Short, J., E. Williams, and B. Christie. 1976. *The Social Psychology of Telecommunications*. John Wiley & Sons Inc. https://resolver-ebscohost-com.proxy.library.ohio.edu/openurl?sid=EBSCO%3afmh&genre=article&issn=00943061&ISBN=&volume=7&issue=1&date=19780101&spage=32&pages=32-33&title=Contemporary+Sociology&atitle=The+Social+Psychology+of+Telecommunications+(Book).&aulast=Parker%2c+Edwin+B.&id=DOI%3a&site=ftf-live.

Siibak, Andra, and Keily Traks. 2019. "The Dark Sides of Sharenting." *Catalan Journal of Communication & Cultural Studies* 11 (1): 115–21. https://doi.org/10.1386/cjcs.11.1.115_1.

"Snap Inc." 2021. Snapchat. 2021. https://www.snap.com/en-US.

Solomon, D. H., and M. E. Roloff. 2018. "Relational Initiation and Growth." In *The Cambridge Handbook of Personal Relationships*, edited by A. L. Vangelisti and D. Perlman, 79–89. Cambridge University Press.

Sprecher, S., and A. J. Hampton. 2017. "Liking and Other Reactions after a Get-Acquainted Interaction: A Comparison of Continuous Face-to-Face Interaction versus Interaction That Progresses from Text Messages to Face-to-Face." *Communication Quarterly* 65: 333–53. https://doi.org/10.1080/01463373.2016.1256334.

Stouthamer-Loeber, Magda, Rolf Loeber, Evelyn Wei, David P. Farrington, and Per-Olof H. Wikström. 2002. "Risk and Promotive Effects in the Explanation of Persistent Serious Delinquency in Boys." *Journal of Consulting and Clinical Psychology* 70 (1): 111. https://doi.org/10.1037/0022-006X.70.1.111.

Suler, John. 2004. "The Online Disinhibition Effect." *CyberPsychology & Behavior* 7: 321–26. https://doi.org/10.1089/1094931041291295.

Thorson, A. R., and H. A. Kranstuber Horstman. 2014. "Buy Now, Pay Later: Family Communication Patterns Theory, Parental Financial Support, and Emerging Adults' Openness about Credit Card Behaviors." *Journal of Family Communication* 14 (1): 53–71. https://doi.org/10.1080/15267431.2013.857324.

Vitak, J. 2014. "Facebook Makes the Heart Grow Fonder: Relationship Maintenance Strategies among Geographically Dispersed and Communication-Restricted Connections." In, 842–53. ACM Press. https://doi.org/10.1145/2531602.2531726.

Walther, J. B. 2011. "Theories of Computer-Mediated Communication and Interpersonal Relations." In *The Handbook of Interpersonal Communication*, edited by M. L. Knapp and J. A. Daly, 443–79. Thousand Oaks, CA: SAGE.

Wang, Man Ping, Joanna TW Chu, Kasisomayajula Viswanath, Alice Wan, Tai Hing Lam, and Sophia S Chan. 2015. "Using Information and Communication Technologies for Family Communication and Its Association With Family Well-Being in Hong Kong: FAMILY Project." *Journal of Medical Internet Research* 17 (8): e207. https://doi.org/10.2196/jmir.4722.

Wang, Ningxin, David J. Roaché, and Kimberly B. Pusateri. 2019. "Associations Between Parents' and Young Adults' Face-to-Face and Technologically Mediated Communication Competence: The Role of Family Communication Patterns." *Communication Research* 46 (8): 1171–96. https://doi.org/10.1177/0093650217750972.

Yu, Shuli, Rebecca Clemens, Hongmei Yang, Xiaoming Li, Bonita Stanton, Lynette Deveaux, Sonja Lunn, Lesley Cottrell, and Carole Harris. 2006. "Youth and Parental Perceptions of Parental Monitoring and Parent-Adolescent Communication, Youth Depression, and Youth Risk Behaviors." *Social Behavior and Personality: An International Journal* 34 (10): 1297–1310. https://doi.org/10.2224/sbp.2006.34.10.1297.

Index

Note: Page numbers in *italics* refer to exhibits and tables.

About the Contributors

Jill K. Burk (PhD, Duquesne University) is an associate teaching professor and program chair of the communication arts and sciences program at Pennsylvania State University, Berks. Dr. Burk studies questions of human communication as practiced in the public discourse of everyday life. She teaches courses in rhetorical theory, communication ethics, community and civic engagement, organizational communication, and public speaking. Additionally, Dr. Burk coordinates the civic and community engagement minor.

Jessica Cherry (MA, Western Kentucky University) is a graduate teaching assistant, working toward her PhD in interpersonal and organizational communication at Ohio University. Her research interests primarily focus on family communication surrounding the end-of-life experience. Her current research projects are centered around the experiences and communication surrounding family caregivers and how individuals and communities cope with traumatic death and loss. Jessica teaches public speaking, introduction to human communication, group communication, interpersonal communication, and nonverbal communication.

Janie Harden Fritz (PhD, University of Wisconsin–Madison) is professor of communication and rhetorical studies at Duquesne University. Her research interests include civility and incivility in professional and personal settings, religious communication, and communication ethics. She is the author of *Professional Civility: Communicative Virtue at Work* (Peter Lang, 2013) and the coauthor or coeditor of several other volumes, as well as multiple scholarly articles and book chapters. Dr. Fritz teaches courses in organizational, intercultural, and interpersonal communication, communication ethics, philosophy of communication, and religious communication and holds the William Patrick Power, C.S.Sp. Endowed Chair in Academic Leadership (2019–2024).

Michael L. Hecht (PhD, University of Illinois) is a distinguished professor emeritus of communication arts and sciences at Pennsylvania State University and co-president of REAL Prevention, LLC. Dr. Hecht specializes in culturally grounded, narrative health message design and evaluation among diverse communities. He has developed evidence-based curricula for adolescent substance use and risky sexual behaviors as well as web-based interventions for the promotion of HPV vaccination among children, women, and men. Hecht current work focuses on digital interventions to improve parenting skills as well as those that impact the opioid epidemic, including an intervention to reverse overdoses and a second to reduce prescription opioid misuse among high school athletes. Among other awards and recognition, Hecht was chosen as the University of Illinois College of the Liberal Arts' 2020 Humanitarian of the Year, 2021 Distinguished Lecture at the Hong Kong Polytechnic University, and the 2012 Pennsylvania Rural Health Leader of the Year.

Angela M. Hosek (PhD, University of Nebraska, Lincoln) is an associate professor in the school of communication studies at Ohio University. Her recent research interests explore women and family's experiences with messages surrounding breastfeeding communication and mothering. Her published research focuses on social identity, privacy and discourse, memorable messages, social media, and student success in the instructional context.

Elizabeth B. Jones (PhD, The Ohio State University) is an associate professor and graduate program director at Asbury University in the School of Communication Arts. Her research occurs at the intersection of communication technology, interpersonal communication, and health communication, often through the lens of life span communication. She teaches courses in digital storytelling, social media, and communication research.

Paul Lucas (PhD, Duquesne University) is an associate professor of communication at the University of Pittsburgh at Johnstown. His research and teaching interests focus primarily on rhetoric, branding, and pop culture.

Christina L. McDowell Marinchak (PhD, Duquesne University) is a senior lecturer of marketing and management communication at Cornell University, in the SC Johnson College of Business Peter and Stephan Nolan School of Hotel Administration. Her research interests start with communicative engagement and emphasizes actively investigating social, civic, economic, and moral problems in the areas of corporate communication, integrated marketing communication (IMC) as well as communication ethics by people and organizations. She has professional experience teaching business/corporate communication and marketing related courses, serving in academic administration roles, delivering professional presentation and workshops in industry, and working in an integrated communication agency setting in account services.

Maryl R. McGinley (PhD, Duquesne University) is an assistant professor at the University of Pittsburgh, Johnstown. Her research focuses on interpersonal communication and communication ethics, with an eye toward the agrarian paradigm/rootedness and the way in which ground influences our communicative framework. She recently published a chapter on the importance of cultivating civility in social spaces and teaches a course named social media strategies that inspired her piece. She also teaches organizational communication, interpersonal communication, business and profession speaking, and public speaking.

Michelle Miller-Day (PhD, Arizona State University) is a professor of communication studies at Chapman University and co-president of REAL Prevention, LLC. Her research has been funded for over 30 years by the United States National Institutes of Health and focuses on developing and evaluating health programs for individuals and families. Her mixed-methods research has led to the development of several evidence-based narrative interventions and health programs including "keepin' it REAL," a social and emotional learning substance use prevention program disseminated to more than 1.5 million youth across 48 countries and five additional m-health and e-learning programs. She has more than 100 published works and is the recipient of several career awards including the 2016 Bernard J. Brommel Award for Outstanding Scholarship and Distinguished Service in Family Communication, 2019 Outstanding Health Communication Scholar Award, and the 2019 Charles Atkin Outstanding Translational Health Communication Scholar Award.

Tiffany Petricini (PhD, Duquesne University) is an Assistant Teaching Professor at Penn State Shenango. She completed her doctoral program at Duquesne University with emphases on communication ethics and the rhetoric of technology. Her research reflects personal interests in media ecology, phenomenology, human development and technology and the works of Walter J. Ong. These interests support her community involvement concerning the rights of children, poverty, domestic violence and human rights.

Anne E. Ray (PhD, Pennsylvania State University) is an assistant professor of health, behavior & society within the University of Kentucky College of Public Health. She is a prevention scientist with research interests in the (1) etiology and prevention of high-risk substance use among adolescent and emerging adult populations, (2) utilization of technology to adapt, improve, and extend the reach of evidenced-based programming, and (3) application of dissemination and implementation science frameworks to scale up evidence-based programming and improve program dissemination for maximum impact.

Tyrell J. Stewart-Harris (PhD, University of Illinois at Chicago) is currently a Lecturer of Management Communication at Cornell University's Nolan School of Hotel Administration, where he teaches business writing for hospitality professionals. Stewart-Harris's research interests include rhetoric, race theory, and housing policy.

Rob Turrisi (PhD, University at Albany, State University of New York) is currently a professor at Penn State University with a joint appointment in the Department of Biobehavioral Health and the Prevention Research Center. Dr. Turrisi also the director of the Prevention Research to Optimize (PRO) Health Lab (https://sites.psu.edu/prcprohealth/). Turrisi's work focuses on developing and evaluating parent and individual-level prevention efforts to reduce alcohol abuse and alcohol-related consequences for adolescents, college students and emerging adults. His prevention research has been supported by funds from the National Institutes of Health, National Institute on Alcohol Abuse and Alcoholism, National Institute on Drug Abuse, and the National Cancer Institute for over 35 years. Turrisi is also the author of *A Parent Handbook for Talking with Students About Alcohol*. The *Parent Handbook* is still the only evidence-based parent-based intervention that has undergone the rigor of 10 well-controlled clinical trials. The research on the *Parent Handbook* has been vetted and reviewed in the most recent Surgeon General's Report as one of the two prevention approaches that met the rigorous criteria to be considered "efficacious" for preventing student drinking and consequences. In addition, the National Institute on Alcohol Abuse and Alcoholism's College AIM Matrix has stated that the *Parent Handbook* is an "effective" intervention to produce changes in attitudes or behaviors related to alcohol use. The data continues to show that the *Parent Handbook* not only prevents students from drinking, but also reduces the drinking of those students with established high-risk drinking habits. These findings are truly unique and extremely important. Turrisi has also developed materials for MADD's Power of Parents program for parents of middle and high school students (https://www.madd.org/the-solution/power-of-parents/).

Anthony M. Wachs (PhD, Duquesne University) is associate professor of rhetoric, communication ethics & the Catholic intellectual tradition and co-director of graduate studies in the department of communication &

rhetorical studies at Duquesne University. His research interests concern the intersections between rhetoric, religion, and technology. He is author of *The New Science of Communication: Reconsidering McLuhan's Message* and co-author of *Age of Anxiety: Meaning, Identity, and Politics in 21st-Century Film and Literature*.

Joel S. Ward (PhD, Duquesne University) is an associate professor of communication at Geneva College in Beaver Falls, PA. He holds a PhD in rhetoric and philosophy from Duquesne University. His research interests include communication technology, family communication, interpersonal communication ethics and communication design. Currently he serves as president of the Pennsylvania Communication Association.

Melissa Rizzo Weller (PhD, Ohio University) where she is currently a visiting assistant professor in the OHIO Honors Program. Her current research focuses on interpersonal communication in various social media. More specifically, she is collaborating on multiple studies exploring how we use social media for supportive communication and relational satisfaction in the contexts of families and online affinity groups. Previous research including investigations into identity and supportive communication perceived by adult adoptees within both their adoptive and birth families. Dr. Rizzo Weller teaches small group communication, family communication, and interpersonal communication.

Patty Wharton-Michael (PhD, Pennsylvania State University) is an associate professor of communication at the University of Pittsburgh at Johnstown. She currently serves as the cochair of the Communication Department at the University of Pittsburgh at Johnstown. Her research areas include media effects and health communication and communication education. Her most recent work includes an investigation of parents' media use—using online search engines and social media—to make health-related choices regarding vaccinations.

www.ingramcontent.com/pod-product-compliance
Lightning Source LLC
Chambersburg PA
CBHW022305280326
41932CB00010B/988